Philip V of Spain

Philip V of Spain

The King who Reigned Twice

Henry Kamen

Yale University Press
New Haven and London

For information about this and other Yale University Press
publications, please contact:
U.S. Office: sales.press@yale.edu   www.yale.edu/yup
Europe Office: sales@yaleup.co.uk   www.yaleup.co.uk

Set in FF Scala by Best-set Typesetter Ltd, Hong Kong
Printed in Great Britain by St Edmundsbury Press

Library of Congress Cataloging-in-Publication Data
Kamen, Henry Arthur Francis.
[Felipe V. English]
Philip V : the king who reigned twice / Henry Kamen.
p.   cm.
Includes bibliographical references and index.
ISBN 0-300-08718-7 (cloth)
1. Philip V, King of Spain, 1683–1746. 2. Spain—History—Philip V, 1700–1745. 3.
Spain—Kings and rulers—Biography. I. Title.
DP194 .K3613   2001
946'.055'092—dc21
[B]
00-067192

A catalogue record for this book is available from the British Library.

2 4 6 8 10 9 7 5 3 1

CONTENTS

ILLUSTRATIONS

Philip V was the first king of the Bourbon dynasty that still rules Spain today. He governed for forty-six years, longer than any other ruler of Spain either before or since, and his reign was one of the most formative epochs of the country's history. After the military and economic problems of the previous Habsburg dynasty, Spain under the Bourbons appeared to promise new life. The early years were traumatic: for the first time since the Arab invasions in the eighth century, the peninsula was occupied by tens of thousands of foreign troops, and in the subsequent peace treaty the monarchy was brutally dismembered. Although the conflict resulted in fundamental political changes without precedent in Spain's history, this did not impede the process of regeneration. Philip V initiated developments – in politics, in imperial policy, in questions of finance, government and the army – that laid the basis of the modern Spanish state. He encouraged trends in literature, the creative arts and music that brought Spanish culture into closer contact with Europe. There were also conflictive issues to address, mainly the autonomy of the provinces of Spain and the role of the monarchy itself.

Despite the importance of all these questions, we know little about Philip's reign and little about the king himself. In English, the most valuable general survey is that of 1989 by John Lynch. Three or four short biographies in Spanish have been published in the last half-century, but none exists in English. In most books, the image that we have of Philip is negative. Non-Spanish historians have referred to him as 'a comic figure', 'stupid, obsessed and indolent, oscillating between lucidity and idiocy', and 'a slave of women'. Spanish scholars have not been more generous: a noted historian, writing half a century ago, saw him as 'a toy in the hands of his authoritarian wife', and as responsible for a regime dedicated to 'authoritarianism, absolutism and centralisation'.

The volume presented here is a short, personal biography of the king; it is based on contemporary sources, both archival and published, and on recent scholarly research. No attempt has been made to offer a history of the reign, which would have required a more extended study. For nearly half a century, Philip's character, decisions and policies affected the destiny of his subjects, and of the whole western world, and therefore deserve examination. In order to present the king within the fuller context of Spain's evolution, my book also gives some attention to aspects of the politics, economy and foreign policy of the first half of the eighteenth century.

Sources are referred to in the notes, and a select bibliography appears at the end. Since the end of the nineteenth century (I take my point of reference from the publication in 1890 of the magisterial work by Mgr Baudrillart) the research of many good historians has begun to shed light on the reign of the first Bourbon. Special mention should be made of the pioneering studies of the distinguished French scholar Yves Bottineau. But much remains to be done, and the task will not be easy. The history of the period is dominated by war and diplomacy, themes that have been almost wholly neglected; and there are few studies on regional or central government.

The reader may note discrepancies between some of the dates given here and those in other books; mine, I believe, are correct. Money is calculated in escudos, the basic unit used by the Spanish government in that period. Except for those that have a well-accepted English equivalent, foreign names are usually given in their original form.

Philip V's reign witnessed a renaissance of critical and historical writings. In 1737 there appeared the *Diario de los Literatos*, a periodical that promised 'to inform with total impartiality'. Later, in 1738, the king extended his patronage to a new institution, the Academy of History, which stated in the first clause of its constitution that its purpose was 'to purge our history of fables, and illuminate it with reliable data'. They are aims that also inspire this brief biography.

Higher Council for Scientific Research, Barcelona

CHAPTER ONE

The Disputed Succession

'I WOULD RATHER GO BACK TO BEING DUKE OF ANJOU, AND I
CAN'T STAND SPAIN!'

PHILIP V, MAY 1701

In the last months of the year 1700, the attention of the western world was centred on the royal palace of the Habsburg kings of Spain. In Madrid on 2 October the mortally ill young monarch, the ashen-faced and rickety Charles II, made the last positive decision of his life and signed a final testament in which he declared that his throne should pass to the French duke of Anjou, grandson of the sovereign of France, Louis XIV. He had previously made two other wills, each favouring a different heir, so that for nearly half a century the shadow of war had loomed over Europe because of the vexed question of the Spanish succession.

Charles II, born in 1661, had become king of Spain in 1665 but suffered throughout his life from serious ill-health and was unable to produce an heir by either of his wives, the second of whom, Mariana of Neuburg, daughter of the Elector Palatine and sister to the wife of Emperor Leopold I, he had married in 1689. The other European powers were anxious that the extensive Spanish empire, if left without an heir, should not fall into the hands of one sole dynasty. To this end various secret agreements were therefore arrived at to divide the empire up. Louis XIV's interest in the throne of Spain dated from his marriage in 1660 to Maria Teresa, daughter of Philip IV. Both the terms of the marriage and the subsequent testament of Philip IV made it clear that Maria Teresa and her descendants were excluded from the throne of Spain. However, at no time did Louis or his advisers take the renunciations seriously. They used, in part, the excuse that the dowry of Maria Teresa had never been paid, and that this automatically made the renunciations invalid. As early as 1668, the Holy Roman Emperor, Leopold I, signed a treaty at Vienna with France, providing for the partition between them of the Spanish territories if Charles were to die heirless. Leopold based his own claim to the Spanish throne on the fact that he was a grandson of Philip III. He had also married, as his first wife, Margarita, daughter of Philip IV. Their daughter, Marie Antonia, married the elector of Bavaria, Maximilian; the couple's son, Joseph Ferdinand, born in 1692, also became a direct candidate for the Spanish throne.

Over the next two decades the interests of England and the United Provinces also came into play, particularly after the union of these two nations under one ruler, William III of Orange, in 1688. When it became apparent in the last years of the century that Charles II was seriously ill, the chief European powers agreed on a secret partition treaty. The treaty, made in October 1698, stated that the throne of Spain would pass to the infant heir of the duke of Bavaria, while France would obtain some Spanish territory as well as Italy, and the Empire would receive Milan. When the news was leaked to Spain, there was indignation. By a testament of 14 September 1693, made during a severe illness, the heirless Charles II had already left his entire monarchy to the Bavarian prince. On receiving news of the October 1698 treaty, the king, with the support of his Council of State, made a secret testament, dated 11 November 1698, in which he named the Bavarian prince sole heir to the crown. The Spaniards were unanimous on one point: there must be no division of the monarchy. The Bavarian prince unexpectedly died three months later, so forcing the powers to draw up yet another treaty (this time without much secrecy but with the participation of the emperor) in March 1700. By this, the monarchy would still be divided up, and Spain would go instead to the emperor's younger son, the Archduke Charles.

The feelings of the Council of State in Madrid were quite clear. Uppermost in the minds of all its ministers was the need to preserve the integrity of the monarchy, and to put it in hands powerful enough to guarantee that integrity. Their view was crystallised in the vote of the marquis del Fresno: 'that Your Majesty cede the whole monarchy to a grandson of the king of France, on the assurance that there will be no unification of the two Crowns'.[1] Following the advice of his ministers, and with his health failing, on 3 October 1700 Charles drew up a final will leaving to the second son of the dauphin of France, Philip duke of Anjou, 'the succession of all my kingdoms and dominions, without exception of any'. If Anjou did not accept, the undivided inheritance was to go to the Archduke Charles. On 29 October Charles appointed Cardinal Portocarrero of Toledo as regent. Just before 3 p.m. on 1 November 1700, All Saints' Day, the last Habsburg king of Spain died. On 6 November, after the customary lying in state, his body was taken to the Escorial and interred the next day.

When the king lay dying, most diplomats in western Europe knew the general terms of his will, for it was in Spain's interest that there be a peaceful transition. The elites of Spain were overwhelmingly in favour of the French candidate. Several years before, the English ambassador Godolphin had reported: 'By all the notices I have of the present temper of this people I am persuaded, if it should happen that the young king dye as things now stand, they would tamely goe into the obedience of France'.[2] Under the last Habsburg king they had watched their empire virtually collapse and they were eager to greet a new dynasty and a new, more promising future. In the great hall of the royal Alcázar of Madrid the nobles, grandees and ambassadors waited for the announcement of the king's death, and the formal statement of the terms of his will. The grandee charged with making that announcement, the duke of Abrantes, emerged from the doors of the antechamber and proceeded towards the two most relevant ambassadors, the count of Blécourt for France and the count of Harrach for Austria. 'Blécourt advanced with the confidence of a man who expected a declaration in his favour; but the Spaniard, casting on him a look of indifference, advanced to Harrach and embraced him with a fervour which announced the most joyful tidings. Maliciously prolonging his compliment, and repeating his embrace, he said, "Sir, it is with the greatest pleasure – Sir, it is with the greatest satisfaction – for my whole life – I take my leave of the most illustrious House of Austria!" '³

In spite of such unequivocal events in Madrid, there was still much doubt in international circles. Louis was bound by the terms of the secret treaty he had made. Would he accept the testament that now placed the entire Spanish empire, the richest and most extensive association of territories on the face of the earth, exclusively in his hands? The king did not hesitate. He received the text of the testament of Charles II on 9 November, at Fontainebleau, and within twenty-four hours, after consulting with his Council of State, had decided to accept it. There would, he was convinced, be war if he accepted the succession under the terms of Charles II's will, and war even if he decided not to accept it, since he would have to take up arms against the emperor in order to enforce the last partition treaty. On 12 November he wrote formally to the queen regent of Spain, Mariana of Neuburg, accepting the crown on behalf of the duke of Anjou. On the 15th he went to Versailles and summoned the Spanish ambassador to attend him the next day.

In the morning of 16 November he staged at Versailles one of the great theatrical acts of his reign. The nobles of the realm and the diplomats of Europe were invited to be present. 'The king', reports the diarist Dangeau, 'summoned to his rooms the Spanish ambassador, then called in the duke of Anjou, who was waiting in the antechamber, and said to the ambassador, "You may address him as your king"'. At precisely 11 a.m. Louis advanced through the throng of guests and opened the inner doors of the palace, through which he led out a shy and somewhat bewildered young man whom he presented to the waiting assembly. 'Gentlemen', he proclaimed, 'the king of Spain! His birth called him to this crown, the whole nation desired it and has pressed me to it, and it is my pleasure to grant my consent.' He then turned to Anjou and said: 'Be a good Spaniard, that is now your first duty, but remember that you were born French in order to uphold the union between the two nations; this is the way to maintain their felicity and to preserve the peace of Europe.'

While diplomats and governments busied themselves trying to sort out the political implications of the decision, the French court tranquilly made preparations for the new king's journey to his kingdom. Officials were designated for his household, and the marquis of Louville was appointed as his tutor. Philip took formal leave of Louis and the French court at Sceaux on 4 December. It was on this occasion that the Sun King uttered one of his most memorable phrases. Philip recalled many years later that Louis, 'full of joy, and taking leave of me with a final embrace, said: "There are now no Pyrenees; two nations that have for so long been rivals will in future be a single people; the lasting peace between them will assure the tranquillity of Europe." '[4] His large retinue of over forty coaches then made its way across country, by way of Orléans and Poitiers, and spent the New Year's holiday in Bordeaux. They passed the second week of January in Bayonne, then crossed the river Bidasoa into Spanish territory on 22 January 1701 and entered Irún. The Spaniards laid on entertainments in every town, but the heavy rains dampened many of the festivities, and cut short a visit that the king made to San Sebastian on the 26th. The royal party took the route through Vitoria, Burgos and Guadalajara. In Vitoria he assisted at his first bullfight on Spanish territory: 'the king was so delighted', reports the *Gaceta de Madrid*, 'that after seeing twenty bulls in action, he asked if there were more'.[5] He spent three days in Burgos, especially to view the impressive cathedral and the convents. The crowds coming to see him grew bigger after he left Guadalajara. On the 18th his coach left Alcalá for Madrid. 'On the news of his approach, so many people came from all parts', it was reported, 'that the like has never been seen in Spain, for the six leagues of the highway were one continuous crowd, and the cheers and cries of *Long live the king* added up to a constant commotion.'[6]

Followed by innumerable carriages and cavalry, he entered the palace of the Buen Retiro on 19 February, stopping first at the shrine of Our Lady of Atocha, 'where the choir of the Royal Chapel were waiting to sing a *Te Deum*, but could not be heard because of the excited cries and acclamations of the public'. At the staircase of the Buen Retiro he was welcomed and had his hand kissed by Cardinal Portocarrero and the grandees of Spain. 'To satisfy all the crowds who wished to see him, he went out on the balcony several times.' There were fireworks that night, but because it was Lent all other celebrations were postponed. The day ended on a note of tragedy, for in the crush of people several were trampled to death in the Puerta de Alcalá; the incident made a lasting impression on Philip, who subsequently always took care to ensure that crowds in his vicinity were controlled.

The young man on whom the world's greatest monarchy had devolved was born on 19 December 1683 and was therefore barely seventeen years old, little more than the age at which his most illustrious predecessor, Charles V, had also succeeded to the throne. Like Charles, the youthful Philip spoke no Spanish and had no personal experience of the Iberian peninsula. Nor had the French much confidence in his capacities. Louis XIV was aware of Philip's limitations and took great, even excessive, care to have experts available at every stage to advise the young king. Second son of Louis XIV's son Louis (known as 'the Great Dauphin') and of Marie Anne of Neuburg, of the ruling house of Bavaria, Philip, with his elder brother the duke of Burgundy (prospective heir to Louis XIV's throne) and his younger the duke of Berry, had been brought up in a completely protected environment where they had little contact with the real world. Their moral and social education was put in the hands of the duke of Beauvilliers and of the archbishop of Cambrai, Fénelon. They were also trained to be soldiers and athletes, with riding and swimming in their repertoire of open-air exercises. Yet despite this rigorous upbringing, Philip appears to have been rather withdrawn. The French foreign minister Torcy observed quite correctly that Philip was 'raised in tutelage and unable to act by himself'.[7] The day he took his leave of Louis XIV at Sceaux, we are told by a contemporary, 'the king of Spain fell into a deep melancholy',[8] brought on certainly by fears of his new role, and an omen of the illnesses that he was later to endure. Madame de Maintenon commented that Philip had 'a hesitant character, an exaggerated lack of confidence in himself, and is slow of speech', but also praised 'his piety, his correct behaviour, his feeling for justice and truth'.[9] Her reading of him was, as we shall see, correct in every detail. Because they were doubtful of his capacities, the French took care that Philip should not have to make any decisions by himself, a policy hardly calculated to help the new king gain any great faith in his own abilities.

Philip's arrival in the palace of Buen Retiro, just outside Madrid, was meant to be a prelude to his formal entry into the capital, which was postponed until after Easter. While notables came every day to pay their respects and homage, the king tried to get used to his unfamiliar surroundings. Finally on 14 April he made the official visit to the capital, despite the fact that it rained all morning and most of the afternoon. His entourage left the Buen Retiro at 3 p.m. and made a slow progress, through packed streets and cheering crowds, first to the Prado, then on to the Puerta del Sol and finally to his destination, the royal palace of the Alcázar. Everywhere there were triumphal arches and throngs of notables dressed in festive clothing. The procession took four hours in all, arriving at the Alcázar shortly before dusk. That night there were lights and torches, and celebrations in the streets.[10] The next day the king made a visit to the church of Our Lady of Atocha, and on his way back to the Alcázar passed through the Plaza Mayor, which had been specially decorated for the occasion.

On 8 May he attended a solemn meeting in the monastery of San Jerónimo. Often described as a Cortes, it was both less and more than that. It was less, because only thirteen of the cities in the Cortes of Castile sent delegates. The government had decided that the meeting would cause excessive expense to the cities, and asked that these send credentials only to delegates who were already in the capital. It was more than a Cortes, because the packed assembly included representatives of all the communities of Castile, from bishops and grandees down to the deputies of provinces and cities. There were also representatives of the Crown of Aragon. All had come to swear allegiance to their new sovereign. The young king's appearance was a triumph, and the people of Madrid were overjoyed. Perhaps the only perplexing event of those days was when Philip declined (on the specific advice of his tutor the marquis of Louville) an invitation to attend an *auto de fe* especially arranged for him by the Inquisition.[11] Northern Europeans had never approved of the ceremony, and the French obviously thought that they should distance themselves from such fanaticism. The French were also unfamiliar with bullfights, but Philip, as we have seen, was immediately converted to them.

The refusal to attend the *auto de fe* was a symbol of the new way in which decisions were going to be made in Madrid. Louis felt that the first requisite was to give the new king access to good advice. Among the documents that Philip had to read in these weeks was a long letter sent to him by his grandfather through the French ambassador Harcourt. Another document of advice reached him from Beauvilliers through his new tutor, Louville. Fénelon also sent, through Louville, a number of counsels. Those who gave advice, whether Frenchmen or Spaniards, all concurred on two main points: the king must change his court, and he must change the manner of government.

The hundreds of French officials who accompanied Philip to Madrid were in agreement that they did not like the court; they shared a dislike of this way of life with which they were completely unfamiliar. The style in clothes, in decoration, in etiquette, in culture, all seemed to the fashionable Versailles courtiers to be relics of a past age. The king, accustomed to a different style of diet, refused to accept food cooked in the Castilian way. The chamberlains issued new instructions to the Spanish cooks in the royal kitchens, but they refused to obey, staged strikes, and even insisted on placing their dishes before the king. In the face of such 'intransigence' Philip had no option but to create a completely new royal household, one in which all the key officials were French and would do things in the French manner. In 1701, Louville was made official head of the French household.

The introduction of radical changes in a society that held its customs and traditions to be immutable created uproar. Some changes were permanent: in 1701, after an incident that displeased the king, the dwarfs and buffoons who had been a part of the way of life at the Habsburg court were expelled from the palace. Other entertainments also irritated the French. Without exception, they thought Madrid comedy and music utterly boring; they therefore took the first steps towards introducing foreign theatre and music into the capital. The question of dress was, inevitably, crucial. The symbol of courtly nobility in seventeenth-century Spain had been the stiff collar known as the *golilla* and the first official portrait of Philip as king, painted while he was still in France by Louis's court painter Hyacinthe Rigaud and now hanging in the Louvre, shows him wearing one. The Bourbons later officially disapproved of the collar, though Philip himself kept on using it until 1703.[12] After the first few months of conflict and resistance within the court, the French became more tolerant of Spanish customs and made an effort to coexist with them.

The same compromises did not, however, occur at the political level. For many years the French ambassadors had been emphasising to Louis XIV that the government of Spain needed a complete overhaul. In 1701, the archbishop of Toledo, Cardinal Portocarrero, submitted to Louis an outline of suggested reforms.[13] Philip's own tutor, Louville, was in favour of abolishing the complete system of government councils.[14] 'The people', he wrote later, 'want an absolute king.' While agreeing with such ideas, Louis XIV arranged for the king to be advised by a select committee of government known as the 'Despacho universal', which had existed in the preceding reign but was now transformed into a sort of cabinet council. From 1701 the Despacho consisted of a handful of leading Spanish advisers, but its most important member was the French ambassador, whose advice rapidly came to dominate. The Spanish advisers were gradually edged out, with consequences that were soon widely felt.

* * *

Two months after arriving in Madrid the new king still felt uneasy; he was alone, isolated and homesick. He was unable to pick up the Spanish language, a failure which aggravated his feeling of isolation (throughout his reign he continued to speak only French). He found the Spanish palaces uncomfortable and the Spanish coaches painful to ride in. The custom of having different living quarters for summer and winter, in the same building, seemed strange to people from the north; and the restricted space in both bedrooms and public areas was a problem. One of the French nobles observed that 'in fact there are no real country houses such as our king has, and it is to be hoped that Philip V will arrange to copy in this country some of the buildings we have in France'. With time, it became possible to carry out changes to his living quarters.

In April 1701 Philip suffered an attack of the periodic depressions that later came to affect his life profoundly. It cannot have been the first such episode, for the documents treat the occurrence as virtually normal, and, as we have seen, he had had a similar attack when he left Sceaux. In all probability, he had been having similar experiences for several years. So low were his spirits that Philip now stated that he wished to return to France and to his family. Indeed, during one of his spells of depression, he informed his tutor that 'I would rather go back to being duke of Anjou, and I can't stand Spain'.[15] Afflicted by chronic shyness and lack of self-confidence, he was afraid to participate in meetings of his ministers although he sincerely wished to. Instead of taking part in the Royal Council, he would listen to the proceedings from behind a curtain. 'I can assure you,' his tutor wrote to Torcy, 'that it is a sad sight.'[16] The Spanish nobles soon realised that the firm government they longed for was lacking. One of them commented sourly: 'Ours is a strange government: a dumb king, a deaf cardinal, a president of the Council with no power, and a French ambassador without goodwill'.[17]

Philip had good intentions. He promised to dedicate four hours a day to affairs of state, to have daily contact with the court nobles, and to have his meals where the public could see him. But with his ill-health he found it difficult to regulate his hours. Council meetings were meant to begin each morning at 9 a.m., yet at 11 a.m. the king was still sleeping. He was meant to have his supper at 8 p.m., but turned up only at 11 p.m. When Spaniards at court found that the king did not fall in with their ways, they were disappointed. In the summer of 1701, thinking no doubt of the conflicts over court customs, the French ambassador reported that 'the great love that the people had for the king has almost entirely vanished'.[18] Like much that the ambassadors reported, it was an exaggerated and incorrect view. Succeeding months would prove that popular loyalty for the monarch increased rather than diminished.

Inevitably, Philip was not allowed to choose his own wife; an affair of such immense significance had to be resolved with great care.

Louis XIV had decided that the right wife for him was Marie Louise, daughter of the duke of Savoy, Vittorio Amedeo II (whose alliance Louis valued) and his spouse, daughter of the duke of Orléans.[19] Accordingly, arrangements were made in Versailles for the new queen's household, which was placed under the direction of an experienced lady of the court, the princess of Ursins. Born in 1642 and widow first of the prince of Chalais, then of the Italian duke Flavio Orsini, Marie Anne de la Trémoille became known by the French form of the latter's family name.[20] As *camarera mayor* (head of the household) of Marie Louise, she would come to play an important part in the government of Spain. The proxy marriage of Philip and his queen was celebrated simultaneously in Versailles and in Turin on 11 September 1701. The noble sent from Madrid to negotiate the marriage terms was the Príncipe Pío, marquis of Castelrodrigo, an Italian resident in Spain. He reported that Marie Louise understood Spanish, and was showing her respect for Spanish customs by wearing 'Castilian dress now and then'.[21] Seven days after the formalities the young princess left for Spain from the port of Nice, where Ursins had joined her.

Meanwhile Louis had also decided that Philip must visit his imperial dominions as soon as possible, particularly Italy. With the uneasy state of international relations that prevailed it was imperative for Philip to ensure the loyalty of his Italian territories. To facilitate the plan, on 1 September a decree was issued in Madrid appointing Cardinal Portocarrero as regent during the proposed royal absence and four days later the royal party left the capital. The king's departure provoked riots of protest from a populace that did not wish its recently acquired king to leave. 'Their love for him reached the stage of fury, even idolatry', observed the French ambassador. Five days after leaving Madrid Philip crossed over into Aragon, where he was greeted with cries of 'Long live the King of Aragon! Long live Philip IV!', since he was the fourth of that name to rule over the realm. He entered Saragossa on Friday the 16th, to great rejoicing, with a bullfight that night. During his short stay he swore an oath of loyalty to the *fueros* of the realm and was recognised officially as king. 'The swearing to the *fueros*', commented an observer, 'gave satisfaction to nearly everybody, and earned the king repeated cheers in public.'[22] He rode through the streets and met the citizens. On the 20th he left the city and headed for Barcelona, passing on the 24th through Lleida, where he swore to observe the laws of Catalonia. On the 30th he arrived in Barcelona, but did not make a formal entrance until two days later.

Philip's stay in Barcelona lasted over six months, and all the signs were favourable, with the Catalans laying on appropriate festivities in his honour. On 2 October he went to the cathedral, where he swore to preserve the constitutions of Catalonia and received the homage of the three estates. On subsequent days, reports a witness, 'he is enjoying himself in Barcelona, going out most afternoons, after meetings of the Despacho, to the castle of Montjuic or hunting near the sea-coast'.[23] On 12 October the Corts of Catalonia assembled in the monastery of Sant Francesc, with the king presiding as Philip's French advisers were anxious to dissipate any negative feelings among the Catalans for their French sovereign. The king's speech expressed the hope that the Corts would attend to 'all that may be profitable, advantageous and just for their better government, preservation and benefit, since my concern for them is motivated by the great personal concern and gracious love that I bear them'. In an atmosphere of mutual good will the king upheld most of the petitions of the Corts and granted several privileges of nobility to members of the Catalan elite. In return the Corts granted him a handsome sum of money for the royal purse.

Philip's satisfaction in Catalonia was made more complete by the arrival of his wife. During the voyage from Nice, Marie Louise had an attack of seasickness so she went ashore at Marseille and made the rest of the journey by land. The young couple met for the first time at Figueres on 3 November. A nuptial mass was celebrated that very evening, to complete the proxy marriages that had already been solemnised.

Marie Louise, born in 1688, fair-haired and blue-eyed, was undoubtedly attractive, lively, and with a personality and determination scarcely to be expected of her thirteen years. From the first, she dominated her husband. Philip was eager on his wedding night in Figueres to consummate the marriage. Marie Louise, however, angry at the way the Spanish servants insisted on serving her Spanish food instead of

French, refused to admit her husband to her rooms. Philip in his turn refused to see her on the second night. On the third night, Marie Louise demonstrated that she was both attainable and quite charmed by her handsome young husband, who fell hopelessly in love with his wife. The unusually long time spent by the royal couple in Catalonia was in effect a prolonged honeymoon. On 8 November, reported the records of the city council of Barcelona, 'His Majesty returned with the queen, they entered in carriages through the Portal del Mar to a royal salvo of guns, then they drove to the palace, where they went out on the balcony so that the people could see them'.[24] His young queen gave the diffident Philip the confidence he needed, and as a result he fulfilled his role as king more faithfully. When the Corts had completed their business, the king and queen together brought the sessions to a close on 14 January 1702. Though there remained many unresolved problems, Philip observed that 'we have examined these papers with attention, and have done what we could, and more than we could; I hope that you will, as good subjects, accept what has been done and be satisfied'.[25] It was possibly the most successful meeting of a Corts ever held in Barcelona. The *braç reial* announced that the king had granted them 'special graces and privileges that have seldom been conceded in past Corts', and a later opponent of Philip's regime would admit that the session had resulted in 'the most favourable laws ever achieved by the province'.

Problems of health, however, resurfaced. In mid-November the Diputats had to suspend a celebration in the queen's honour because she had a severe attack of migraine. But the more serious case was that of the king. On 20 December he began to have fever and was confined to bed by his doctors. It is possible that this was another attack of his depressive disorder, but the available documents speak only of 'fever' and it seems unlikely that a newly married young man would have been depressed. He remained unwell and in bed until the end of the first week in January, while the anxious city authorities sent representatives every day to enquire after his health. For the rest of January he was well, thus fortunately able to attend the closing of the Corts. Then on 8 February it was announced that his doctors had bled him, which meant that something was wrong but that they had not the slightest idea what it was. On 9 February they reported 'that His Majesty has the smallpox', then two days later they stated 'that His Majesty has the measles'.[26] The day after, they admitted that neither diagnosis was correct, and that he simply had 'a bit of fever'. Whatever the cause of his renewed illness, the king was on his feet again in two weeks, and in the last days of February he and the queen went out for drives in their coach up and down the Rambla, to the delight of the public. These days also coincided with Carnival; Philip and Marie Louise took part 'in the many celebrations held inside and outside the palace, as well as in masques, and popular entertainments'.[27]

Louis XIV, meanwhile, feared that Philip was spending too much time among the Catalans and with his wife. In October he reminded the king of the purpose of his journey: 'I continue to believe that you must go to Italy next spring'. In the course of 1701 the French king had successfully occupied, in the name of his grandson, the Spanish possessions in northern Italy. War was almost inevitable, and Louis wished to secure all the available fortresses in good time. However, Marshal Catinat, the French commander, was unable to prevent the successful entry into Italy in May that year of an army of the emperor, commanded by one of the most renowned generals of the time, Prince Eugène of Savoy-Carignan.

Philip eventually left the port of Barcelona in the afternoon of 8 April 1702, in a fleet of nine French warships that headed for the kingdom of Naples. His wife remained behind, and immediately dedicated herself with vigour to the role of queen. She left Barcelona on the 10th for Saragossa where she opened the meeting of the Aragonese Cortes on 26 April. Her stay in the Aragonese capital was a long one – eight weeks – but did not serve to expedite the Cortes, where the *brazo* of lesser nobility delayed business because of its internal disputes. The queen swore to preserve the *fueros*, and was granted in return a substantial subsidy. Unfinished business was postponed for a proposed further session to be held in two years' time, but this never took place. On 17 June she left the Aragonese capital and made her way to Madrid. The only realm of the Crown of Aragon to have no meeting of its Cortes was Valencia. 'The rumour in Madrid that the queen is going to Valencia to hold the Cortes there', Ursins wrote to Torcy in May, 'is entirely baseless. We have no instructions in that respect.'[28] The advent of war, in effect, made it impossible for any further Cortes to be held. Apart from a visit he made much later, in May 1719, Philip seems never to have visited the city of Valencia.

* * *

Philip's empire had never been an empire in real terms, and Spaniards had usually referred to it as a 'monarchy'. Essentially it was a vast confederation that covered the globe. The seat of government was in Madrid, the principal city of the Castilian realms that covered two-thirds of Spain and included three-fourths of its population. The Crown of Castile included within its political area wholly autonomous units such as the kingdom of Navarre and the Basque communities of Vizcaya, Guipúzcoa and Álava. 'Autonomy' at this period involved accepting the final authority of the king, but keeping all local affairs separate from Castilian control, and retaining the territory's own laws, coinage, Cortes and customs posts. Even in Castilian realms that were not wholly autonomous, such as Galicia or Asturias, effective daily government was exercised at local level rather than from above, a factor that came to be of some importance in subsequent years. The remaining realms of Spain were grouped in the Crown of Aragon, which consisted of the three mainland realms of Aragon, Catalonia and Valencia, together with the Balearic Islands. Though associated with Castile since the reign of Ferdinand and Isabella in the fifteenth century, the realms of the Crown of Aragon were wholly autonomous from Castile and from each other. In addition the king of Spain ruled over extensive territories outside the peninsula that were all, in some measure, autonomous. In Italy these included the duchy of Milan (in Spain's control since the mid-sixteenth century) and the kingdoms of Naples and Sicily, together with the island of Sardinia. In northern Europe, Spain controlled the provinces of the southern Netherlands, with their capital at Brussels. Over and above these territories, the Spanish crown possessed extensive colonies that enjoyed no political autonomy and were ruled directly by the king: they included the Canary

Islands, the whole of South and Central America, the Philippine Islands, and a handful of fortified towns on the north African coast.

The list of possessions would be longer were it not for the continuous wars that France had waged against Spain in the later seventeenth century. From the 1670s to the 1690s, thanks in great measure to French expansionism, Spain had lost the whole of Franche-Comté, much of its territory in the southern Netherlands, and almost all its major possessions in the Caribbean. Consciousness of their country's weakness weighed heavy on Spanish minds, both then and later. 'The present state of the realm', wrote a Castilian grandee, the duke of Escalona, marquis of Villena, to Louis XIV in 1700, 'is the saddest in the world, for the feeble government of the last few kings has produced a horrible disorder in affairs: justice is abandoned, income spent, resources sold, the people oppressed, and love and respect for the sovereign lost.'[29] 'What was the whole of Spain before the august House of Bourbon came to the throne?' proclaimed a later writer. 'A corpse, without spirit or strength to feel its own debility.'[30]

Spaniards were second to none in exaggerating their own disasters. Since the mid-seventeenth century, when the writers known as *arbitristas* had analysed economic problems and suggested solutions, it had become a dogma that Spain was in ruins. The truth is that all the pessimistic analyses referred to Castile rather than to the peninsula as a whole, and to the politics of Madrid rather than to the life of the provinces. There were of course many serious problems. Just before the end of the seventeenth century, both the English and the French ambassadors were agreed in their verdict on the condition of Spain. Louis XIV was particularly impressed by a report from his ambassador in 1689 informing him that 'what is needed is a complete revolution before establishing good order in this state. Such a revolution can be found only by changing the form of government.'[31] Was Spain truly in such a terrible state?

From the point of view of the government in Madrid, it undoubtedly was. The advisers of the new king looked for three principal things when they came to Spain. They sought an effective administrative machinery to help them rule; an army with which to defend the country; and money with which to finance both administration and army. They found that none of the three was available. Coming from a France that had an extensive bureaucracy, an enormous army (the biggest in Europe), and a generous budget, they were bitterly disillusioned. But from the point of view of the people of Spain, there were very many promising signs in the opening era of the eighteenth century, nor did the evidence necessarily point to a country in total disarray. Certainly, there had been times of crisis in previous decades,[32] but they were now past.[33] In Castile inflation was subsiding, the currency was stable. Throughout the peninsula, as a sign of healthier times, the population had been increasing since the 1680s and the dreaded plague had disappeared. If citizens had complained in the past of the burden of taxes, they had not done so for a generation. The reign of Charles II was the only one in the Habsburg era when no new taxation was imposed on the people, when changes were attempted in the system of tax collection, and when inflation was decisively checked by government policy. In all the major seaports commerce was increasing prior to 1700. In Bilbao the Basques were beginning a period of success, in Andalucia the port of Cadiz was beginning to supplant that of Seville. In the last decades of the seventeenth century the harvests were rich. For Valencians it was a time of opulence in food and wine.[34] All along Spain's Mediterranean coast, the people were optimistic and the commercial elite thriving. These were the years when the Catalan lawyer Narcís Feliu de la Penya and his friends began to dream of resuscitating the economic vitality of their province.

* * *

Philip left his Spanish realms at a particularly inopportune moment. There were rumours of war in Europe, and his Spanish advisers were very unhappy that he should leave when he was most needed. There circulated in Madrid at this time a pamphlet, dated February 1702, which expressed Spanish dissatisfaction: 'The absence of His Majesty from Spain is open to irremediable hazards and mischiefs. What greater glory could we Spaniards have than to see our king traversing the whole land with his triumphant banners?'[35] After years of uncertainty about the succession, Spaniards felt that the new king should dedicate himself to consolidating his territories in the peninsula.

But Louis XIV, perhaps quite rightly, felt that the delicate international situation required a positive gesture towards Italy by the new king. Versailles was faced by a hostile military alliance, agreed upon at the end of 1701 between England, the United Provinces and the emperor. Louis was left with the support in Germany of only two princes, the duke of Bavaria and the elector of Cologne. In the summer of 1701 he had also managed to secure a treaty of alliance with Portugal. But his other allies deserted him, the most notable defector being the duke of Savoy, who allied with the emperor in October 1701, at virtually the same moment that his daughter was joining Philip in Barcelona.

Philip's visit to Italy confirmed what Louis XIV had feared, that many Italians had little sympathy for the new dynasty or indeed for Spain. In September 1701 the authorities in Naples uncovered an extensive conspiracy, led by a group of nobles, to stage an uprising in favour of Archduke Charles and assassinate the viceroy. Those involved were arrested and some were executed. The entire Italian visit would be plagued by political instability. However, when the king arrived in the port of Naples on 18 April, he seemed satisfied with his reception. 'They did not think I would come', he wrote to Louis.[36] That same day he visited the cathedral, where the phial containing the dried blood of St Gennaro duly performed the miracle of liquefying for the king. Among the entertainments put on for him early in May were a concert of music by the famous composer Alessandro Scarlatti and the same composer's opera *Tiberio*. The experience, which confirmed elements of his education in France, infused in him a taste for Italian music that lasted all his life. Later in the month, on 20 May, a formal royal entry was made into the city, accompanied by festivities and fireworks.

Philip soon found that the kingdom of Naples was a sea of troubles. The Habsburgs had carefully cultivated the loyalty both of Spanish officials there and of the provincial Neapolitan nobility. While Philip was in Naples, the allied European powers (England, the United

Provinces and the Empire) simultaneously declared war on Louis on 15 May 1702, thereby setting in motion the War of the Spanish Succession. The dynastic conflict immediately raised political problems for Philip V, who had looked forward to visiting the pope and paying his respects but was now told by his grandfather that he must put the idea out of his head. Naples was by tradition a feudal possession of the papacy and Philip could not formally use the title of king of Naples until the pope had confirmed the feudal tenure. Pope Clement XI's position, trapped between the claims of the major Catholic powers, was unenviably difficult, and he tried his best to make no decisions of any sort. However, his inaction was understandably interpreted as hostility by the effective ruler of the Spanish empire, Philip V, and would lead several years later to a break in relations between Spain and the papacy.

After six weeks in the kingdom of Naples, Philip prepared to travel to his duchy of Milan. He had wished to make a visit to Sicily, where there had been an insurrection against Spain in the previous reign, but was persuaded by Versailles that he would do the Sicilians a favour by sparing them the cost of a royal presence there. Before departing, as a courtesy to the pope he sent his ambassador to convey his greetings. Then on 2 June his fleet of twenty galleys set sail northwards. They spent a day in the port of Livorno, where Italian notables came out to the royal ship to pay their respects. The same happened in the port of Genoa. Eventually on 11 June the fleet entered its destination, the port of Finale, on the coast of Liguria. For the next seven days the king and his large group travelled overland towards Milan. For Philip the journey was by no means uncomfortable: part of it was done by coach, and when the roads became difficult he was carried on a litter. Only when conditions were good was he allowed to ride on horseback. Four days after leaving Finale, he was joined by his father-in-law the duke of Savoy, who accompanied him for the rest of the journey until they entered the city of Milan on 18 June. Milan, for over two hundred years the most hotly contested territory in all Italy because of its strategic position, was on a war footing.

The few weeks that he spent in northern Italy were of decisive importance for Philip. For one thing, the symptoms of the illness that was to change his entire life became more pronounced. In Naples, he had suffered attacks that lasted several days and incapacitated him almost entirely. 'For some days now', he wrote to Louis in May 1702, 'I have been suffering from vapours that prevent me writing to you.'[37] His formal entry into the city of Naples was, for example, delayed by five days because he was confined to the palace by bouts of depression. Immediately after the festivities of the entry, he was again confined to bed for a couple of days, and was bled by his doctors.[38] The way in which the private problems of his illness affected the public role that he was supposed to play in affairs of state can be seen in one small example. In response to a question from his grandfather, he confessed that many of his letters had not really been written by him but by his tutor Louville, who accompanied him in Italy. 'I didn't have much confidence in myself and was not yet used to writing official letters, but at present I am getting more used to it.' The 'vapours' that he reported to Louis XIV took the form of intense depression, a wish for isolation and headaches that left him unable to do anything but retire to bed, where he refused to see anybody except his doctors. The indisposition would last for several days and affect only his mental and psychological condition, but not his physical health. The symptoms had disappeared by the end of his Naples visit but recurred in Milan, where during the festivities for his arrival he retired to his rooms, would speak to no one and was willing to see only the faces he knew. He reported feeling that he was about to die, that his head was empty and was about to fall off his shoulders.

The Milan visit was particularly important as it was Philip's first contact with war. Undoubtedly he shared in the military ethic that his grandfather had done so much to cultivate, but paradoxically war also had for him a specially therapeutic role. It presented a challenge that helped him almost at once to overcome his depressions. It transformed him at a stroke from a condition of extreme indolence to one of highly charged activity. These lows and highs became, for the rest of his life, the two poles between which his spirits oscillated. 'He appears to have', a French diplomat reported from Milan, 'more of a taste for war than for any other activity.'[39] Less than two weeks after arriving, Philip left for the front. It is easy to imagine the excitement that his first military campaign aroused in the breast of the 18-year-old king. His conduct during the Italian campaign shows his total enthusiasm for the war, and affords us an unusual insight into his character.

The Franco-Spanish forces in Milan were commanded by the duke of Vendôme, Louis-Joseph de Bourbon, one of France's leading generals who knew the Spanish peninsula and had in 1697 led an army that captured Barcelona. On 12 July, Philip's group joined Vendôme. The king spent the next few days inspecting the troops and the military positions in the area of Cremona. 'Everywhere there was acclaim and applause for the king', according to an official, 'and the troops cheered him continuously.'[40] On the 23rd he presided over a council of war in what was a purely formal role, for the real commanders were Vendôme and Marshal Villeroy. However, Philip took an active part in the first successful military engagement, at a place called Santa Vittoria, where the Bourbon forces were victorious. The king was 'on horseback more than fourteen hours, but displayed such ardour that all were encouraged by his energy and enthusiasm'.[41] It was reported that he threw himself into the fighting without any concern for his own safety. The principal battle took place on 15 August before the town of Luzzara where Prince Eugène had his camp, and despite a high number of casualties, was indecisive. The French later claimed that it was a victory, because they took possession of the town of Luzzara. Philip had commanded one of the detachments and when criticised for placing his life in jeopardy during the battle he retorted, 'All are risking their lives for me, reason enough that mine should not be counted of any greater importance than theirs'.[42] The risk was very real (there are reports of casualties right next to him), but provided him with the stimulation he needed. His dedication explains not only his later participation in the campaigns of the peninsula, but also the considerable importance that he gave to war as a method of resolving political problems.

On 2 October he left the front and returned to Milan. While he was there one of the most famous incidents of the war occurred in Spain. News reached Philip that the English and Dutch fleets had attacked the Spanish treasure ships from America while they were anchored in Vigo harbour in October 1702, captured all the silver on board and destroyed all the vessels. A soldier accompanying the king, who was later ennobled as the marquis of San Felipe and wrote a famous history of the reign, was appalled.[43] The truth, as the king found out when he returned to Spain, was quite different from the news he had received.

*   *   *

The king left Milan early in November and took ship in Genoa on the 17th of the month. That same day the fleet put in at Monaco, where notables came on board to greet him. Bad weather the next day, however, made him decide to put ashore at Antibes, and the royal party made the rest of the journey overland. Philip was content to be on French soil once more. However, though invited to go to Paris, he preferred to continue towards Spain, after spending three days in Marseille. He arrived in Perpignan on 15 December and on Wednesday, 20 December, at 4 in the afternoon, entered Barcelona on horseback. It was a triumphant homecoming. He and his retinue went directly to the cathedral, where they assisted at a solemn *Te Deum* to give thanks for his safe return. After three days of ceremony and entertainment Philip left Barcelona on the Saturday, but then went to Montserrat, where he chose to spend Christmas. The day after Christmas, he resumed his route homeward. On a cold rainy night in mid-January 1703 he was met at Guadalajara by Marie Louise, and together they returned to Madrid on the 17th. The *Gaceta de Madrid* reported how 'all admired our victorious King, full of vitality and energy, and unaffected by the long journey, as he received the acclamations of the public all the way to the palace'.[44] Philip had certainly matured considerably during his stay in Italy, but had also missed his wife. Their reunion restored his sense of well-being and reinforced his new-found confidence; he no longer had headaches. Endorsing this positive note, the *Gaceta* reported in February that 'Their Majesties are in perfect health and during these days of Lent entertain themselves with Spanish and Italian theatre plays'.

But the members of his court, particularly his French advisers, recognised immediately that with Marie Louise at his side there was no way that they could control the king. Philip's tutor Louville was particularly resentful. He presented to his superiors in Versailles a portrait of a king

Europe in the Reign of Philip V

who spent excessive time in his queen's arms. The couple remained closely attached to each other, and refused to go to any of the palaces outside Madrid. 'Not just the Escorial and Aranjuez but even the Pardo remain unknown to the queen', the marquis of Louville complained.[45] It was quite true; for example, the queen saw the Escorial for the first time only in 1705. And since she herself was controlled by her *camarera mayor*, the princess of Ursins, it was the latter who came to be regarded by many advisers as the real power behind the throne. It was a typical scenario of personal rivalries and factional struggles. Ursins herself always denied that she was exercising undue influence. Whether real or imagined, these power games played a significant part in the politics of the court of Madrid.

During her husband's absence in Italy, in the months that she was regent, Marie Louise began to make improvements in the living conditions in the palaces.[46] She took charge of changes in the furnishings of the royal Alcázar: 'I am going to touch up my palace a bit', she noted in July 1702, 'that is, in ways that will not lead to great expense'.[47] She took account too of Philip's complaints about his lodgings, for the king, Ursins wrote to a friend, 'has said many times to the queen that his apartments do not please him because they are too melancholy. She has decided to do him a small favour and to open a chimney in his bedroom and make three of the doors bigger.' Little money was available, but essential changes were carried out and in the Alcázar all the antechambers and corridors connecting with the royal apartments were opened out and broadened. The royal bedrooms were altered to allow more light in, and the decoration was changed by the introduction of tapestries and furniture more in accord with French taste. The queen also imposed a palace etiquette similar to that practised at Versailles.[48] Marie Louise, meanwhile, could not overcome the resistance of the palace cooks, and had to make her own meals. In 1707, she was still making 'onion soup' in her private chambers because the kitchens refused to do so.[49]

During Philip's nine-month absence from Spain, the situation in Castile had deteriorated rapidly. Members of the ruling Castilian elite fought bitterly with each other for a place in an administration that was changing radically. The presence of French officials at court provided the biggest source of conflict since many Castilian grandees, accustomed to a system in which they had always enjoyed precedence at court, objected to the protocol privileges granted to French nobles and diplomats. In July 1701 a small group of them, led by the dukes of Alba and Arcos, sent directly to Louis XIV a memorial in which they claimed that their blood and privileges gave them precedence over the nobles of France.[50] 'The decision that has been taken', they protested, 'offends the most lofty and exalted body in the Spanish Nation.' Their memorial was immediately replied to by a group of French nobles.

In the same month, the former chief minister of Charles II, the count of Oropesa, expressed his disappointment that the new French-dominated regime in Madrid could find no place for his services. Bit by bit, important sections of the Madrid elite began to separate themselves from the government, their disenchantment fuelled by thwarted ambitions and personal resentment. But there was too a stirring of old attachments of honour to the house of Austria, as in the case of Oropesa. Other grandees also drifted towards expressing their sympathies for the house of Austria and their hostility to the Bourbon government. The most startling case was that of the admiral of Castile, Juan Tomás Enríquez de Cabrera, duke of Rioseco and count of Melgar.[51] Concealing his dissatisfaction with the regime, he accepted from Portocarrero's hands the post of ambassador to France, leaving Madrid in September 1702 with an unprecedentedly large retinue of 300 attendants and 150 personal carriages. Instead of heading for Paris, however, he suddenly changed direction and fled to Portugal, where he denounced the Madrid government and entered the service of the archduke. It was an ominous defection, and one accompanied by that of the count de la Corzana, Diego Hurtado de Mendoza, a former viceroy of Catalonia and friend of the admiral, who complained that 'the ministers in power are not favourable to me'. Mendoza also left in 1702 to offer his services to the archduke.[52] From 1704 he served as a commander of the allied forces based in Portugal.

During these months the Madrid government received a secret report that 'it has been learned through a reliable source that there have been meetings between the dukes of Medinaceli, Montalto, and

Infantado, the Constable, the marquis of Leganés . . . and other gentlemen, gathering regularly in the house of Medinaceli, where they hold
long and secret talks'.[53] In fact, there was no secret about the grandees'
antagonism, which could be seen clearly in the meetings of the councils. In one such meeting, the marquis of Villafranca complained
angrily that decisions of the king in Italy were being made by the
French while at another the count of Montalto, on being reminded that
France was giving help to Spain, retorted that it was also helping to
ruin Spain.[54] Disillusion ran much deeper than this in parts of Castile,
where during 1704 an important conspiracy was uncovered in Andalucia. 'In the kingdom of Granada there were movements to bring in
the archduke. It was said that on the day of Corpus in 1705, the plotters would seize the Alhambra and proclaim the archduke [king].'[55] The
plot's leader was the count of Cifuentes (see Chapter 2); included
among the conspirators was the count of Eril, who was reported to have
stated that 'he is a faithful subject of His Majesty, but the French are
dogs'.[56] Eril and other accused nobles were arrested and confined in
the Alhambra.

Dissatisfaction among the nobility was widespread. Louis XIV was
committed to changing totally the form of government in Castile by
reducing all the old Habsburg councils down to one alone and concentrating decision-making in the Despacho, a policy calculated to
antagonise the whole Castilian political class. The famous Council of
State, theoretically the most important in the monarchy, ceased to function. 'It disappeared shortly after the king's arrival', according to the
duke of Saint-Simon in his *Mémoires*, 'and has not been used since.'[57]
Likewise, in 1702 the council of Flanders, which had dealt with the
affairs of the Netherlands, was suppressed, because the French were
in firm control of that country and did not see the need for the council.
Even in the Despacho, decisions tended to be made not by the
Spaniards present but by the French. According to the marquis of San
Felipe, the French ambassador 'made the principal decisions, and left
Portocarrero nothing to do. This made him greatly discontented, he
spoke ill of the French and said that they should not usurp control that
belonged to the Spaniards.'[58] Indeed, during Philip's absence in Italy,
'the ministers complained that they have their hands tied, that on the

smallest matters they have to await the decision of the king, who makes no decisions without consulting his grandfather, and that all this wastes a lot of time'.[59]

Louis XIV had no intention of modifying his policy. In 1702 he told his ambassador that 'it is to be wished that one could carry out a general reform in all the different states of the monarchy. But as this idea is too vast, he [ambassador Marcin] must try as far as possible to remedy the most pressing evils and think principally of enabling the king of Spain to contribute in some way to the war that the king [of France] is preparing to endure.'[60] A whole team of French administrative experts and military officers descended on Madrid. Among them was an official called Jean Orry, who arrived in 1702 and was entrusted with the formidable task of revising the state of the monarchy's finances. By the summer of that year, then, the direction of affairs in Madrid was firmly in French hands. The French ambassador controlled decisions in the Despacho, and the princess of Ursins in the name of the queen made general policy decisions. In practice, there was continuous conflict between the ambassadors and the princess, a situation that was agreeable to neither and least of all to the Spaniards. Ursins was a dominant figure who played, in effect, the role of chief minister, since she corresponded directly with Louis XIV and her approval was essential to all government decisions. Although her quarrels with the ambassadors were serious, she managed to retain the confidence of France, remaining at her post in Spain for nearly thirteen years.

When Philip returned to Madrid in 1703, he found that the government was functioning smoothly, despite conflicts and tensions. Cardinal Portocarrero left the government and the king took control personally, working principally with Orry and other advisers. He assisted at meetings of the Despacho, where he issued instructions to the two administrative secretaries, the marquis of Ribas and the marquis of Canales. 'This method of working', he informed Louis XIV that September, 'is very satisfactory to me, because I can in this way receive all the explanations I need and can make decisions on each matter with full information.'[61] Throughout the war years, Philip continued to be an active and conscientious king, the French

ambassador Amelot reporting in 1705 that he 'sends me every day the
memoirs and reports regarding war and finance, and after I have
examined them with Orry I take him the replies or the orders that I
have drawn up. He usually approves them and then sends them on
to be put into effect'.[62] Philip may have lacked experience, but not
ideas or the will to work. At the first Despacho that Amelot attended in
May of that year, the king agreed that a certain matter be referred to a
council, 'and turning to me,' Amelot reported, 'he added that there
were some matters on which two hundred councils needed to be
consulted before making a decision, but there were others on which
none need be consulted'.[63]

It was the misfortune of the young and inexperienced 18-year-old
king that he was trapped in a complex political situation which had
few parallels in the history of Europe. His sponsors, the French,
who wished to make the creaking machinery of the Spanish empire
work adequately, were committed to major administrative changes
that threatened to provoke widespread opposition. His subjects, the
Spaniards, nurtured grievances that brought them into conflict with
him, with the French, and even with each other. Finally, his international neighbours were insisting that he abandon power and allow
them to take over. No ruler of Spain had ever faced such formidable
obstacles. Philip's personal capacity for survival was, apparently with
good reason, doubted by all who had known him as a young man in
France. Even his old tutor Fénelon had serious misgivings, later
expressing the opinion (in 1710) that the only way to achieve peace in
Spain was for Philip to abdicate the throne. Yet, against all odds, Philip
would demonstrate in the end that he had the capacity to outlast all his
critics and all his enemies. Only factors beyond his control frustrated
his early promise.

* * *

Though the European phase of the War of Succession had commenced,
the peninsula had not yet been seriously affected. Allied propaganda
was insistent that the war had been engineered and provoked by Louis
XIV, an accusation that was in some measure true. According to the

allies, Louis had reneged on his agreements in the partition treaty and so had made conflict inevitable. He also took measures that seemed calculated to provoke the English. In September 1701, he had recognised the title of the Old Pretender, James III, as 'king of England'. Worst of all, he seemed to be contemplating the eventual union of Spain with France, a step that would make him the most powerful ruler on earth. His intervention in government in Madrid could be interpreted in no other way. Louis, of course, would have put a different interpretation on each of these matters, but that was less important than the view taken by the other European powers.

Were the allies defending the peace and security of Europe against an expansionist France? Though the fate of the peninsula was of considerable importance to England, the United Provinces and Austria, the three powers were more immediately concerned with power politics in their part of Europe. This explains why the major campaigns of the war were all fought in northern Europe, where the most famous generals – the duke of Marlborough and Prince Eugène, neither of whom ever visited the peninsula – were employed. The conflict over the Spanish throne was in reality more than a dynastic one; it formed one crucial part of a larger struggle: for domination in Europe and in Europe's overseas markets.

The War of the Succession developed into a virtual world war, with military and economic repercussions that stretched from Russia to Peru. In the English colonies of North America, where the conflict against contiguous Spanish colonies took on serious proportions, it was known as 'Queen Anne's War'. We may consider briefly the objectives of each of the participants in Europe. Emperor Leopold I claimed for his Habsburg dynasty the entire Spanish empire, and had sent (as we have seen) his troops into Italy long before the outbreak of hostilities. His principal logistical weakness was that Austria had no navy of its own, and therefore relied entirely on the English and Dutch for maritime support. The Dutch had been fighting for thirty years against France, and refused to accept any political arrangement that gave Louis XIV control over western Europe. They therefore insisted on the complete separation of France and Spain, favoured the division of the Spanish empire, and above all maintained as absolutely necessary the creation of a line of military fortresses (a so-called 'barrier') between France and the southern Netherlands. The British, who until 1702 had the same ruler as the United Provinces, William III of Orange, shared Dutch aims, but were particularly interested in securing commercial privileges (and possibly territory) in America.

Once the war became inevitable, Louis could afford to express his real intentions. He was determined, he told Philip, to protect the latter's inheritance. He wished to leave his grandson in control of a stable and prosperous kingdom, and therefore never ceased to give him advice. Further, Louis was concerned to keep the riches of America out of the hands of the English and Dutch. The French were obviously also interested in exploiting their good fortune in obtaining control of Spain. 'One could gain great benefits for French trade', a merchant of Nantes reported to the government. 'The principal means would be to make the peoples of this monarchy, both in America and in Europe, cast off their black clothing in order to adopt our fashions and dress in the French way'.[64] The instructions given by the French government to their ambassadors after 1701 reflect this interest: they 'must pay particular attention to maintaining and increasing the trade that the French do there'.[65] The report of a French official speaks for itself: 'Spain united with France brings us so many benefits that we must make every effort to support the king of Spain'.[66] Above all, the French government was interested in trade with America and the possibility of obtaining American silver. 'On the accession of Philip V to the crown', a later ambassador reported, 'the French saw the lack of action in the Spanish court, and wished to have their share in the profits from this rich trade'.[67] Louis's own view, as expressed to his ambassador in Madrid, was quite clear: 'the main objective of the present war is the commerce of the Indies and the wealth that they produce'.[68]

Apart from commercial interest, Louis XIV was keen to ensure the integrity of the Spanish monarchy, a policy that entailed serious sacrifices on the part of France. In 1701 French troops were sent into the Spanish Netherlands and into northern Italy to secure Spanish possessions while the French navy was equipped to maximum strength to resist the known superiority at sea of the English and Dutch. All of this involved immense expense, and Louis could feel justified in asking Spain to cover part of the cost.

* * *

The first military moves in the peninsula consisted of efforts by the English to seize Cadiz, not only because it controlled trade to America but also because it would be a convenient base from which to launch an invasion of Spain. In July 1702 a joint naval expedition, totalling fifty English and Dutch vessels under the command of Sir George Rooke, invested Cadiz. On board was a landing force of about 14,000 men, under the duke of Ormond, who intended to secure a land base that might serve as a point of entry for an invasion force. But after a month in the area, during which smaller towns such as Puerto Santa Maria were occupied, the admirals and the military commanders could not agree on a policy.[69] In addition, fierce resistance from a rather poorly garrisoned Cadiz made its capture impossible, and sea conditions made ship manoeuvres hazardous. Facing certain failure, Rooke re-embarked the troops and set sail at the end of August.

The disappointment at Cadiz was soon forgotten at news that the Spanish silver fleet, due from America under the escort of the French admiral Chateaurenaud, had arrived off the coast of Galicia. The English had already sent out a fleet under Admiral Sir Cloudesley Shovell to attack the galleons, and Rooke was at the same time informed of the situation. The latter instantly sailed to Vigo Bay, where the silver fleet had taken shelter, and proceeded to land Ormond's troops. In an engagement between the allied and French ships on 23 September, most of the Franco-Spanish fleet was destroyed, many prizes taken, and much merchandise sent to the bottom. The booty taken was substantial.

Both then and since, the episode of Vigo was viewed as a disaster for Spain. But Philip arrived back in Madrid in time to receive a report about what had really happened. The silver fleet from America had indeed been destroyed: of the three galleons and thirteen vessels in the fleet, all were burnt and destroyed except for six that were taken by the enemy. The French naval escort with the fleet was also

annihilated: of the fifteen French warships and one frigate, all were
destroyed except for six that were captured and integrated into the
English navy. The crucial fact for the Spanish government, however,
was that none of the vessels belonged to it. Much merchandise was
destroyed at Vigo – pepper, cacao, hides, cochineal – but none of that
belonged to the government either. What it really owned, the silver
from America, had in fact been unloaded from the ships long
before the English and Dutch attacked, and deposited for safety in the
castle of Segovia. In February 1703, after consulting with a committee
of theologians, Philip issued a decree stating that in view of the crim-
inal attack of the allied warships on the Spanish fleet, he had decided
by way of reprisal to confiscate all the silver that had come on the fleet
for English and Dutch traders. In addition, he intended to take as a
loan part of the silver that had come for Spanish traders and the
Consulate of Seville.[70] In total, he managed to keep for the government nearly 7 million pesos, representing over 50 per cent of the silver
from the fleet and the biggest sum in history ever obtained from the
American trade by any Spanish king. It was a magnificent outcome to
an episode that had seemed to be a disaster.[71]

Despite these military actions, the war for the moment was limited
to northern Europe and Italy. Louis XIV was busy preparing defences
on France's northern frontier, where (as he foresaw correctly) the
principal military campaigns would take place. By an agreement
with the Madrid government, France took over complete control of the
southern Netherlands, which till then had been nominally under
Spanish rule, and became responsible for defence there. Despite
the naval attacks on Cadiz and Vigo, the allies were planning no
military action in the Iberian peninsula, and awaited the proposals of
the emperor.

During the year 1703, however, the war moved towards Spain, an
event precipitated by Portugal's change of alliances. From April 1702
a new English minister in Lisbon, John Methuen, began attempts to
attract the Portuguese away from their alliance with Spain. In October,
the arrival of the defecting admiral of Castile helped to advance negotiations. Finally, in May 1703 Methuen's son Paul, who was active in

the same mission, succeeded in accomplishing one of the greatest diplomatic triumphs of the century, a treaty that was very favourable to Portugal's pretensions and that bound the country firmly to support the forthcoming allied military campaigns.[72] The allied cause was further strengthened by the defection of Vittorio Amedeo of Savoy from his alliance with France; Marie Louise's pleading letters to her father did nothing to change his mind.

In September 1703 the Austrian claimant to the Spanish throne, the archduke Charles of Habsburg, second son of Emperor Leopold I and only eighteen years old, was proclaimed king of Spain in Vienna. He then left for England, and in January 1704 (now known by his supporters as Charles III of Spain) paid a visit to Anne, queen of England, at Windsor. The Whigs, who formed the government in London, were ardently in favour of the war and hoped to gain substantial economic benefits from it. Accordingly, in February Charles was accompanied to Lisbon by a fleet under Sir George Rooke. On board were 300 German troops, 4,000 English and 2,000 Dutch. Charles disembarked in the Portuguese capital on 7 March, amid great celebrations. Early in May, news was received in Lisbon that Spanish forces had crossed the frontier into Portugal. The war in the peninsula had commenced.

Philip, who had matured considerably since his accession to the throne, was fully prepared to play his part. Although he was still actively engaged in his studies, and was developing an interest in literature and the theatre,[73] by 1703, he was having classes in the art of fortification. All his lessons, directed by Louville, were given in French. His hours of leisure were spent in riding and above all in his favourite occupation, hunting. Ursins commented that 'everybody admired the king for his skill and elegance' on horseback. The portraits of him painted at this time present him as he clearly was: an elegant and handsome young aristocrat, cultured and refined, supreme ruler of the biggest empire on earth.

CHAPTER TWO

The War in the Peninsula, 1704–1709

'ALL ARE RISKING THEIR LIVES FOR ME, REASON ENOUGH THAT
MINE SHOULD NOT BE COUNTED OF ANY GREATER IMPORTANCE
THAN THEIRS.'

PHILIP V, AT THE BATTLE OF LUZZARA (1702)

The realities of war soon broke in on the refinement of court life. It would prove to be an unprecedented scenario. For the first time in history the peninsula was invaded by foreign troops, half of them Protestant, their specific aim to overthrow the ruling dynasty. Nor was there any way for Spain to defend itself adequately: because of the country's constitutional system there was no national army and no navy. In 1704, Philip's advisers in Madrid were discovering to their horror that Spain did not have the resources to wage a war.

In the 1690s a government report claimed that Spain had 'insufficient ships and soldiers for our defence' and was, indeed, completely exposed from the sea. In 1702 there were no royal warships in the Mediterranean, only galleys; in the Atlantic and America there were in theory twenty warships, four of which were reserved for the protection of shipping from the Americas. On land, the fortresses of the peninsula were badly equipped and poorly manned. In the whole of Spain in 1703 the crown had at its disposal just over 10,000 infantry soldiers and 5,000 cavalry,[1] but both lacked adequate armament and were therefore ill-equipped to fight. Most of our information on the condition of Spain comes from the detailed reports drawn up by Jean Orry, who had been sent by Louis XIV to check to what extent the country could contribute to the war effort. Orry arrived in Madrid in June 1702, and began to draw up the biggest catalogue of the resources of the Spanish monarchy ever to have been attempted.[2] He confirmed that in terms of finance, in 1704 only 3.5 million escudos a year were available for the war, when perhaps 12 million were needed.[3] The situation was clearly desperate.

The first task was to make sure that Spanish resources could be identified and this was what Orry, with the close collaboration of the king, set out to achieve. He found that the government of Castile could count on only half the money that it normally collected in taxes (the other half went to creditors); that the treasury received virtually no silver from America; that the soldiers of Spain had outdated military equipment and no uniforms; and that 'in 1701 the king of Spain received almost no gunpowder from the realm'.[4] He took steps to subsidise the establishment of factories to produce munitions, which in the meantime had to be bought from France. 'The king of Spain', wrote the French minister of war Chamillart in 1704, 'needs gunpowder, arms, bullets, explosives and other munitions. His Majesty will be happy to supply him, on payment of the price obtaining in France.'[5] A fundamental change in government accounting was also adopted, with the establishment in 1703 of a new War Treasury, which gradually began to replace the old Council of Finance as the principal body for the collection of state revenue.

It was evident that France had to supply everything that was lacking in Spain. 'Spain is entirely your responsibility,' Louville wrote to Chamillart, 'without troops, without money, without a navy, in a word lacking in everything that pertains to the defence of a monarchy as extensive as this.'[6] Since it was Louis XIV's intention to send French soldiers to fight at the side of the Spaniards, it made sense to standardise equipment wherever possible. To this end, in January 1703 the

Madrid government was persuaded to abolish all its antiquated weaponry (the arquebus, the pike) and to adopt the French flintlock with bayonet. In March that year a directive ordered the conscription of 1 per cent of the male population. In September 1704 the old *tercios*, dating back to the early sixteenth century, were abolished and substituted by regiments. For the first time, an order was issued in 1703 that all soldiers wear a standard French-style military uniform. The war effort, effectively, was put into French hands. French industry benefited from the tens of thousands of pistols, swords, flintlocks, bullets, uniforms and tents that now flowed across the frontier.[7]

French advisers in Madrid, however, were busy quarrelling among themselves about the direction of the war effort. The dominant voice was that of the princess of Ursins, who was strongly backed by Marie Louise and the king. But she incurred the enmity of all the French ambassadors, one of whom succeeded in having Louis recall her and Orry to France in July 1704, against the express wishes of Philip. Indeed, the French foreign minister Torcy complained that 'quarrels among the French have done more harm to affairs in Spain than all the plotting of the disaffected'.[8] The king and queen refused to accept the absence of Ursins, insisting to Louis that he send the princess back, and she returned triumphant to Madrid in August 1705. Orry had meanwhile also returned, in May. For the next ten years, through her close friendship with both Louis XIV and Madame de Maintenon, as well as through her influence over Marie Louise, Ursins played an important role in the formation of policy in Madrid. Her real influence may, however, have been exaggerated, both at that time and by later historians. Her own view, expressed in a letter dated 1703, was that 'both my friends and my enemies imagine that I govern everything. I really would like those who share this opinion to have the weight of the government of Spain on their heads, they would admit quickly enough that only a crazy person would take on such a burden voluntarily.'[9]

Just three months before her return, a new French ambassador also arrived in the shape of Michel-Jean Amelot. He not only managed to work amicably with the princess, but also won the confidence of the king and queen, becoming in effect the founder of the new Bourbon state. Amelot, marquis of Gournay since 1693, was an eminent diplomat who had served as ambassador in Venice, Portugal and Switzerland. He had strict principles of conduct, and political beliefs that won him respect in some quarters but hostility in others. Never depressed by opposition, he worked his way methodically towards a rational system of government in Spain, his most useful long-term achievement perhaps being the encouragement he gave to the careers of young Spaniards anxious to serve the crown, among them the jurist Melchor de Macanaz.

* * *

The first detachments of French troops sent to help the king entered the peninsula in February 1704, under the command of the marquis of Puységur and the duke of Berwick. A month later the entire royal army, comprising both French and Spanish troops, and numbering 18,000 infantry and 8,000 cavalry, left Madrid for the Portuguese frontier with the king and Berwick at their head. James FitzJames, 1st duke of Berwick, was the illegitimate son of the last Catholic king of England, James II, and of the sister of the duke of Marlborough. Now aged thirty-four, he had been in the service of France as a general since 1693. As for Philip, his role was similar to that he had played during the Italian campaign in 1702; he would take part in all the engagements of the next few years. He left Madrid on horseback in the afternoon of 4 March, like a hero, cheered by the crowds, and a short way outside the city changed to a coach which took him by way of Talavera to the front.

The army marched first against the Portuguese garrison in the border town of Salvatierra, which capitulated in May. The aim was to capture Lisbon and thereby eliminate the military threat to the penin-sula. Berwick and the king were to advance down the right bank of the Tajo as far as Villa Velha, while the rest of the forces, commanded by the Netherlands general the prince of T'Serclaes Tilly,[10] were to follow the left bank and occupy Portalegre. Other small expeditionary forces were sent in: Francisco de Ronquillo[11] was to invade Beira, the duke of

Hijar northern Portugal, and the marquis of Villadarias was to invade from Andalucia.

The strategy worked excellently. T'Serclaes captured Portalegre and the king presided personally over the capture of Castel-Branco. There were, however, problems with supplies of food and munitions. It was the first real military campaign to be undertaken within Spain for half a century, and deficiencies soon became apparent. 'I see such great shortages among the troops', Philip reported, 'because of lack of bread and non-payment of wages, that it appears as though the money I got from the Vigo fleet has not served for much, since troops are deserting on all sides.'[12] Louville in those months confirmed that the Spanish troops were 'neither paid nor lodged, and the bread they receive is worthless'.

But the coming of the summer heat made it impossible to continue with the campaign. The Spaniards held their positions, and Philip went home, reaching Madrid on 16 July. He was greeted in the capital like a conqueror, the celebrations continuing for six days. The summer heat, however, did not affect the war at sea, where the allies were in a position of strength. The fleet under Rooke, which included thirty English and nineteen Dutch warships, moved into the Mediterranean and made a half-hearted attack on Barcelona (30 May), then set sail for Italy. On finding that the main French naval forces under the count of Toulouse and Admiral d'Estrées were stationed at Toulon, Rooke decided it was safer to return to Portugal, where his force was augmented by twenty-three warships under Admiral Shovell. The allied admirals considered the possibility of once again attacking Cadiz, Spain's main port for trade with the Americas, but rejected the idea as impracticable because of the lack of support from land forces. Eventually in July they accepted the advice of Prince George of Hesse-Darmstadt, former viceroy of Catalonia for the last Habsburg king and now commander-in-chief of allied forces in the peninsula, that it might be worth assaulting Gibraltar.

On 1 August 1704 Rooke positioned his ships in the bay of Gibraltar. That afternoon the forces disembarked and cut off communications between the fortress and the mainland by occupying the isthmus. Despite his tiny garrison and poor defences, the governor of the city rejected a call to surrender. Thereupon, on the morning of 2 August the allied ships drew up in the bay, preparatory to an attack. Early next day they began their bombardment. By the evening the governor agreed to capitulate, terms were agreed, and three days' grace was given. On 6 August, Darmstadt occupied the city in the name of Charles III, though effective possession remained with the English.

That same month the battle of Málaga, the biggest naval engagement of the war, took place. The count of Toulouse with the French fleet was known to be in the vicinity of Gibraltar, so Rooke kept his forces on the defensive, and in mid-August he was joined by Shovell. On the 23rd the count of Toulouse was sighted off Málaga, and an engagement became inevitable. On the morning of the 24th the combatants took up battle positions. On each side the countries' principal naval forces had been committed, making the outcome a matter of great importance. The French fleet under Toulouse and d'Estrées consisted of 96 vessels; on the allied side there were over 68 vessels, commanded by Admirals Rooke and Shovell, Vice-admiral Sir John Leake, and two Dutch admirals. The battle, which began in mid-morning, lasted for thirteen hours and wreaked severe damage to both sides. It was, Rooke commented later, 'the sharpest day's service I ever saw'. Though not a single ship on either side was taken or destroyed, numerous vessels were seriously incapacitated, several high-ranking officers were killed, many others (including Toulouse[13] himself) were wounded, and the casualties on both sides ran into thousands. The effective stalemate made both parties unwilling to prolong the conflict, and next morning they steered away from each other. The remainder of the war in the peninsula saw no further naval engagements of importance, and the respective navies were employed principally in giving support to land campaigns.

Meanwhile the allies had decided to use Portugal as their base for the invasion of Spain. By spring 1704 the total allied commitment in Portugal was about 20,300 foot and 700 horse, with the English detachments under the command of the duke of Schomberg, second son of the famous French marshal of that name.[14] The commanders-in-chief of the Portuguese and allied forces were two Portuguese generals, the count of Las Galveas, aged over eighty years, and Antonio Luis de

Souza, marquis of Das Minas, aged sixty. Their campaigns in early 1704 were purely defensive ones against the highly successful Bourbon forces. When Berwick retired in July, however, some readjustments for the autumn campaign were carried out. Schomberg was recalled to England and replaced by another eminent French exile, Henri de Ruvigny, count of Galway, who joined the allied forces late in August. Minas was made supreme commander of the troops.

These changes were mirrored by others that took place in Philip's camp. News of the fall of Gibraltar had made the authorities in Madrid concerned about the safety of Andalucia, and Berwick had been asked to divert his troops to the south. Aware of the allied build-up across the Portuguese border, he had refused to move. Consequently he was replaced by the marshal count of Tessé and ordered to return to France. Marie Louise, a friend of Tessé, supported the change, in part because she hoped to obtain the return of Ursins through Tessé's influence in France, in part also because she felt that Berwick was 'a great dry devil of an Englishman, who always goes his own way'.[15] Berwick, suitably rewarded with the Order of the Golden Fleece, returned to France. Meanwhile, in February the king and queen made their first visit to the Escorial, where they assisted at a *Te Deum* and afterwards went hunting.

Tessé's first task was to recover Gibraltar. In February 1705 he arrived before the Rock and began measures to recover a fortress whose loss had seriously hurt Spanish prestige. A Spanish force, commanded by the marquis of Villadarias, had been conducting a siege of the place since October 1704. However, attempts to recover the town failed and the idea of a blockade seemed impractical. Tessé finally received permission to raise the siege from Philip, who had always insisted on the need to recover the fortress. The Bourbon troops struck camp at the end of April and retired to the north. The case of Gibraltar is of some significance. As was to happen subsequently with whole provinces of the monarchy, the allies succeeded in their conquests because they encountered inadequate defences. By contrast, the Bourbons had difficulty regaining territory because the allies took care to garrison and equip places they had occupied. The parlous defences of Spain, rather than any preference of the people for Charles III, explained in great measure the success of the allies. In Gibraltar, a small but efficient garrison of 2,000 English, 400 Dutch and 70 Catalans successfully resisted a besieging Franco-Spanish army of 18,000 men for eight months. English naval support also made it impossible for the French to attack from the sea. The successful defence of Gibraltar had a very important consequence. The city had no strategic or commercial value, and had initially been captured only as a place from which to mount an invasion. The dramatic siege now suddenly enhanced its importance in English eyes.[16] Gibraltar became a symbol of victory that no British government would contemplate relinquishing.

In the first half of 1705, there was little military activity outside the Gibraltar area. In April the allies, from their base in Portugal, tried to launch an invasion of Spain by laying siege to Badajoz, but Tessé, who arrived from Gibraltar in May, prepared to defend the city. When the allies resumed the siege in October after the summer season, the French general forced them to retreat to Portugal. The count of Galway lost his right arm during the military operations, and had to be attended to by surgeons sent by Tessé. Allied successes in 1705 were made possible only by sea operations.

The contacts maintained with several Catalan leaders by Darmstadt – their last Habsburg viceroy – influenced the English government to send an invasion fleet to the Mediterranean coast of the peninsula. An expeditionary force for Catalonia was formed. Since Darmstadt was a Catholic and therefore ineligible for service under the English crown, command of the force was given to the earl of Peterborough (who was not a soldier), while the naval contingent was entrusted to Shovell. On 26 July 1705 the English ships set sail from Lisbon, with Archduke Charles on board. At Gibraltar on 4 August more troops were embarked, and six days later the fleet put in at the port of Altea, in Valencia. Altea joined the allies, thereby beginning the movement of civil disturbance in Valencia. On 22 August, the fleet anchored off Barcelona.

At Altea the allies put ashore an exiled Valencian soldier, General Basset, together with a small force of Spanish troops. While Basset devoted himself to raising Valencia for Charles III, the allies were besieging Barcelona for the second time. On this occasion they were completely successful. No attack was made against the city for three weeks, during which time the allies were in regular touch with their friends in Catalonia. Then on 13 September a surprise night attack was made by a small force of 1,000 men who scaled the walls of Montjuic. Prince George of Darmstadt was killed in the assault, but the garrison surrendered. The allies then fortified Montjuic and used it as a base to direct fire against Barcelona. On 9 October the city capitulated. Two months later, on 16 December, Basset entered Valencia city in his sovereign's name and by the end of 1705, the provinces of Catalonia and Valencia were largely in allied hands. The unpopular viceroy of Catalonia, Francisco of Velasco, was hurried on board the English ships when an anti-Bourbon riot broke out in the streets of the Catalan capital.

*   *   *

The relative ease with which the allies gained the advantage in the eastern territories of the peninsula had a tremendous impact on the government in Madrid. Supporters of Philip V were quick to use the term 'rebellion', but the situation was far more complicated than that. 'All these malcontents one sees in the kingdoms of Valencia and Catalonia', a correspondent of the French minister of war wrote from Spain in 1705, 'cannot complain of the king, for he demands nothing of them; so that all their grievances arise only from the harshness of their lords who crush them with taxes and tributes'.[17] In the course of that year, internal events in the territories of the Crown of Aragon prepared the way for allied military successes.

The energetic resistance of Barcelona to allied attack in September 1705 demonstrated that the Catalans were by no means in favour of rebellion. Yet there were seeds of discontent. Catalan commitment to the cause of the allies was given substance by an agreement made at Genoa in June 1705 between a small group of discontented Catalans and agents representing the English government. In return for Catalan support of the archduke, the English would supply men and weapons, and protect the *fueros* of Catalonia.

Those who made the 1705 agreement did not by any means speak for all Catalans. As in other parts of the peninsula, people in Catalonia had differing opinions on the arguments for supporting Philip V or the archduke. Barcelona had excellent memories of Philip's visit in 1701, when the Corts wrung concessions from the king that were 'the most favourable laws ever achieved by the province'.[18] But in certain parts of the province there was strong anti-French feeling among both the elite and the common people rooted in their experiences during preceding decades. There were also echoes of past social conflicts. In the area of Vic, epicentre of support for the archduke, the rebel leaders in 1705 were 'the same people who were responsible for the revolt of the Barretines',[19] an important uprising that had shaken the region sixteen years before. Barcelona, for its part, had bitter memories of the savage sea-bombardment of the city by the French in 1697, when Vendôme directed the siege. 'This siege', the high court, the Audiencia, reported to Madrid at that time, 'has witnessed more blood and fire than any seen in our time, the bombs ruined a great part of the city.'[20] Another witness was more precise: 'The city was left in ruins, with the destruction of 2,500 houses'.[21] It was probably Barcelona's worst disaster of the century. When the city surrendered to Vendôme many Catalans, including a lawyer named Feliu de la Penya, left Barcelona rather than live under French rule. It was Feliu and his friends who now in 1705 refused to accept the French dynasty. They linked up with a small popular movement that had begun in the area of Vic and by October that year was dominant in many other areas of the principality.[22] At this stage, the conflict in Catalonia was more in the nature of a little civil war among Catalans themselves than a deliberate rejection of the Bourbon regime.

In Aragon, the loyalty of the people to their new king was counterbalanced by a long-standing hostility to the French, based mainly on proximity and on commercial rivalry; indeed, the people were, according to a distinguished Aragonese historian of the time, 'natural enemies of the French'.[23] In 1704 the Madrid government was busy uncovering a plot whose central figure was an Aragonese noble, Fernando de Silva Meneses y Zapata, count of Cifuentes. According to one accomplice, Cifuentes had declared that 'the king was no king but only a viceroy through whom his grandfather dominates us', and that 'he was bound in duty to hate the French, for they killed his father and his brothers'.[24] Cifuentes was detained in Madrid in November 1704 but escaped to his estates in Aragon. In Saragossa, 'the people rioted in his favour' and he used his influence during the year 1705 to stir up popular opinion against the French dynasty.[25] He then went on to Barcelona, where he joined the archduke, leaving behind him a realm in turmoil.

Three important issues tried the patience of the Aragonese in that year 1705. First, the king asked the estates of the realm for a grant of money (a 'free gift') to help with the costs of war, since Castile had paid all the costs so far. In response, the viceroy, the archbishop of Saragossa, reminded the king that 'this kingdom is so privileged by its *fueros* that no individual pays any tax whatsoever without the approval of the general Cortes'.[26] But Philip had no intention of calling a Cortes in the middle of a war. Second, in the autumn the king replaced the viceroy by a Castilian, the count of San Esteban de Gormaz, an appointment that infringed the spirit of the *fueros* which gave the Aragonese the right to have one of their own nation as viceroy. Third, in November the government despatched troops across Aragon to Catalonia. There was a novel presence of French soldiers among them which gave rise to serious incidents. On 28 December 1705 the first two battalions of a French regiment under the command of Marshal Tessé began to enter the city of Saragossa, when suddenly the gates were shut fast by the inhabitants and rioting broke out. Taken utterly by surprise, the soldiers were set upon and beaten, some killed, by the populace to cries of 'Protect our *fueros* and liberties!' Tessé had to seek refuge in the viceroy's residence. San Esteban jumped on his horse and rode through the streets in an attempt to pacify the mob. Everywhere he went there were cries of 'Long live our viceroy!' and 'Protect our *fueros* and leave no Frenchman alive!'[27] Similar uprisings occurred at about the same time in other parts of the realm. It was clear that Aragon had ceased to be secure for the royal cause.

Hostility to the French was likewise a very important factor in disturbances in Valencia. Father José Miñana, whose *De bello rustico valentino*, written in Latin between 1707 and 1723, is an invaluable contemporary analysis, reported that 'hatred was aggravated by traders and the very great number of other Frenchmen'.[28] It is possible also that the failure to hold any Cortes of the realm in Valencia had an effect on the governing classes. But the real cause of the rebellion had its roots in events that had shaken Valencia over a decade previously, when in 1693 a peasant rebellion was suppressed but not extinguished.[29] When the allied fleet appeared off the Valencian coast in the late summer of 1705, it met few military obstacles. The coast was defenceless so that on 10 August the allies took the coastal town of Altea without any trouble. There they set ashore Francisco García, one of the leaders of the rebellion of 1693. His task, which he fulfilled brilliantly, was to raise the Valencian peasants as he had raised them in 1693, with promises of freedom from taxation. The fleet also disembarked (as we have seen) another Valencian exile, Juan Bautista Basset y Ramos, who had served as a general in the Imperial armies in Milan and Hungary, and was now put in charge of the allied campaign in Valencia. Between them, these two Valencians helped to win a good part of the population over for the archduke.

In Valencia, the first objective of the invaders was the strategic fortress and town of Denia, which capitulated on 17 August. The fall of Denia threw the capital city, Valencia, into confusion. Aware of its own lack of defences, on 21 August the city sent a letter to Philip V asking for the dispatch of troops. Philip replied the same week, saying he intended to send cavalry immediately. Meanwhile, the threat to Barcelona, which fell to the archduke on 9 October, began to absorb most of the king's attention. In these circumstances, the defence of Valencia was relegated to second place, and the government ordered the few troops available in Valencia to proceed at once towards Catalonia. The order created consternation in the city council of Valencia: not only had Philip not sent the troops he promised, he was now withdrawing the few that remained in the province. The situation became considerably worse when in December 1705 one of the two cavalry regiments in Valencia, commanded by a Catalan, Rafael Nebot, rebelled and declared for the archduke. Nebot's defection was heavily influenced by the fact that his brother, Josep Nebot, was one of the commanders of the rebels in Catalonia, and had succeeded (with

English naval help) in capturing the cities of Tortosa and Tarragona for
the allies in September 1705. On 15 December the three estates of the
Cortes of Valencia sent an appeal to Philip V emphasising their complete lack of defence. It was all in vain. That night some of the city's
leaders seized the viceroy, took from him the keys to the main gate,
and let the enemy in. Valencia fell, in the words of the viceroy, the
marquis of Villagarcía, 'without a single shot being fired from the
walls'.[30] The city was taken over by the peasants and the rebels. Then,
on 2 February, English and Catalan troops under the command of the
earl of Peterborough entered Valencia. It was a good base from which
to extend allied control of the province.

A narrative of the complaints of the people in the Crown of Aragon
is not in itself sufficient explanation for the ease with which those territories passed into the control of the allies. The most notable aspect of
allied success is that the people offered little resistance. For supporters
of Philip V this demonstrated beyond doubt the guilt of the Aragonese.
The facts, however, can be read a different way. We have seen that
the peninsula was almost wholly lacking in adequate defences. In
Catalonia, as in Aragon and Valencia, many towns and cities fell into
allied hands for the simple reason that they lacked armaments. In
Catalonia the key fortress of Girona discovered in July 1705 that its
artillery was insufficient for resistance, and decided to capitulate to the
allies because it had no alternative. Lleida in September 1705 found
that it was virtually defenceless; the citadel had only twenty-five soldiers
for its protection, and in the current military situation there was no
hope of outside help. To make matters worse, the inhabitants were
growing restive and had lost faith in the city's ability to defend itself.
In a very serious popular disturbance on the 15th of the month, the
rioters demanded that Lleida make its submission to the obviously
superior forces of the archduke.[31] These examples, which can be multi-
plied indefinitely, demonstrate that the decisive factor in the War of
Succession was not the political preference of peoples, but the military
capacity of the contending armies.

Of considerable importance in Aragon, too, was the role of many
parish priests, who supported their parishioners' rebellion to such
an extent that the archbishop of Saragossa could claim in 1706, if

somewhat exaggeratedly, that 'the greater part of the clergy of this realm have been rebels'. Similar allegations were made about the clergy in Valencia. In Catalonia at a later date the bishop of Barcelona and the abbot of Poblet were among those suspected of treason. There is no incontrovertible evidence to explain any possible infidelity among the clergy, but it is true that many were eventually forced to flee from Bourbon Spain. It was reported from Rome in 1713 that over 3,000 exiled Spanish clergy had taken refuge there.[32]

When all is said and done, the many possible explanations for alleged rebellion in Catalonia, Aragon and Valencia fail to answer the fundamental question: Why did it happen? One fact, and one fact alone, triggered everything else. As a historian has observed, 'there is nothing to show that there would have been a rebellion without the presence of the allied fleet'.[33] It was the English fleet that provoked the fall of Gibraltar, the rising of the Valencian peasants and the defection of part of Catalan society. The British imposed the War of Succession on Spain. Would they remain faithful to the Spaniards whom they had incited to civil war?

*   *   *

By the beginning of 1706, the two chief Mediterranean cities, Barcelona and Valencia, were in allied hands. Their loss was a major blow to the Bourbon cause, and Louis XIV put all his resources at the disposal of his grandson.

Philip wished to emphasise the importance of the coming year's campaign, and accompanied his troops in person. In the first week of December 1705, he and the queen went out every day to Carabanchel, just outside Madrid, to watch the army exercises. Meanwhile, in response to appeals from his grandson, in February 1706 Louis XIV created Berwick a marshal of France and sent him back to Spain to conduct the campaign against the Portuguese. The king left his capital on 23 February, escorted by a large following of nobles. 'There is no time to be lost in advancing to Barcelona', he wrote to Berwick four days later. 'I can tell you', he wrote to the marshal from Belchite at the beginning of March, 'that I prefer to go straight on to Caspe, in order to be closer to the army, for I have an enormous impatience to be at its head.'[34] Accordingly, on 12 March he arrived at Tessé's camp at Caspe. The decision was taken to head straight for Barcelona, bypassing Lleida and other towns that had given their obedience to the archduke. At Barcelona, Tessé would be joined by more French troops from Roussillon and would be supported by the French navy from its base at Toulon. Philip evidently enjoyed his role as a soldier and leader, but the marshal was unhappy about having a superior authority at his side who might question his decisions. 'The king's presence', he grumbled to Louis XIV, 'does more harm to his service than if he had stayed in Madrid.'[35]

On 3 April Tessé and Philip arrived before Barcelona, where two days before the French fleet from Toulon, commanded by Toulouse, had dropped anchor. North of the city, a French force under Marshal Noailles that had entered through Roussillon also invested Barcelona. The entire besieging force was French. Meanwhile the count of Cifuentes, who commanded a small Catalan force that had occupied the routes behind the French and cut off any chance of retreat, made sorties against Tessé's camp. On 5 April Cifuentes made a daring night raid on the quarters of the king, who narrowly escaped capture but lost his household plate and personal goods. After this incident, Philip preferred to spend his nights on board the French fleet.[36] At the end of April Montjuic was taken, and it seemed that the city must fall. At this juncture, on 7 May Vice-admiral Leake arrived with a fleet of 39 English and 13 Dutch ships, together with military reinforcements, forcing Tessé to abandon the siege.

That same day the French fleet quietly withdrew, and on the night of 11 May Tessé struck camp and retired north towards Montcada. The siege represented a very high cost to the French: they lost 6,000 men (including wounded and deserters) and a large amount of military stores which they had to leave behind. It was a singular and memorable occurrence that, not long after daybreak on the morning of the retreat, at 9 a.m. on Wednesday, 12 May there was a total eclipse of the sun.[37] The phenomenon lasted two hours in all,[38] bringing with it a strange lowering of the light, a short period of total darkness and a sharp drop in temperature. Since the sun was the symbol of Louis XIV, its eclipse at this moment was taken as a good omen by the allies. The event was also clearly visible in the city of Valencia, where the sudden darkness in daylight hours caused consternation among the population,[39] who were already in a state of high tension after four months of occupation by the archduke's forces.

Philip, of course, was extremely unhappy about the decision to withdraw; 'the resolution did not please him', commented the marquis of San Felipe, 'not only because it appeared unfitting but also because it called into question his own capabilities.'[40] The presence of allied forces in Aragon made it necessary for him to cross the frontier, and he arrived in Perpignan in France in the last week of May. From here he followed a route that took him through Narbonne, Carcassonne, Toulouse, Pau, Saint-Jean Pied-de-Port, Roncesvalles and Pamplona, returning in this way to Spain through Navarre. As he travelled through the Pyrenees, the young king was able to evaluate his situation and his responsibilities, and his letters to his grandfather at this point reveal his growing maturity and determination. 'I cannot express to you my grief', he wrote to Louis on 20 May, 'at having to leave the archduke in Barcelona, and I shall have no rest until I fight him wherever he is.' Seven days later he wrote from Narbonne: 'This morning I left Perpignan in the carriage, and I plan to continue my route, in the belief that there is nothing more important than to return as soon as possible to Spain, nor can I get there soon enough to defend it personally against the efforts of my enemies'. On the 31st he wrote from Navarreux: 'I believe that there is nothing more dangerous in this situation than to show a lack of confidence in the Castilians, when they on their side have shown so much fidelity and zeal. The best way for me to confirm them in their good intentions, in so delicate a time as this, is to throw myself into their arms with complete confidence. I have decided to take the direct route through Pamplona rather than that through Bayonne.'[41]

On 6 June Philip was back in Madrid, but his position appeared to be desperate. He was losing the war and, as he found when he returned to Madrid, he was also losing the support of many among the ruling class in Castile. Marshal Tessé was witness to the disorder in the political direction of the struggle. 'The king', he wrote, 'will

never have troops or an army so long as there is no prime minister
to rule over the other ministers and do in Spain what Cardinal
Richelieu did in France. . . . Spain needs a king who wishes to be
master or who will select a chief minister in whom he invests full
authority.'[42]

*   *   *

The crisis in the capital was intense. During the early years of the war,
major innovations were being carried out in the government, provok-
ing alarm and outright hostility among the ruling classes. We know of
the fundamental constitutional changes that took place later in the
Crown of Aragon, but their importance has tended to overshadow the
very significant changes that were also taking place in Castile. In reality,
the new regime altered the constitutions of Castile several years before
it destroyed those of Aragon. The innovations represented little threat
to traditional power structures, and even strengthened Castilian state
authority; the seriousness of what took place has therefore not been
recognised. But profound changes did occur, and many Castilians did
not like them.

Within the royal court, tensions developed quickly. One of the
main areas of conflict was the royal guard. A royal cavalry guard had
existed since the previous reign,[43] but after his return from Italy
Philip carried out various changes and finally in a decree of June 1704
created, on the basis of plans drawn up by Orry and approved by Louis
XIV, a royal guard consisting of four companies of 200 men each.
The great novelty was the introduction of non-Spanish soldiers.
While two of the new companies were Spanish, commanded by
the count of Lemos and the duke of Sessa, one was Italian, under the
duke of Popoli, and one Flemish, under the prince of T'Serclaes
Tilly. The Castilian grandees objected fiercely to the foreign guards,
whose presence they considered an insult to their own ability to
protect the king. In August 1705 the duty captain of the bodyguard,
T'Serclaes Tilly, was given the task of standing immediately behind
the king at mass in the royal chapel, so conferring on Tilly apparent
precedence over the grandees of Spain. In consequence, the nobles

of the household refused in a body to attend mass. The 'strike of the grandees' caused a major scandal. T'Serclaes Tilly was created a grandee of the first class in order to circumvent opposition; the two Spanish grandee captains, Lemos and Sessa, were dismissed and sent to do military service in the Netherlands; and the presidents of the Councils of Castile and Aragon were sacked.

Fundamental changes were also taking place in the administration. The instruments of change were the French officials and notably the ambassadors, of whom the most important was Amelot, who since 1699 had also been one of the directors of French commercial policy. He stayed in Madrid from May 1705 to September 1709, and his term of office marked the apex of French influence in the Spanish capital. The changes, all directly related to the war, affected every branch of government. The entire war machine of Castile was put into the hands of the French, who came to a country that had been accustomed for two centuries to fight its wars abroad rather than at home. The commanders now appointed to direct the war in the peninsula were largely French. The leading generals of Philip V – the marquis of Bay, the count del Valle, the prince of T'Serclaes Tilly, the marquis of Castelrodrigo, the duke of Popoli – were all foreigners, and their superiors were, like the dukes of Vendôme and of Berwick, always French. Only French control could make it possible to co-ordinate military and naval strategy, in a theatre where support from the sea was of immense importance. Spanish armies benefited from foreign advice, which rationalised their methods of recruitment, organisation and equipment, and supplied the war material needed to fill the enormous shortfalls in Spanish equipment and resources.[44]

The entire administration of the Castilian state was entrusted to French advisers.[45] The conciliar system of the Habsburg dynasty was in practice abandoned, and the Despacho turned into a cabinet council staffed by French. The ruling elite of grandees was excluded from power. Louis XIV wrote to Amelot in 1705: 'the principle you are to lay down with regard to the grandees is a valid one. It is necessary to preserve all the external prerogatives of their rank, and at the same time to exclude them from cognisance of all matters of government'.[46] It was not, of course, possible to exclude the grandees from a nominal role in government, but Amelot found that most of them were incompetent, reporting to Louis XIV that 'it is depressing to have to choose between such people'.[47] The grandees were excluded from consultation, with the result that when Barcelona fell into allied hands in October 1705, the disaster was blamed on the Francophile government, and released a flood of fury among the nobility in Madrid. The Council of State met in special session on 9 November, and the fourteen councillors present denounced the mismanagement of the war. The meeting was opened by Cardinal Portocarrero, who regretted that the council had not been consulted on the defence of Barcelona. After him, each speaker in turn delivered a bitter and hostile speech, the count of Fuensalida going so far as to say that the Catalans had rebelled only because they had been treated badly. The council formally demanded 'a good understanding between the king of Spain and his Councils, by which alone he can defend his realms; they should have cognisance of everything, to give their opinion; and the king of Spain must endeavour to make himself loved. . . . This is the way to defend the realms. . . . As for the expenses of war, it is necessary to consult the Councils.'[48]

In 1706 Amelot tried to placate and encourage a special meeting of the grandees, but his words provoked a sharp response. 'The duke of Medinaceli spoke up and said that if there was anything that could give offence to the nation and cause it to be not as faithful to its prince as it had been to all its other kings since the establishment of the monarchy, that could arise only from the contempt shown to it, seeing [as] how the armies were commanded by foreigners, secret councils were held without the participation of the principal leaders, a number of people had come into the realm only to plunder it, and these reasons were only too powerful in causing divisions and making people lend an ear to propaganda that the enemies of the two crowns had distributed.'[49] Finally, the Cortes of Castile was completely superseded, being summoned only once during the war years, in April 1709, to take the oath of loyalty to the heir, the Infante Luis. The king needed neither its consent nor its money.

Discontent continued to spread among the higher nobility. On 10 June 1705 the marquis of Leganés, suspected of heading a conspiracy, was detained by T'Serclaes Tilly in his capacity as captain of the royal guard, and escorted to the fortress of Pamplona. From there he was later transferred to France, where he died in the fortress of Vincennes, outside Paris, in February 1711. Other grandees were involved in the plot, which had ringleaders in Cadiz, Málaga and Badajoz. The centre of the conspiracy was Granada, in particular the Alhambra, where those who had been arrested the year before managed to correspond freely with the outside world. The authorities intercepted letters to Prince George of Hesse-Darmstadt which implicated various nobles as well as canons of the cathedral of Granada. On this evidence all the conspirators were arrested and several of them executed.[50] When the government ordered the rest of the grandees to take an oath of loyalty to the government many refused to do so, because it obviously called into question their personal honour. By 1706, the loyalty of several nobles was near breaking point.

* * *

Philip's return to his capital in June 1706 was timely. In Portugal the armed forces of the allies, considerably superior in numbers and equipment to those of Spain, were preparing to invade Castile under their Portuguese commander, the marquis of Das Minas.

At the beginning of April the allies crossed the Portuguese border, and Berwick was unable to prevent them breaking through successfully to capture Alcántara, on the Tajo. The only troops he commanded were 15,000 Spaniards; the French in the peninsula were all occupied besieging Barcelona. For the next few weeks, the marshal was obliged to stand by helplessly while the enemy pushed successfully through Castile. On 28 April Plasencia fell, on 26 May Ciudad Rodrigo, on 7 June Salamanca. Madrid was now threatened. On 20 June the queen, the court and all the government departments left the capital and retired north, first to Guadalajara and then later to Burgos. When Philip returned from his long detour through France, he put himself at the head of 3,300 soldiers and joined Berwick's troops. But instead of offering battle to the Portuguese, these withdrew to Alcalá de Henares on 25 June. Then, from Madrid, a group of disaffected grandees invited the allies to take possession of the city; on 25 July a troop of 2,000 cavalry under the marquis of Villaverde entered. Two days later the main allied force under Galway and Minas arrived in Madrid.

The fall of Madrid appeared to be a resounding victory for Minas. The Portuguese troops could hardly believe that they had defeated Spain; it all seemed like a dream.[51] Charles III (at the time in Barcelona) was proclaimed king, the dowager queen of Charles II, Mariana of Neuburg, sent her submission from Toledo, and several nobles joined the Habsburg cause. In Toledo the aged Cardinal Portocarrero, who had been pushed out of government by the king's French advisers, celebrated a *Te Deum* for Charles III. News also arrived that on 23 June Spain's chief naval base, Cartagena, had fallen into allied hands with the help of Luis Manuel Fernández de Córdoba, count of Santa Cruz, commander of the galleys of Spain. Two days after the fall of Madrid, Saragossa also fell to the allies and the archduke was proclaimed king there.

In Madrid, a number of discontented nobles took the opportunity to desert the cause of Philip V. At the beginning of the year, three of the four gentlemen of the royal chamber were deprived of their keys for refusing to follow the king to the army at Burgos.[52] Now several grandees came forward to swear loyalty to Charles III, among them the count of Oropesa,[53] the duke of Nájera, the marquis of Mondéjar and the counts of Cardona and Santa Cruz.[54] The count of Lemos, former captain of the royal guard, together with his wife, sister of the duke del Infantado, attempted to join them, but they were detained by loyal supporters of the king and sent as prisoners to Pamplona.

On the whole the people in Madrid, and in virtually the whole of Castile, refused to accept the allied troops. Amelot informed Louis XIV of a few typical instances of the welcome the troops received:[55] a convoy of 800 soldiers from Portugal was attacked by the common people led by their parish priests, leaving eighty of the soldiers dead; enemy couriers could not get through the countryside because the peasants captured them and brought their letters to the royal camp; the villagers of La Mancha put to flight 700 Portuguese soldiers who had been sent to punish them; in occupied Madrid nobody dared cry 'Long live Charles III!', the populace forcing the Portuguese soldiers to shout 'Long live Philip V!' instead. Even bishops took the field against the enemy. The best-known instance was that of the bishop of Murcia, Luis de Belluga; but Amelot was also able to report that 'the bishop of Calahorra mounted his horse at the head of 1,500 clergy of his diocese, all armed and on horseback'.[56] As testimony to the loyalty of the people, San Felipe mentions that in occupied Madrid 'the prostitutes deliberately took special care to entertain and thereby to finish off the army; they went out in groups at night through the camp, and spread their infection that ended the lives of a great many, for in the hospitals there were more than 6,000 afflicted, of whom the greater part died'.[57] Yet, so long as the allied troops could not join forces with the troops in Aragon, or place adequate garrisons in Castile to consolidate their gains, the conquests remained illusory.

However, enthusiasm for their success remained high. After the capture of Saragossa, the allied invaders were in control of the four chief cities of Spain and it only remained for them to consolidate their position. Galway and the Portuguese halted beyond Madrid, in Guadalajara, and waited for Charles to arrive, a delay which allowed Louis XIV to send reinforcements of infantry and cavalry, a total of 12,000 troops, through Navarre to join Berwick. The two forces met at Xidrueque, and their junction sealed the fate of the hitherto triumphant allies.

Though some of the allied generals advised that the archduke should go to Madrid to establish his authority, or else to Valencia, after some hesitation Charles decided to make his base in Saragossa. He entered the city on 15 July, staying in the Aragonese capital till the 24th, on which day he left and made his way to the allied camp at Guadalajara, arriving there on 6 August. His troops reinforced Galway's numbers, but the Bourbon army had already made inroads into territory occupied by them, and a month later, on 4 October, Philip V returned to Madrid unopposed. He wrote to his grandfather: 'I can assure you that I very much regret leaving the front, since there is nothing I have so ardently desired during the whole campaign than to come to grips with the enemy'.[58]

When the court and government returned to the capital, the civil governor of Madrid, Pedro Ronquillo, began enquiries into the conduct of all those who had either recognised the archduke or collaborated with his government while a royal decree of 16 September arranged for the punishment of officials who had participated in the administration set up there by the archduke. Such cases apart, two grandees – the marquis del Carpio and the count of Palma (the latter was a nephew of Cardinal Portocarrero) – were banished from Madrid, the first to Oviedo and the second to San Sebastián. At the same time Philip's restored government took several radical measures. The membership of the councils was reduced so as to increase efficiency: the Council of Castile was reduced from 20 members to 6, that of Finance from 28 members to 10, that of the Indies from 24 to 8. It was a bad omen for the councils, as well as for the bureaucratic class as a whole. The government was using the war as a means to reform the administration. In November a decree extended certain financial reforms to the nobility, and plans were made to collect a special loan from the Church.

Very many nobles had tried to keep a foot in both camps, or else had collaborated only to a minimal degree. Philip had no intention of victimising anybody, and either tolerated the collaborators or allowed them to make their own decisions. He overlooked the conduct of Portocarrero in view of the cardinal's well-known services to the monarchy. Mariana of Neuburg, however, besides being aunt to the archduke was an important symbol and might be used again by the allies. The king therefore sent an armed guard to escort her out of the realm to Bayonne, assuring her that she would find greater security there than in war-torn Toledo. Mariana lived in Bayonne and was allowed to return to Spain eventually in 1739, when she took up residence in the ducal palace at Guadalajara.[59] Despite the few who had wavered, Madrid and the people of Castile remained loyal. 'It has been obvious on this occasion', Marie Louise wrote to Madame de Maintenon, 'that, after God, it is to the people that we owe the crown. We could count only on them, but thank God they count for everything!'[60]

* * *

The recovery of Madrid was of little comfort to Philip, who during the year 1706 also lost control of the whole of northern Italy as a result of allied military triumphs. After a successful march into Lombardy, Prince Eugène joined forces with Vittorio Amedeo and won the magnificent victory of Turin in September. The French commander died in battle, and the remaining French troops withdrew across the Alps. Philip's power in the western Mediterranean was almost completely wiped out, as the victorious allies, aided at every stage by local nobility, went on to occupy strategic points. Although in each case the rebels were small in number, as they had been in Valencia, the presence of naval power facilitated their defection. English ships made possible the capture of the key fortress of Alicante early in September 1706 after a siege of ten weeks. In September too Leake's fleet presented itself before Mallorca, carrying on board the rebel Mallorcan noble, the count of Sevallà, the archduke's nominee as viceroy of the island. The city's fortress resisted for only one day. The capture of Mallorca proved to be of inestimable help in the later stages of the war, since the rebels in Barcelona were able to rely on the island for supplies and armaments. Only Sicily held out for Spain.

In the eastern half of the peninsula, the forces of the archduke were still unassailable. Their situation in Castile, by contrast, was not so favourable. Communications between the allied army and Portugal had been broken by the fall of Madrid into the hands of Philip V, and Galway and Minas had of necessity to rely on their bases off the Levant coast. Accordingly a retreat towards Valencia was ordered. The army crossed the Tajo at Dueñas and marched towards Valverde on the river Júcar. At Vélez on 17 September they were met by English troops that had captured Requena (in July) and the fortress of Cuenca (in August) during their march westwards. Galway pushed on through the valley of the Júcar and crossed the river Gabriel on the 25th. All this while, Berwick had been harassing the allied rear but failed to prevent them crossing into Valencia. On 1 October the archduke entered the city, which he made his capital for the next five months.

The Bourbon cause improved rapidly after this allied retreat, and the last months of the year saw the turn of the tide. On 8 October Berwick sent a detachment to recapture Cuenca, a task that was fulfilled after only two days' resistance. On the 11th Spanish troops commanded in part by the militant bishop of Murcia, Luis Belluga, captured Orihuela, and on the 21st the duke of Berwick entered the town of Elche, an event that was followed, one month later, by the fall of Cartagena. By these successes the territories of Castile, Murcia and the south of the kingdom of Valencia returned to the Bourbon obedience and were used as winter quarters for the royal armies. Aragon was still largely under allied control, but in Extremadura the marquis of Bay, Alexandre Maître, a French general in the service of Spain, had recaptured Alcántara in December.

The strategy now adopted by the allies in Valencia, and one that went against the wishes of the English generals and government, was to divide the available forces and defend gains already made. In accordance with this decision, Charles left Valencia in early March 1707 and went to Barcelona, taking a number of Dutch and Catalan troops with him. Galway and Minas stayed behind to defend Valencia.

*   *   *

Louis XIV had in the meantime decided to send another general to Spain, in the shape of his nephew, Philip of Bourbon, duke of Orléans. Aged thirty-three when he was appointed head of the royal armies in Spain, he had previously been in command of the French troops in Italy and he was destined to play a significant role in the history of his nephew, the king of Spain.

Orléans arrived in Madrid on 10 April 1707, and the troops under him were sent ahead to join the forces of Berwick, camped at Yecla in Murcia. In the belief that a junction of the two French armies had not yet been made, Minas and Galway decided to march into Murcia and attack Berwick's forces before Orléans arrived. On 18 April the king wrote to Louis XIV: 'I wait in anticipation of a battle, so Your Majesty can understand the apprehension I feel, though I have been assured by everybody that our troops are superior in number and in quality'.[61] On 25 April, the opposing armies met on the plains before the town of Almansa. The Franco-Spanish forces, commanded by Berwick, Popoli and d'Asfeld, amounted to somewhat over 25,000 men; half were French, there was also an Irish regiment, and the rest were Spanish. Galway and Minas had a considerably smaller force of about 15,500 men, of whom half were Portuguese, one-third English and the rest Dutch, Huguenot and German; there were no Spaniards. The battle, which began early in the afternoon and went on for two hours, resulted in the total defeat of Galway's forces. The allies lost 4,000 killed (mostly English, Dutch and Huguenots) and 3,000 prisoners, losses which would have been higher but for the flight of most of the Portuguese at an early stage in the fighting. Berwick's total casualties in dead and wounded were also substantial, about 5,000 men. Orléans arrived the day after the victory, too late to share its glory.

The importance of Almansa, the one decisive battle of the War of the Succession in the peninsula, is beyond dispute. By it, Valencia was permanently recovered for Philip V, the principal allied army was shattered, vital moral initiative was regained and the archduke was compelled to rely solely on the resources of his Catalan supporters. At Almansa, the marshal duke of Berwick saved the Bourbon succession. Years later, Frederick the Great of Prussia described it as the most impressive battle of the century.

A grateful Philip suitably rewarded Berwick. 'Immediately after the battle', the duke wrote in his memoirs, 'the king bestowed on me the towns of Liria and Jérica with all their dependencies. He raised them into a dukedom, with the title of grandee of the first class, for me and my descendants.'[62] In addition to these honours, he received from Louis XIV the post of honorary governor of the province of Limousin in France.

The task of recovering the rest of Spain was yet to be done. To that end, subsequent months witnessed a number of sieges throughout Valencia and on the borders of Aragon and Catalonia. Valencia city was taken on 8 May. Orléans now split forces with Berwick, and marched northwards to reconquer Aragon. Within the kingdom of Valencia, the French commander Jacques-Vincent Bidal, *chevalier* d'Asfeld and later marshal of France, reduced the city of Xàtiva. Meanwhile on 26 May, Orléans had successfully retaken Saragossa. With these gains, most of Valencia and Aragon were returned to the obedience of Philip V. After the summer break, Orléans united his forces with those of Berwick and laid siege to the important fortress of Lleida. The city fell on 14 October, but the garrison in the citadel (mainly English and Catalan) kept up resistance for another month, capitulating only on 14 November. It was the first Catalan city to fall into royalist hands since the abolition of the *fueros*, but Orléans did not touch its privileges, and only changed the members of the municipality. In Castile during this period, Ciudad Rodrigo was recovered from the Portuguese on 4 October. The year 1707 ended with the Bourbons on a victorious offensive.

At the royal palace, too, it was a happy summer. In June, the military standards captured from the allies at Almansa were placed with ceremony in the chapel of Atocha in Madrid. And it was not the only triumph of the year. On the morning of 25 August the queen, now aged nineteen, gave birth to Luis Fernando, who received the title of prince of Asturias and became heir to the throne. He was baptised immediately, though a formal baptism ceremony was held later, on 8 December, with Cardinal Portocarrero and two other bishops officiating, in the presence of the grandees, the royal family and the duke of Orléans. The Bourbon succession in Spain had an heir. On the day that Louis was born, reports the *Gaceta*, 'the king very generously wished to show the crowds the new-born prince from a balcony, giving rise to great applause and tears, followed by celebrations, illuminations, fireworks and other demonstrations of joy'.[63] 'Now the Spaniards saw the crown confirmed in a Spanish prince', commented San Felipe, 'and they were more committed to supporting the rule of King Philip.'[64] Not until 7 April 1709, in a special session of the Cortes of Spain where representatives from the Crown of Aragon joined those from Castile, was he officially recognised as successor to the throne. Over 200 delegates and officials took part in the short ceremony.

The following year, 1708, Berwick was recalled by Louis XIV, who needed his services elsewhere. The duke left Valencia in January, passed through Saragossa in February and left the country in March. He did not even have time to take his leave of the king, who was deeply disappointed by the marshal's departure. 'The king and queen', Ursins wrote to the French foreign minister Torcy, 'cannot imagine why one should take from them a general whom they had asked for, who is necessary to them, whom the Spaniards like, and who has made himself fully acquainted with everything concerning the war in this country.'[65]

Orléans was left to take on the siege of Tortosa. Similar changes took place in the allied command. An Imperial marshal, the Austrian count of Starhemberg, was appointed commander-in-chief in Spain, and General James Stanhope – the English envoy to Charles III – replaced Galway at the head of the English troops. Their first concern was to relieve the pressure on Tortosa, but the foreign reinforcements arrived from Italy too late, and on 11 July 1708 the city capitulated to the Bourbon army. It was the second Catalan city to fall into royalist hands, and remained royalist for the rest of the war. Its municipal privileges were abolished the following February, when new city councillors were appointed to replace the old ones, and 'the observance, practice and style of the laws of Castile' were introduced in what was a clear warning to the rest of Catalan territory. Other successes marked the Bourbon campaign in Valencia: on 17 November, the town and port of Denia fell to Spanish troops, and on 7 December the town of Alicante was occupied by d'Asfeld, although its garrison continued to hold out.

That autumn, the duke of Orléans returned to France. Philip had admired the duke as a general in Italy, and had personally requested that he be sent to Spain. But in the peninsula tensions arose between the two. Philip's lack of an heir at that time made Orléans into a likely successor to the Spanish throne; the king felt threatened by this. Moreover, Orléans got on well with the Spaniards, which created further tensions. His successful campaigns in the Crown of Aragon helped to increase suspicions. The day that the city of Valencia surrendered, 8 May 1707, on his own initiative as commander-in-chief Orléans issued a decree pardoning the inhabitants for their act of rebellion, an action he repeated on entering Saragossa at the end of the month. These measures gave rise to the suspicion that he was attempting to win favour in the Crown of Aragon for his claims to the Spanish throne. As if to endorse such fears, in 1709, the year after he had left for France, two of his secretaries, Regnault and Flotte, were arrested in Spain for allegedly taking part in a plot to assassinate Philip V. They had also been in touch with a group of grandees who appear to have promised Orléans their support as possible king of Spain in place of Philip. 'He told me', the duke of Saint-Simon wrote later, 'that many grandees of

Spain and other notables had told him that the king of Spain could not persevere, and had proposed hastening his fall and putting himself in his place'.[66] Further arrests were made two weeks after those of Regnault and Flotte, when the marquis of Villaroel, a general who had served under Orléans, was detained in Saragossa. Significantly, Villaroel later deserted the Bourbon side and joined the archduke in Barcelona. The king, always prone to suspicions, continued for many years to harbour fears of a personal threat to himself from the duke. Louis XIV, well aware of the conflicts within his family, commented in April 1709: 'I have found excuses for not sending my nephew back to Spain this year'.

Philip's correspondence with his grandfather over these months shows that he had matured greatly since the early days of his reign. Instead of obediently accepting all the decisions made by France, he now questioned them. In July 1707 he protested his complete loyalty to Louis XIV but added: 'I confess to you that I don't have the same confidence in your ministers'. And in August 1708, aware of the pressure being put on Louis by the allied diplomats, he affirmed a sentiment which he would later repeat on various occasions: 'I shall never give Spain up so long as I have life, I am not capable of stepping down from the throne to which God has elevated me'.[67]

That same August the archduke's betrothed, Elisabeth von Wolfenbüttel, arrived in Barcelona with the English fleet and married Charles. Also in that month, the presence of the fleet was exploited in order to carry out the conquest of Sardinia, where Cifuentes was installed as viceroy. Minorca was invaded in September by Stanhope and Leake, and reduced after just over a week, its strategic importance being immediately recognised by Stanhope, who wrote to his government that 'England ought never to part with this island, which will give the law to the Mediterranean both in time of war and of peace'.[68]

* * *

The most important consequence of the victory at Almansa was the revocation of the *fueros* (or autonomous laws) of the realms of Aragon and Valencia. Even before the whole of Valencia had been recovered, the possibility of abolishing them was being considered. The decree of pardon issued by Orléans on 8 May 1707 was strongly resented by the government in Madrid because it conflicted with other decisions being made in the capital. Philip and his advisers, however, had no fixed policy or any firm decision about abolition. The duke of Berwick, for example, wrote to Amelot that 'as to the *fueros*, I have always been of the opinion that they should be suspended, but that nothing be said of their extinction'.[69] Both Berwick and Orléans shared the view that it was too early to take such a radical step.

There were, of course, no doubts about the *principle* of abolition, something on which Philip, his French advisers, his generals, and many of his Spanish ministers were all agreed. On the day he issued his pardon in Valencia, Orléans remarked: 'I shall not omit to burn all the archives and all the *fueros*'. Three days after entering Saragossa he wrote that 'it is absolutely necessary to subject Aragon to the laws of Castile'.[70] Louis XIV's advice to the Spanish govern-ment also followed the same lines. Indeed, it is important to bear in mind that the sentiments of Louis and of Philip's other advisers were in no sense directed only against the Crown of Aragon. As we have already seen, the French had strong criticisms of the entire Spanish style of government; they had begun to reform the Castilian system and were now interested in changing that of Aragon. Nor, on the allied side, was the attitude of Archduke Charles radically different.[71] Amelot shared these views completely, and at the time of the conquest of Valencia had in mind a scheme to alter the constitu-tion not only of Valencia but of all Spain: 'after introducing the change in this realm, one would do the same in Aragon and Catalonia, and if there were no problems the same system would be introduced in other realms and provinces of Spain'.[72] The suppression of the *fueros* would be the first step towards reorganising the administration of the whole of Spain, including Castile.

These radical proposals had little to do with any theory of absolutism. The ministers were interested in crown control, military security and, in the words of Louis XIV, 'the expenses of the state'. In June 1707 Louis XIV wrote to Amelot that 'I have always been convinced that the best procedure for the king of Spain, after reducing the realms of

Aragon and Valencia to his obedience, was to suppress the privileges they enjoyed until their revolt. Maintenance of these privileges has been a perpetual obstacle to royal authority, and a pretext by which these peoples have always been exempt from contributing to the expenses of the state.'[73] The cost of the war was immense. In 1704 it was estimated that to feed, clothe and pay the Spanish troops a minimum of 7 million escudos a year was needed, without counting other items that would bring the total to 10 million.[74] At that period the annual revenue of the Spanish crown was relatively low at 9.7 million escudos, of which perhaps only a third could be made available for the war. Expenses continued to rise. Apart from maintaining his own forces, Philip had to contribute to the upkeep of the French troops who were helping him. There were constant disputes about this between Spain and France, although in practice Philip's government paid a high proportion of French costs in the peninsula.

The need for more money was not, of course, the reason given for the constitutional changes proposed by the government in the Crown of Aragon. There had to be a firm theoretical justification. At this juncture a little-known secretary of the Council of Castile, Melchor de Macanaz, drew up several memoranda which he presented to the government. In these and other writings Macanaz, a native of Murcia, emerged as the theorist and architect of the new regime in the Crown of Aragon. And in reality the main supporters of abolition were Spaniards; a majority of the Castilian advisers of the crown were in favour of it. After the recovery of Aragon in 1707 the archbishop of Saragossa wrote to Philip V advising him to 'make a complete change in the political government of Aragon, by establishing the laws of Castile'.[75] The desire to establish Castilian law in the Crown of Aragon had a very long history that went back at least to the days of Philip II.[76] Opposition to the *fueros* may be identified more with a trend in Spanish – and not simply Castilian – political thinking than with any influence of French absolutism.

On 29 June 1707, in a famous decree, Philip V abolished the *fueros* of Aragon and Valencia. Two principal reasons were given. Firstly, the realms 'and all their inhabitants' had defected from 'the oath of loyalty they swore to me', and were therefore guilty of 'rebellion'. Secondly, the royal armies had exerted 'the just right of conquest'. Accordingly, the crown had considered it correct to exercise 'one of the principal attributes of sovereignty', namely the power to change the laws. Wishing therefore to 'reduce all the realms of Spain to the uniformity of the same laws . . . I abolish all the *fueros* and usages observed until now in the kingdoms of Aragon and Valencia'.[77]

There were immediate protests on all sides. Orléans stated that the decree was both mistaken and hasty, and he proved to be right. What, he said, of 'all the nobility of Aragon who did not accept the archduke and who abandoned their estates in the service of the king?' The archbishop of Saragossa, who was also viceroy of Aragon, made the same objection. The accusation that 'all the inhabitants' had been rebels was, he said, false: 'for it is certain that nearly all the nobility, gentlemen and leading persons have been faithful', as well as a great number of towns.[78] The following month, therefore, Philip V issued a new decree, dated 29 July, in which he revised the judgment he had passed on the loyalty of his subjects in Valencia and Aragon. 'The greater part of the nobility', stated the decree, 'and other good subjects, and many and entire towns in both realms, have preserved their loyalty pure and blameless, giving way only to the irresistible force of enemy arms.' At the same time the king confirmed many of the local laws, and in another decree guaranteed the Church possession of its property, 'for the Church is not judged to be guilty of rebellion, and cannot lose what is its own through crimes committed by its individual members'.

Once the crown had recognised the fact that nearly all the upper classes and clergy, and many cities and towns, had supported the Bourbons, it made little sense to talk of 'the crime of rebellion'. The abolition of the *fueros*, which in Valencia was followed immediately by extensive changes in the government of the province (in Saragossa the changes came much later, in 1711), was based on a fiction. The allies had deliberately exploited social tensions for their own ends, with the help of a handful of discontented nobles and many of the common people. In their turn the royal forces deliberately exploited the resistance of the towns in order to carry out a radical change in the administration. Both sides in the war invented their own version of the facts;

as in all wars, it was the truth that suffered.[79] They also began to invent labels with which to identify their opponents. Officials spoke of rebellion and civil war, disregarding the circumstances that had provoked the conflict in Spain. In essence, this must have been the view of two of the chief citizens of Valencia, both of them loyal to Philip V, Pere Luis Blanquer the *jurat en cap*, and Josep Orti the secretary of the Diputació, who in September 1707 drew up an appeal for the restoration of the *fueros*. They were immediately imprisoned and then transferred two days later to the citadel of Pamplona.

Philip's government, in short, had made its first important mistake. It used the war as an excuse to extend the competence of the central government in administration and taxation but in the process alienated many of its subjects. Very few of the upper or middle classes in the towns had been rebels, and the realms of Valencia and Aragon as a whole had been more loyal than seditious. Yet they were now, after 1708, occupied by a foreign army, subjected to foreign laws, and forced to obey foreign officials. The Bourbon troops occupying Valencia in 1712 numbered 16,000 infantry and cavalry.[80] As a result, in 1714 the governor of the province reported to the government that 'in the kingdom of Valencia the people clamour with persistence for their privileges'.[81]

Subsequent generations harboured bitter memories of the events of those months, but few evoked such a reaction as the sack of the town of Xàtiva. The fate of the town made it into a symbol of the 'rebellion' of Valencia, and moved the marquis of San Felipe, a firm supporter of the king, to perhaps his only outright condemnation of the Bourbon cause. 'Both Frenchmen and Spaniards', he wrote, 'committed so many outrages, pillages, oppressions and injustices, that we could write an entire book on the travails that Valencia suffered, even though the king knew nothing of what was going on.'[82]

Lieutenant-general d'Asfeld appeared before Xàtiva on 5 May 1707 with about 3,500 men. The town, with a garrison of 700 English soldiers as well as some Catalans, put up a fierce resistance; the siege lasted a month. When the citadel finally capitulated, the English troops were allowed to march out, but royalist losses here had been very high, and Berwick ordered an exemplary punishment for the town. 'To impress terror, and by a severe example to prevent similar obstinacy, I caused the town to be razed, and sent all the inhabitants into Castile, under a prohibition never to return to their native country.' He also recommended to the government that if possible the inhabitants should be deported to America.[83] In fact not all the town was razed; several public buildings, including churches, monasteries and the hospital, as well as homes belonging to supporters of the king, were spared.[84] It was one of the most regrettable events of the war. But Xàtiva, like many aspects of this cruel conflict, also became in time a myth. Like most Valencian towns, it had also supported Philip V; when the allies occupied the area, General Basset had 'ordered many of all social classes to be imprisoned, among them nearly all the nobles and over 120 friars, for the crime of being supporters of the king'.[85] When d'Asfeld besieged the town, reported the *Gaceta de Madrid* that week, 'the town councillors came to give their obedience, from which it is clear that it is the foreigners who are putting up the resistance'.[86] As in most wars, the citizens were victims, and the violence was perpetrated by both sides. Later generations, in both Valencia and Aragon, looked on the brutality at Xàtiva and the abolition of the *fueros* as part of a single systematic policy carried out by the Bourbon government. The reality was much more complex.

Opposition to the disappearance of the *fueros* was just as strong in Madrid as in Valencia and Saragossa. One result of abolition was the dissolution on 15 July that year of the Council of Aragon, which had lost its *raison d'être* with the end of Aragonese autonomy. The members of the council, in particular its president the count of Aguilar and his colleagues the counts of Montalto, Montellano and Monterrey, were firm opponents both of the abolition of the *fueros* and of the suppression of the council. Undoubtedly, they took the view that the threat to Valencia and Aragon was equally a threat to Castile, and continued in opposition to the government for years. In 1709 Amelot informed Louis XIV that the same nobles were involved in a plot to restore the *fueros*.[87] 'The residence of Montellano', it was reported, 'became the resort of all those who were discontented with the government.' Perhaps the grandee who was most actively opposed to the revocation was the duke of Medinaceli, the greatest landowner of Valencia, whose intrigues and opposition were to have a fatal outcome.

The problem was that though Philip's advisers were agreed on abolishing the *fueros*, they had little idea of what to do next. Amelot left matters entirely in the hands of Macanaz, who over the next two years played a crucial role in the internal affairs of Valencia and Aragon.[88]

*   *   *

In 1708, both Spain and France suffered serious climatic problems that affected their economy and their military activity. 'There had not in mortal memory been cold as severe as that of this year', San Felipe wrote of the winter of 1708/9. 'Many rivers froze, and the intense cold shrivelled the trees. Crops failed, and the countries with most cold began to suffer famine.'[89] The harvest of 1708 was very bad, particularly in Andalucia, and the Spanish authorities had to import grain. After the cold weather came the spring rains. It rained copiously in spring 1709, wiping out any possible harvest and presaging a year of great hunger. Murcia, La Mancha and Andalucia had severe food shortages in the first half of the year, and Seville had floods followed by famine; the hunger, misery and death experienced in this city reached unimaginable proportions. Epidemics were reported in Seville, Jérez and Córdoba. The harvest of 1709 was bad in Aragon, Valencia and parts of Castile. By a decree of 24 October 1709 Philip V opened the ports of Spain to all vessels, enemy or neutral, that could bring grain to the peninsula, granting them permission to introduce all hitherto forbidden goods except the textiles of England and Holland. The crisis continued through many parts of Spain during a good part of 1710.

The year 1709 proved even more disastrous for France, where bad weather brought misery and famine and was accompanied by extensive epidemics of plague. The military situation became desperate, and no money was available to pay the troops. In April 1709 a collapse of credit occurred among French bankers in Lyon; 'for the last four months', the Controller General of Finances reported in August, 'money has been unobtainable.' The French troops in Catalonia, under the command of Marshal Noailles, were in a particularly desperate situation; in May 1709 Ursins recognised that the soldiers 'would be dead of starvation or would have deserted if they had not been able to live at the expense of the people'. Noailles admitted that the French were being forced to seize crops from the population. If the peasants revolted, he wrote, so much the better, for that would justify the seizure of their grain.

Meanwhile, Louis XIV's armies in northern Europe were suffering very serious reverses. In December 1708, after the surrender of the nation's powerful frontier fortress at Lille, the way into France lay wide open to the armies of the duke of Marlborough. Louis XIV sent his foreign minister Torcy to The Hague, in disguise, to seek peace terms, but he was offered humiliating conditions. Negotiations continued and then, in September 1709, the allies inflicted on the French army the bloody defeat of Malplaquet.

These decisive events placed the case of the peninsula in perspective. There was little enthusiasm on either side for continuing to fight. The Bourbon forces in Spain gained a few advantages. In April 1709 the English garrison in Alicante finally capitulated and was allowed to march out and leave on English warships waiting in the harbour. Then in early May the marquis of Bay won a significant victory over Anglo-Portuguese troops at the Portuguese border. But from the viewpoint of Versailles these gains were incomparably less important than the bleak military situation in northern Europe. Allied diplomats easily persuaded Louis that peace terms must be agreed.

There was further pressure on the Bourbons from the pope. Since the beginning of the war, Clement XI had refused to ally with either the Bourbons or the Habsburgs, but the military supremacy of the Habsburgs in Italy, where they threatened to deprive the papacy of some of its states and contested its authority in others, finally forced him to give way. On 15 January 1709 he issued a declaration recognising the archduke as 'Catholic king', but without implying that he was calling into question the title of Philip V. For his part, Philip reacted to the measure with anger and disappointment. After consulting a committee of ministers and theologians, on 22 April he retaliated, issuing a decree expelling the papal nuncio; he prohibited the sending of funds to Rome, seized papal revenues, and forbade the clergy to use papal bulls. It was, in effect, a complete legal break with Rome, and lasted until 1717.[90] In some degree the rupture was play-acting; Philip knew that the pope was under pressure and therefore continued to accept the spiritual role of the papacy, but on the assumption that the pope was a prisoner. The king also had to contend with the protests of those among his bishops who were ardent papalists, notably Luis Belluga, the militant bishop of Murcia.

France's desperate situation, and the pressure of the allies, now drove Louis XIV to one of the most painful decisions of his life. By personal letter as well as through his ambassador the French king informed his grandson that he had decided to withdraw his forces from Spain as a first step towards agreeing to peace. 'I am obliged', he wrote to Amelot on 3 June, 'to recall immediately all the troops that I now have in Spain.'[91] In subsequent letters he explained why: 'The state of my kingdom does not permit me advancing further help to Spain'; and elsewhere, 'the famine, the war and the flooding of the rivers' were among the many reasons he cited. The news was received in Madrid with stupefaction. Unwilling to leave Philip entirely unprotected, Louis ordered several battalions to remain in the peninsula, but on a defensive footing only; all other forces and all French generals were recalled to France. In September 1709 the last link was cut, with the departure from Madrid of the French ambassador, a gesture by which Louis hoped a fair diplomatic agreement could be reached with the allies, while still preserving Philip on the throne.

Amelot's departure, Ursins reported, 'leaves the king of Spain in a very serious situation, since he does not know whom to entrust with the many affairs that the ambassador had taken care of. The king is at the moment going to take charge by himself'.[92] Philip changed all the ministers in his council in order to allow himself a more active part in deliberations. Amelot's loss was severely felt. In Castile he was revered as few Spanish ministers of the crown had ever been. Years later, in 1714, when a pamphleteer chose to vent his wrath on the activity of foreign advisers, he made an exception of 'Monsieur Amelot, who was more intimately attached to the advice and policy of Spaniards'.[93] Even in 1722 when Saint-Simon came to Madrid as French ambassador, he spoke of 'this great reputation that after so many years is still revered in Spain'.[94] On the day that Amelot left the capital, 2 September, Philip also did so. The previous day, Ursins wrote to Madame de Maintenon that 'the king is preparing to leave tomorrow to put himself at the head of the army, for he is determined to die rather than be covered in infamy'.[95] Philip went directly to the front, where he assumed command of the troops. The defence of the monarchy was now in his hands alone.

CHAPTER THREE

The Later War Years, 1709–1715

'GOD HAS PLACED THE CROWN OF SPAIN ON MY HEAD. I SHALL
MAINTAIN IT SO LONG AS I HAVE A DROP OF BLOOD IN MY VEINS.'

PHILIP V TO LOUIS XIV, 17 APRIL 1709

Philip's character rose to the occasion. When presented with a real challenge, of whatever sort, he cast off his melancholy and took on new life. He became now what many Spaniards would later remember him to have been: 'el Animoso', the valiant king, the hero of his people. When he received from Louis XIV in the spring of 1709 the news of the intended withdrawal, he affirmed to his grandfather that he would never betray Spain. 'God has placed the crown of Spain on my head; I shall maintain it so long as I have a drop of blood in my veins. I owe it to my conscience, to my honour and to the love I receive from my subjects. . . . I shall never give Spain up so long as I have life, I would rather perish fighting for every piece of its soil, at the head of my troops.' When Amelot, who revised the letter for him, commented that 'it seems to me extremely strong' because it implied criticism of Louis XIV, Philip replied, 'those are my true feelings'.[1]

The fears of France and the hopes of the allies centred on the performance of the soldiers now available to Philip. The Spanish troops were not wholly alone. Louis XIV left twenty-five French battalions in the peninsula, as well as French garrisons in Rosas, Pamplona, Fuenterrabía, San Sebastián and Los Pasajes.[2] Their costs were to be met wholly by Spain, they were to play a defensive role only and not engage in battle.

To emphasise that he was now independent of outside help, Philip made a direct approach to the allies who were negotiating with France at The Hague. In a letter that contained one of the most significant statements to come from Philip in this period, he ordered his finance minister in Flanders, the count of Bergeyck, to 'persuade the Dutch that my interests now are different from those of France. Try to obtain a treaty with them. The Spaniards do not wish France to collaborate in the government of Spain, and I am wholly in agreement with them.'[3] In March 1710, he informed Bergeyck that 'if I could see the slightest inclination on the part of the allies to make a treaty, I would give them the firmest guarantees',[4] a clear indication that Philip was willing to identify himself with Spanish interests, to the extent of dissociating himself completely from French help. The statement also raises fundamental questions of what might have happened in Catalonia if a general peace had been reached in 1709 rather than four years later, in 1713.

The campaign of spring 1710 was conducted principally in Aragon, where the marquis of Villadarias, formerly commander in Andalucia, directed operations. On 3 May Philip left Madrid to join this army. Unfortunately, the summer was not a successful one for the Spaniards. After facing each other and manoeuvring for two months by the river Segre near Lleida, on 27 July the opposing armies joined battle near Almenar, by the river Noguera. The allies, commanded by General James Stanhope and by Starhemberg, were also led by the archduke, who had joined his forces early in June. Both armies therefore had their kings to lead them. Philip, who risked his life in the engagement, was rescued by his cavalry, but the allied forces won the day: they suffered 400 casualties, but the Spaniards lost nearly 1,000 dead and over 300 prisoners. Philip V was forced to withdraw towards Lleida. Although a limited engagement, their defeat seriously depressed Bourbon hopes, and the king immediately replaced Villadarias by the marquis of Bay, who arrived on 15 August from Extremadura.

The royal troops continued their retreat to Saragossa, encamping outside the city where the pursuing allies under Starhemberg caught up with them. At 8 a.m. on 20 August, they again entered into combat. Gunfire was exchanged from dawn, but the battle proper did not begin until midday, whereupon Philip 'went through the ranks, encouraging the soldiers, then withdrew to a promontory in the middle of the zone from which he could see and direct the action'.[5] The Bourbon army numbered under 20,000 men, all Spaniards, while the slightly superior allied army of over 23,000 was a mixed force, as usual, that included nearly 14,000 Germans. The defeat at Almenar was repeated, this time with a vengeance. By early afternoon the Spaniards were in full retreat, having suffered about 3,000 casualties and the loss of some 4,000 prisoners. On the 21st the archduke entered Saragossa and stayed there five days; most of Aragon now returned to allied control.

After the reversal, Philip withdrew to Castile, his crown once more in peril. The allies reached Calatayud on 4 September, and debated whether they should take Madrid or continue the campaign in the field. The archduke was opposed to occupying the capital, but the generals felt it was advisable and overruled him. As in 1706, the Bourbons decided to evacuate Madrid. On 9 September the royal family left, arriving at Valladolid on the 16th. The king set out surrounded by crowds of citizens who shouted their support. His departure was the signal for a general emigration. On the 28th, Charles III entered Madrid, a week after his forces had taken possession of it. He found the city hostile, and few nobles came forward to support him. 'Madrid is deserted', he complained in disgust. By contrast, Philip was met with enthusiasm in Valladolid. 'I am very pleased', he told the French ambassador, 'that the English have brought the archduke to Madrid; he will have occasion to see the disposition of the people in my capital.'[6] The king and queen were visibly heartened by the enormous popular support they received in Castile. 'If ever we had to abandon Spain', Marie Louise said resolutely, 'we would emigrate to America and establish the throne in Peru.' Because of the potential threat to Valladolid and possibly also because of the severe food shortages experienced that year in the city (bread was rationed), the government transferred itself to Vitoria and the queen went to Corella. Philip went to join the Spanish forces, which were assembled in Navarre under the command of the marquis of Bay.

The military defeats in Aragon gave rise during the year 1710 to further desertions among the higher nobility. The most startling case was that of Luis Francisco de la Cerda, 9th duke of Medinaceli, the most prominent and active of all the grandees. A man of great wealth and influence both in Castile and Valencia, and a resolute opponent of the abolition of the *fueros*, he was among those most feared by the French advisers to the crown. Arrested suddenly on 15 April 1710, he was tried in secret on charges that were never made public,[7] and sentenced to imprisonment. He was confined first in Segovia and then in Pamplona, where he died in 1711. During the archduke's occupation of Madrid, the three principal defectors were the count of Palma, the count of Paredes and the duke of Hijar. In these weeks the duke of Uceda, who had till 1708 been ambassador in Rome, also transferred allegiance to the archduke. In 1710 he kept up a secret correspondence with the duke of Medinaceli, even while the latter was in prison in Segovia, and in August that year we find Uceda complaining that 'I have never received any satisfaction, while all the others who are my enemies receive inflated honours'.[8] With Barcelona, Madrid and Saragossa in enemy hands and his nobles continuing to desert him, the position of the king of Spain looked hopeless.

*   *   *

In these circumstances, Louis XIV had no alternative but to intervene. The peace proposals put forward by the English during the negotiations in 1710 at Geertruidenberg, in the United Provinces, were wholly unacceptable. Not satisfied with Louis XIV's offer to withdraw his support from Philip, they insisted that he declare war on Spain. According to the Tory opposition in England, the English government's negotiators had no real intention of ending the war, because of the profits being made out of it by Marlborough and the Whigs. They knew that Louis would reject the proposal of going to war against his own grandson, and it was indeed thrown out by Louis's Royal Council in May 1710. In July the foreign secretary Torcy reported that 'the king's intention now is to achieve a closer relationship than ever with the king his grandson'. In July the peace negotiations were suspended. A grateful Marie Louise thanked Louis XIV for rejecting the 'barbarous proposals' of the allies, and asked him to send the duke of Vendôme to command the army in Catalonia.[9]

The most urgent problem now was to remedy the error of having deserted Philip. In August 1710 the marshal duke of Vendôme, who knew Spain well and, as we have seen, had conquered Barcelona in 1697, left Paris in order to put himself at the head of the troops in the peninsula. French soldiers and supplies once more flowed into Spain and in September Vendôme and the duke of Noailles arrived at Valladolid to confer with Philip V. It was decided to let Bay defend Extremadura against the Portuguese, while Vendôme held the centre of the peninsula and Noailles went to Roussillon to attack Catalonia from the north.

Starhemberg, for his part, considered it inadvisable to seek winter quarters in the hostile territories of Castile, and it was decided to retire to Catalonia. The allied position was made difficult not only by the obvious hostility of the people of Madrid but, more threateningly, by the fact that Vendôme had an army of over 25,000 encamped at Talavera de la Reina. Charles III left to journey eastwards, reaching Barcelona in mid-November. In the same month the allies under Starhemberg began their retreat towards Aragon, and on 3 December Philip V returned to Madrid. His first action was to pay homage at the shrine of the Virgin of Atocha, then he headed on horseback towards the royal palace, but found his way blocked by the cheering crowds. 'It took many hours for his triumphal carriage to pass through the main streets, since the crowds were immense.'[10] The houses were hung with banners and flags and at night the whole city was lit up. The excited king stayed in his capital only two days. On 6 December he went to join the army under Vendôme.

The retreating allied forces moved in national detachments. On the night of 6 December the English, commanded by Stanhope, arrived at the town of Brihuega and took up quarters there. Believing that

Vendôme was still some distance away, Stanhope delayed in the town for a couple of days, allowing time for a forward detachment from the Bourbon army to reach Brihuega on the afternoon of the 8th. By that evening Vendôme had surrounded the town with troops and artillery and by the next morning the French marshal called on the English to capitulate. When this was refused, the French began to bombard the town. At 6 p.m. Stanhope ordered a general surrender. The English had lost, according to their own figures, 300 dead, 300 wounded, and over 3,000 taken prisoner including Stanhope himself and all his principal officers.

Starhemberg hurried back from Cifuentes when he heard of the siege at Brihuega. On the 9th he took up a position nearby at Villaviciosa, quite unaware of Stanhope's surrender. Then, on the morning of the 10th, Vendôme was joined by the rest of his army and they took up positions against the allies. Against the 20,000 men under him and Philip V were ranged about 14,000 under the Austrian general. The engagement began in the early afternoon and con- tinued until nightfall; the first attack was launched by the right wing of the Bourbon army, commanded by Philip. Conflicting versions of the battle do not alter the fact that it was a Bourbon victory. Starhemberg retreated swiftly through Aragon and reached Barcelona on 6 January, the pursuing Bourbon troops recapturing Aragon and its cities as they went. At Villaviciosa, Vendôme had permanently saved the Bourbon cause. The battle, in Torcy's words, 'placed the crown on the head of the Catholic king'. The desultory campaigns of the next two years did nothing to dent the supremacy of Philip V in Castile and Aragon.

Meanwhile Noailles had been preparing his campaign in Roussillon. Despite the wintry conditions, on 15 December the French forces laid siege to the important fortress of Girona, the surrender of which on 25 January 1711 opened the way for the capture of the plain of Vic and the Val d'Arán. Vendôme in the meantime established his base in Cervera. The allies were now reduced to the area enclosed by Igualada, Tarragona and Barcelona. Everywhere else in pen- insular Spain the Bourbon cause was triumphant. But the well- defended Catalan triangle, supported from the sea, proved extremely difficult to reduce, and the generals had perforce to wait on events elsewhere in Europe. To celebrate the successes of the campaign, Philip decided to visit Saragossa, where he went with Marie Louise in the middle of January. The king could not resist prolonging his stay in order to participate in the ceremonies of Carnival and several other popular celebrations.[11] At the same time, he gave his approval to the appointment of Melchor de Macanaz as intendant of Aragon, and prepared the new measures that, in the form of a decree of 3 April, reformed the entire administration of the city and realm of Aragon. The changes in this province were meant to be purely temporary. However, they appear to have provoked considerable confusion, Philip explaining later that 'I have formed the government here on a temporal basis; it may be continued or changed according to what I consider suitable'.[12]

The king's personal success in the campaigns of these years was fundamental in establishing his image among his people. The marquis of San Felipe was but one witness to the way in which the Madrid public greeted their hero when he returned to the capital on 15 November 1711: 'the cheers and applause were never-ending; their eyes and hearts, accustomed to seeing a king who was always unwell, emaciated, and gloomy [the reference is to the last Habsburg ruler, Charles II], were delighted by the sight of a gallant young prince'.[13] The *Gaceta* reported how 'the whole town was ablaze with lights, and the streets full of people who never ceased demonstrating their satisfaction with continuous applause'.[14] Supported by a forceful wife, sustained by an enthusiastic people, constantly excited by the challenge of war, Philip had evolved into a personality that far exceeded the limited promise of his early years. The image that became engraved on the public mind found its way into official art when, many years later, the court artist Jean Ranc, a Frenchman, produced an equestrian portrait of the king that reflected the new Bourbon style and was also a complete departure from the stiff and formulaic court likenesses of previous monarchs of Spain.[15] In the portrait, Philip rides gloriously into conflict with signs of battle all around him, and with Victory as his guide. The rich imagery of a warrior king emerged also in a pamphlet issued in Granada in 1709, which explained that 'the vigour and valour of our king is that of a true soldier, of a Mars, of another Alexander, always victorious, never vanquished'.[16]

* * *

Despite the failure of the talks at Geertruidenberg, peace was made inevitable by two circumstances. In the English general elections of 1710 a Tory ministry, committed to end the war, had come into power. And in April 1711 Emperor Joseph died, after a brief reign of only six years, leaving the Imperial crown to his brother Archduke Charles. Those who had been opposed to the union of the crowns of France and Spain now found themselves in the unwelcome position of supporting a war that would unite the crowns of Austria and Spain, and thereby revive the empire of Charles V.

Military actions in Spain now hung on decisions reached in European diplomatic circles. On 27 September 1711 the new emperor, Charles VI, departed from Barcelona on board an English ship, leaving his wife Elisabeth behind as his official representative. A month later the British government resumed peace talks with the French, and in December removed Marlborough from his command. In January 1712 a peace conference between the maritime powers and France opened in Utrecht. That summer, in June, Vendôme died in Vinaroz after an attack of apoplexy during a lunch. His sudden demise was a severe blow to the Spaniards, but the approach of peace was soon to perfect the work he had so brilliantly begun.

Meanwhile, another obstacle to the peace process appeared. The dauphin, son and prospective successor of Louis XIV, died in 1711. During the year 1712 other members of his family also died (as we shall see below, in Chapter 6), leaving as the one and sole surviving heir to the crown a two-year-old child; if he too were to die, the throne of France would pass to Philip V. Since the war had been fought to prevent a union of the thrones of France and Spain, a solution became urgent. Fortunately, in May 1712 Philip formally renounced his rights to the French throne, a renunciation that was made, said Louis XIV, 'of his own volition and against my advice',[17] for the French had hoped that Philip would give up Spain and accept

the Italian territories of the monarchy, with the near certainty of succeeding to the French throne.

In August 1712 hostilities between Great Britain, the United
Provinces, Portugal, France and Spain were suspended, and on 11
April 1713 the treaty of Utrecht was formally concluded. By its terms,
Spain and the Indies were guaranteed to Philip V who, in turn,
reaffirmed the renunciation of all his rights to the French throne. For
the rest, Utrecht was fundamentally an English peace, and Britain
emerged with all the honours. It received from France several territories in America, and recognition of the Hanoverian dynasty. From
Spain it received the *asiento* for the slave trade to America (March 1713),
and possession of Minorca and Gibraltar (July 1713). While Spanish territorial losses in Europe were humiliating, they were not politically
or economically disadvantageous. Louis XIV had long been aware of
the need to make concessions, but his problem had been to try and
convince his grandson. As early as October 1706 he was warning
Amelot that 'the king of Spain must be prepared for great dismem-
berments of the monarchy'. Even more forcibly, in 1711, when Philip
was refusing to accept the loss of Gibraltar and Minorca, Louis told his
grandson directly that 'there are occasions when one must know how
to lose'.[18] The Spanish Netherlands were given to the emperor, and
Sicily to the duke of Savoy. Spain made peace with the Dutch in June
1713, with the British and Savoy in July the same year, and with Portugal in February 1715.

The year after Utrecht, on 6 March 1714, France and the Habsburg
Empire agreed peace terms in the treaty of Rastatt. By it, the French,
whose forces were in possession of the relevant territories, handed over
to the emperor all Spanish territory in Italy, including Naples, Sardinia,
Milan and the fortresses of Tuscany. With Minorca and Gibraltar in
English hands, and Italy under Austrian control, Spain found itself
deprived at one blow of its control of the western Mediterranean.
Utrecht and Rastatt opened a new era in Spanish history. Relieved of
the dead weight of its possessions in northern Europe, the monarchy
could now devote its resources to internal regeneration. Foreign policy,
however, still remained at the head of the agenda. The conditions
imposed at Utrecht were to remain in force for a century, and in theory

regulated the relations between the great powers. But it was a system that had been imposed by force on Spain, which therefore made repeated attempts to overturn it. No peace treaty existed between the Empire and Spain, leaving the latter free to question the new arrangements in the Mediterranean. Over the next half-century, the two powers continued to fight for control of Italy.

Those who felt they knew what Utrecht signified were bitterly disappointed. A street satire of 1714 went:[19]

> España está pereciendo,
> Nuestro rey la está mirando,
> Los españoles llorando,
> La reina se está muriendo;
> Los grandes acoquinados.
> Los consejos aturdidos,
> Los franceses asistidos,
> Los soldados mal pagados.

(Spain is perishing, our king is looking on, Spaniards are weeping, the queen is dying, the grandees are cowed, the councils are bewildered, the French are favoured, the soldiers unpaid.)

To the year 1714 belongs a significant pamphlet entitled *Reply of a friend to one who asks when our ills in Spain will end*.[20] After lamenting Spain's losses – 'the Netherlands lost, as well as all Italy, the Mediterranean and the islands, part of Catalonia, Gibraltar, and our trade in the Indies' – the author concludes that 'the main cause for our lament is that innate hostility with which all foreigners have always looked on Spain', a hostility responsible for 'the complete subversion and destruction of our way of government'.

* * *

The old Habsburg system of governing an empire through councils resident in Madrid had collapsed during the war as the territories of the monarchy one after another altered their status. The Council of Flanders was abolished on 29 March 1702, that of Aragon on 15 July

1707. In 1706 an important reduction in the size of the Councils of State, War and the Indies was made.[21] Yet these moves were only the beginning of serious constitutional changes. Later, in 1712, a session of the Cortes, representing this time not only Castile but also the whole of Bourbon Spain,[22] was convoked in Madrid in order to deal principally with the king's renunciation of the French throne (see Chapter 6), to witness which act the English envoy to Utrecht, Lexington, came especially to Spain.

The Cortes of 1712 was asked to approve a change in the law of succession. The intention was to make it impossible for the issue of future marriages of Spanish princesses with the royal houses of Savoy and of Austria – at that time enemies of Spain – to succeed to the throne. In effect, by allowing succession only through the male line, this introduced the French Salic law into Castile. Despite the strong opposition of leading members of the Council of Castile, where the proposal was first debated, the law was approved by the Cortes and issued as a decree on 10 May 1713. Four weeks later the Cortes was dissolved. The opposition of the Council of Castile to the law was used by ministers as an excuse to reform the structure and role of the councils. At this period the major changes in government were carried out by two ministers, Melchor de Macanaz and Jean Orry, the latter having returned to Madrid in April 1713 after an absence in France of seven years. Macanaz took charge of the reforms (called a '*nueva planta*' in the vocabulary of the time), designed in fact by Orry and put in train by a royal decree of 10 November 1713. The changes affected the Councils of Castile, Finance, Orders, and the Indies; a subsequent decree of 23 April 1714 also added the Council of War.[23] The apparent intention was to achieve greater efficiency in administration, but the decree served in fact to demonstrate that the crown could when it wished alter the entire traditional system of government. In effect, the administrative innovations of 1713 and 1714 unleashed an unprecedented flood of propaganda leaflets against the regime and its principal symbols, Orry, Macanaz and Ursins. 'These *plantas* in Castile', said a verse in one pamphlet, playing on the words '*planta*' and 'plant', 'will produce Catalans'. The discontent among the Castilian ruling class was immense. Early in February 1714 a new structure was given to the cabinet or Despacho, and more grandees were nominated to sit on it. But they were allotted no effective part in decisions. At one of the sessions of the new Despacho, the count of Frigiliana exclaimed angrily: 'Gentlemen, this is only to have more witnesses to the fact that nothing is decided here!'[24]

The success of Macanaz in carrying out changes in the state structure reached its peak when he attempted to attack the Inquisition. The matter arose when Louis XIV offered to mediate between the papacy and Philip V, to resolve the rupture since 1709 of relations between the Holy See and Spain. Talks began in Paris for which Philip asked Macanaz to prepare a memorandum covering the various issues involved. The latter drew up an aggressive document, dated 19 December 1713, which was presented to the Council of Castile for its approval.[25] In this startling memorial, which was in part influenced by the policy of the government of France, Macanaz argued that the crown had full powers over all aspects of the national Church, and that the jurisdiction of the pope was limited. Philip V was pleased with the report, and the council accepted it after a few protests. Nothing happened for several months.

Then in August 1714 the Inquisitor General, Cardinal Giudice, who was at the time in France where he had been serving since April that year as ambassador to Louis XIV, issued a condemnation of Macanaz's memorial. The king reacted as firmly as he had in 1709. He ordered Giudice back to Spain, sacked him from his posts, and ordered the Inquisition to suspend the condemnation. At the same time he asked Macanaz to draw up another report, this time on the Inquisition itself and whether it needed to be reformed. Macanaz presented his findings on 3 November. His conclusion, based on a long-standing 'regalist'[26] tradition, was that the Inquisition should be restricted exclusively to a spiritual role, and that its temporal jurisdiction – above all its power to prohibit and censor books – should be transferred to the crown.[27] Many years later, explaining his ideas on the matter, Macanaz informed a government minister that his motive in writing the memorial had been 'so that Spain may shed the erroneous idea (which it entertains because of fear of the Inquisition) that the king cannot interfere in anything that the inquisitors do'.[28] The king accepted the document approvingly.

This astonishing series of proposals by Macanaz would, if put into effect, have represented a revolution in the government of ecclesiastical affairs in Spain and it is of considerable significance that the king was entirely in agreement with them. He had been formed in the tradition of Louis XIV, who would never have tolerated an Inquisition and who had little patience with papal pretensions.

*   *   *

After the peace treaties, the only outstanding matter was the case of the Catalans.

The War of Succession created many myths, and nowhere more than over the conflict in Catalonia. It was easy at the time to fall into the simplified image of loyalists and rebels. For the royalists, everyone who supported the allies was a rebel. We have already seen that in the case of Aragon and Valencia these simple categories are not applicable and indeed it is significant that two of the chief Bourbon commanders, Berwick and Orléans, both strongly criticised royalist attempts to condemn opposition as 'rebellion'. In Castile, in Aragon and throughout the peninsula nearly all the elite and populace supported the side which they knew: this happened to be the side of King Philip. But they were also willing to adapt to political realities that took the irresistible form of an occupying army. People followed the tide of military events.

At the same time, the war acted as an external pressure that aggravated existing divisions among Spaniards and, in that sense, it provoked many civil conflicts. Groups and, families supported one side because their enemies supported another. Under cover of war, individuals and communities eliminated rivals. Villages went to war against rival villages. Elites in city councils were split down the middle. Social conflicts, of the type that occurred in Valencia, took place right across the peninsula. All of these circumstances could be found in Catalonia, where the rebel movements of 1705 (to which we have referred above) provoked a veritable civil war. 'The entire principality', observed San Felipe, 'took up arms against itself.' Many Catalans fled the territory when the archduke took over. The dispute over the new dynasty precipitated conflicts that had long been latent among Catalans, Castilians and other Spaniards. Moreover, at no stage was there unanimous or even majority support in Catalonia for the archduke.[29] During the course of the next few years, however, the existence of a strong pressure group of rebels inside the province, together with the superior allied military and naval presence in Barcelona, forced many towns to decide – often very reluctantly – for the archduke. Tarragona, for example, joined the archduke because it was bombarded from the sea by allied ships and attacked from land by the forces of Colonel Nebot.

The rebel movements of 1705 had certainly helped to polarise opinion in Catalonia. In the cities and towns, there were some groups that preferred Philip V and others that preferred the archduke. As in the other realms of the Crown of Aragon, a good part of the upper classes – in Barcelona, Tortosa, Reus and other towns – favoured the existing regime (of Philip V).[30] But they did not make decisions until military events forced them to do so.[31] Though many Catalans served in the allied army, there was no general movement of rebellion; the image, cultivated later by romantic historiography, of a national uprising against Castile, has no foundation in reality. In many cases, the relevant documentation was destroyed at the end of the war and it will always be difficult to determine exactly how people reacted. Certainly, the idea that towns like Cervera were solidly Philippist is based on little conclusive evidence. The troops of both sides devastated the countryside and were equally detested by Catalans. 'They marched continuously', reports a contemporary, 'across the principality, eating and drinking, sacking and burning'.[32] As a consequence, the people resisted whichever troops happened to be in their area. Their situation was reflected in a verse that circulated in Valencia at the time:

Entre Philip Quinto
Y Charles Tercero
Nos quedamos desnudos
Y sin dinero.

(Between Philip V and Charles III, we are left naked and penniless.)

Pro-Bourbon historians such as San Felipe represented the Catalans as separatists and rebels. In fact, the Catalan movement was neither in its origins nor its nature separatist or anti-Castilian.[33] But a fundamental change occurred in the movements in Catalonia between 1705 and 1713.[34] The groups that wanted to continue the war because they had the firm support of Austria and England could point with reason to the evidence that Castile and Aragon were subject to a regime that had changed their laws and driven many of their nobles into prison or exile. A flood of pamphlets in Catalonia presented a picture of 'the nation crushed, and the cities, towns and villages of Castile, Aragon and Valencia left with no option but to live under tyranny'.[35] Seven years after the revocation of the *fueros* of Valencia, it was perfectly clear to many of the elite that Catalonia faced the loss of its historic constitutions. When all possibility of agreement with Philip V vanished, Catalan ideology also changed. It was not significantly anti-Spanish and could not be, since many of those who had taken refuge in Barcelona were Castilian, Valencian and Aragonese opponents of the Bourbon regime. In the last stages of the defence of Barcelona, the authorities called on the people to fight 'for your honour, for the fatherland, and for the liberty of all Spain'. The 'fatherland' was seen as an entity within the context of 'Spain'; the Catalan rebels were fighting for a free Spain, not for their independence from Spain. But at the same time they were fighting for their laws, as they made clear in the later attempts at negotiating with Berwick. They now excluded the Bourbon king definitively from this concept of their '*pàtria*'; their appeals now were to '*la terra*' ('the land', a traditional Catalan invocation).

The siege of Barcelona was, for the government of Madrid, a matter of detail. The greater part of Catalonia had long since been recovered: Lleida was captured in 1707 and again in 1711, Tortosa in 1708, Girona in 1711. Since the end of 1712 the issue over Barcelona was whether it would surrender, as both the allies and France hoped, or whether it would resist to the end. There was very little mention of the political privileges of the Catalans. Although the Archduke Charles had always disliked the *fueros*, he continued to insist to diplomats that they be preserved; but there was little support anywhere else. When in January 1713 the new British ambassador in Madrid, Lord Lexington, raised the matter with Philip, the king retorted that he would 'never grant privileges to these blackguards and scoundrels, the Catalans, for he would no longer be king if he did. We hope that the queen [Anne] will no longer require anything of the sort from us, for we think that we have already done very much in allowing them to keep their property and their lives.'[36]

The agreements at Utrecht had in fact made it clear that the British were going to abandon the Catalans: Lord Bolingbroke, writing from England, informed the diplomats at Utrecht that 'it is not to the interest of England to preserve the Catalan liberties'.[37] In March 1713, one month before the signing of Utrecht, the Empress Elisabeth sailed from Barcelona. 'This is the saddest day in my life,' she said in a speech to the city authorities, 'and I shall not see another like it.' Starhemberg and the Austrian troops followed her. Thereafter, the most pressing problem for Spain early in 1714 was agreement on details of the peace with the Dutch. Louis XIV wrote to Philip: 'I will not give you any fresh help towards reducing Barcelona until you have signed this peace. As soon as you have concluded the treaty with Holland my troops in Roussillon will be at your disposal.' Since Philip knew that he could not reduce Barcelona without French help, he gave way. The French troops under Berwick duly crossed the frontier in June and headed for Barcelona.

The crucial problem for Barcelona was that the British reneged on their promise to protect it, a failure which provoked discord among groups in the Parliament in London. The House of Lords petitioned Queen Anne, and she promised to help. But the peace treaties made it impossible to return to a war footing. Philip V told the British ambassador: 'You need a peace no less than we do, and will not wish to fight with us over a trifle'.[38] After France had signed the peace of Rastatt the intervention of French forces also became possible. In these difficult circumstances, the Catalans tried to reach a decision and at a special meeting of the Corts in June 1713 in the hall of Sant Jordi in the palace of the Diputació, two of the three *braços* – a majority – voted at first to submit and surrender. After objections and further votes, two of the *braços* finally voted to fight, and war was declared against Philip V on 9 July 1713, a decision, it has been pointed out, that 'defied reason and set the Catalans on a suicidal course'.[39] But at no stage had the king given any hint that he might respect the privileges of Catalonia; indeed, the intention to abolish the *fueros* had been common knowledge since the decrees of 1707 that affected Aragon and Valencia. The only hope held out by the instructions given to Berwick by the king lay in the mercy of the king, who would adopt measures (he said) at his 'discretion'. Few Catalans were willing to risk leaving all to this discretion.

Just as he had criticised the hasty abolition of the *fueros* in 1707, so now in 1714 Berwick was critical of the instructions he received from Madrid. He found the harsh terms laid down by Madrid to be *peu chrétien* ('unchristian') for by them he was ordered to treat the city of Barcelona with extreme severity if it did not surrender immediately, and to substitute all its laws with those of Castile, instructions which contradicted the practice of the authorities up to that date. The privileges of Lleida had not been touched when it was recovered in 1708, and on its recovery in 1711 no formal abolition of privileges was made. Even more strikingly, when the duke of Noailles occupied Girona in 1711, he expressly confirmed the city's privileges.

The Spanish ministers, Berwick felt, were responsible for their own problems because of their uncompromising attitude towards the supporters of the archduke. 'If the ministers and generals of the king of Spain', he wrote in his memoirs, 'had been more moderate in their language, Barcelona would have capitulated immediately after the departure of the Imperialists [in 1711]; but as they talked of nothing else publicly but of sacking and executions, the people became furious and desperate.'[40] Writing to the king from Perpignan in June 1714, he strongly urged him to guarantee the people of Barcelona not only their lives (which Philip had done) but also all their property: 'I beg Your Majesty to give me orders on this matter'.[41] In fact, Philip modified his instructions at the end of July, but Berwick continued to believe that they were too harsh. As late as August 1714, Louis XIV was also advising the king to treat the Catalans with clemency, to reach reasonable terms of capitulation, and to preserve the municipal laws and institutions of Catalonia. 'I believe that it is in your interest', he wrote, 'to moderate the severity that you wish to use with the inhabitants, for although they are your subjects you should be as a father to them, chastising them without losing them.'[42] Philip promised Louis that he would preserve the municipal laws and the civil law,[43] but said that he would make 'no other concession'.

Berwick's forces arrived before the city in July 1714. Though he wished to offer terms of capitulation, the Barcelona representatives refused to accept them because Berwick would not guarantee the *fueros*. The siege of Barcelona was the final heroic episode of a war which saw many episodes of heroism. An immensely superior French and Spanish army (35,000 infantry and 5,000 cavalry) faced a city defended by 16,000 soldiers and by its citizens.[44] A considerable Catalan force was also active in the countryside, but there was no possibility of help for the city from the sea. Though the attackers carried out a vigorous siege, the defending forces, commanded by General Villaroel, resisted successfully for over a year. By September 1714 the situation of Barcelona was desperate, and Berwick offered to receive a deputation in the hope that the city would capitulate. The deputation, which was led by the *conseller en cap*, Rafael Casanova, and deliberately excluded military men, came to see him on 4 September but refused to discuss terms of surrender. Villaroel saw the decision as senseless, and resigned his command. The leaders of the city promptly appointed the Virgin of Mercy, whose banner was taken into meetings, as their commander. The last and hopeless defence took place, with much loss of life, on 11 September. Shortly after midday on the 12th, Berwick accepted the surrender of Barcelona, and that afternoon his troops began to enter.

The siege had cost more lives than Berwick considered acceptable. In his memoirs he estimated that 6,000 defenders had died, a figure that coincides with that suggested by recent historians.[45] He also calculated that his own army had lost 10,000 men. Angry at the unnecessary deaths,[46] when the city lay within his grasp he considered himself no longer bound by any possible capitulation. He curtly dismissed the delegation sent to see him on 13 September, two days after the fall of the city. On the 16th orders were issued in his name suppressing the city council (the Consell de Cent), and the government of the principality (the Diputació).

The last stage of the Catalan story was the recovery of Mallorca, which surrendered in June 1715 to an army of 10,000 under the command of d'Asfeld. The lives and property of the besieged were guaranteed, and a general pardon was issued. It was the final episode of the War of the Succession.

As Berwick had feared, it was the repression in Catalonia that eventually created the negative image that people would retain of Philip V. But repression was inevitable, and continued for many years.[47] Peace had arrived but Catalonia, more than any other realm that had rebelled, remained a province under martial law.

* * *

The war helped considerably further to mature Philip. In 1701 he had been a timid young man with no experience whatever of the world and none whatever of ruling. Unlike the higher nobility of the time, he had not travelled before his arrival in the peninsula and, as we have seen, his own tutor, Louville, and his French advisers all had negative opinions about his capacity. The short trip to Italy was fundamental in forming his character because it enabled him to take a direct part in decision-making, in political correspondence, and above all in warfare. For a while after 1703 he was his own chief minister.

His biggest support was Marie Louise. Despite her thirteen years when she became queen, she quickly showed that she had an independence and ability rare in one of her age. We have seen that she immediately dominated her inexperienced husband. She made active efforts to dissuade her father from his decision to support the allies. When that failed, she committed herself wholeheartedly to the Bourbon cause. 'It is important to show in every way and everywhere, that the house of France rules in this monarchy', she announced. 'We must convince some through tact, and others through force.'[48] These were the sentiments of an experienced politician. During Philip's absence in Italy, she conscientiously fulfilled her role of governor of the realm. She presided over the Cortes in Saragossa and as regent of Spain during her husband's absence, she regularly attended meetings of the Royal Council in Madrid. 'The queen', the *Gaceta* announced in

July 1702, 'every day attends the Committee of Government, which is held daily from ten to twelve, as well as sometimes in the afternoon.'[49] 'On some days', she informed Louis XIV, 'I spend six hours a day in the Council. I also spend a similar amount of time giving public audiences.'[50] Nor did she neglect her civic role; she went for rides regularly through the city, and made contact with the people.

It is not surprising that some diplomats and politicians resented her activity. Their criticisms were often in part directed against Ursins, whom they felt to be the real person in authority because she was presumed to influence the queen. Women, they believed, should not meddle in government, which was the concern of men alone, a mindset about which Louis XIV's wife, Madame de Maintenon, warned Ursins in one of her letters. 'On n'aime pas ici', she wrote, with a strong hint of displeasure, 'que les dames s'occupent d'affaires.' But resentment also centred on the very real bonds between Philip and his wife. Philip was passionately in love with Marie Louise. She also reciprocated his feelings. 'Farewell, my dearest king', she wrote to him when he went to Italy, 'I do not doubt that when the campaigns are over you will find nothing else to occupy you, but will come back to your own little wife who loves you a hundred times more than she loves herself.'[51] She never deviated from these sentiments, which she often expressed in her private letters. Some years later, writing to her grandmother in Savoy, she referred to the close physical bond with Philip: 'I have the happiness to have a husband who, over and above the qualities he possesses, has those which are necessary to make a woman into the happiest person in the world.'[52]

The French and Spanish advisers surrounding Philip soon discovered that the queen was an implacable obstacle to their efforts to dominate the king. A typically despairing complaint came from the French ambassador, the duke of Gramont, in 1705. 'The king of Spain', he reported, 'is timid, weak and excessively indolent. As long as the king has this queen, he will be a mere six-year-old child and never a man.' In his despatches, Gramont was particularly resentful of a queen who instead of doing her needlework was busying herself in politics. 'At sixteen years', he wrote, 'she is not interested in music or in the theatre or in conversation or in going out for walks or in hunting.

All she wants is to dominate, and to have the king always in her arms.'[53] Gramont's conviction, quite obviously, was that women have no place in politics. Bitterly opposed to the return of Ursins to the peninsula, he faced defeat when in spring 1705 Louis allowed the princess to resume her position. 'Sire,' he wrote to Versailles, 'recall me promptly from here.'

The bond with Marie Louise gave strength to Philip's troubled character. A constant male tradition in western culture had always insinuated that men should not love, or at least should not publicly display their love for, their wives. Philip clearly violated the tradition. His relation to the queen was one of complete dependence, personal, emotional and psychological. It was expressed through the channel of matrimony and love, but outside observers saw only the sexual context and not the clinical problems behind it. Their reports, copied faithfully by later historians,[54] insisted always on the insatiable sexual demands of the king (we shall return to this subject in the next chapter). It is consequently important to insist that Philip's sexual needs were neither abnormal nor insatiable, and that he had none outside his marriage to the queen. In 1711 when Marie Louise was ill the French ambassador Noailles and the count of Aguilar attempted to separate the couple by suggesting to Philip that it would be better for them to sleep apart, and that if the king needed a temporary bed-mate it would be easy to find him one. Philip became furious and promptly told both Marie Louise and Ursins. The latter complained to Madame de Maintenon, and the ambassador's strategy was quickly dropped.

The constant complaints, by both Spaniards and French, of the excessive influence of Marie Louise and Ursins, were well founded, indeed, the French foreign minister's summary of the situation in 1711 was exact: 'Philip deliberates and decides with the help of the queen and the princess, and this inner council is what determines matters of state; the other councils are a mere formality'. It was of great importance, for Philip at that time was refusing to accept the French conditions for a peace settlement. The marquis of Bonnac, Torcy's ambassador in 1711, could only confirm what his instructions had told him: 'The king does not make decisions alone, the queen is absolute mistress of Philip's heart and soul', he wrote to Torcy.[55] It was clearly humiliating for an experienced noble and diplomat like Bonnac to be outmanoeuvred by a young girl. Yet Marie Louise possessed a dynamism that was not restricted only to her relationship with her husband. She knew how to communicate with the people, and did so during the war. When she had to move to Burgos in 1704 with the court, while her husband was away at the front, she responded to the cheers of 'Long live the king and queen!' with her own cries of 'Long live the people of Castile!' To encourage by her example, she publicly sold her jewels to pay for the costs of the war. She was the only Bourbon queen not to be the subject of satirical attacks by pamphleteers,[56] with Saint-Simon even going so far as to say, several years later, that it was the affection of the Spaniards for her that preserved the crown for Philip V.[57] Louis XIV was agreeably surprised by Marie Louise's maturity, and her fortitude during the evacuation from Madrid in 1706. 'I would be surprised by all the qualities that you have displayed at such a difficult time', he wrote to her in May 1706, 'were I to take account only of your age and your limited experience, but you have accustomed me to discount the years when considering your wisdom and your talents.' 'I know', he wrote later, 'that Spain places you already in the ranks of its greatest queens.'[58] Marie Louise's correspondence allows us to see some of the astonishing qualities that so impressed the Sun King. One of her letters to her father, Vittorio Amedeo of Savoy, in 1708, is a minor masterpiece. She begins by chiding him for waging war against his own children. 'You are doing your best to deprive me of my crown, and thereby display none of the marks of the love you should have for me. How long, dear papa, are you going to persecute your children? Nothing is more cruel than having to endure war against oneself. Give me the love that I deserve, you alone can make me the happiest princess in the world.' After several more pleas for kindness, her letter changes its tone and offers him a direct bribe, promising him possession of the state of Milan as well as the title of king of Lombardy if he lays down arms.[59]

The queen's second son, Philip, was born prematurely on 2 July 1709 and died six days later. Marie Louise's illnesses and fevers became severe in 1710, but she had been unwell for some time before; 'for four years', she informed Louis XIV in November 1710, 'I have tried all sorts of remedy'.[60] The problem of her ill-health became serious in 1711, serving as an excuse for the attempt, mentioned above, to separate the king and queen. That spring, plans were made to take her to Corella, in Navarre, in order to recuperate in the mountain air, and she was accompanied there in June by Philip, who used the opportunity to hold discussions with French diplomats over the terms of the proposed peace treaty. The royal couple returned to Madrid in November after a short stay in Aranjuez, but Marie Louise was both ill and pregnant. In May 1712 the *Gaceta de Madrid* reported that she 'does not attend public functions'. Her third child, Felipe Pedro, was born on 7 July 1712 in the Alcázar and outlived his mother (he died in December 1719). The royal family in the Alcázar celebrated the Carnival of 1713 with great festivities, but the queen was not present. Marie Louise had no difficulty with the birth of the Infante Ferdinand on 23 September 1713. In January 1714 her illness – since diagnosed as tuberculosis[61] – was accompanied by continuous fever, and she died on 14 February. The loss, we are told by his tutor Louville, affected the king very severely,[62] and there is absolutely no reason to accept the distorted image given by Saint-Simon, who in any case was not there at the time, of a king who remained indifferent to his wife's death.[63] Her body was displayed for three days in the main hall of the Alcázar, and on Sunday the 18th was taken in state to be buried in the monastery of the Escorial.

Immediately a search was begun for a new queen. The possibilities reduced themselves to just two: the daughter of the king of Poland, and the niece of the duke of Parma. Advisers both in Versailles and in Madrid opted for Parma, whose ruling family, the Farnese, had historic links with Spain and moreover had important territorial interests in Italy that might one day become Spanish. The candidate, Elizabeth Farnese, born in 1692, was daughter of Dorothea Sophia of Neuburg, sister of the last queen of Habsburg Spain, Mariana of Neuburg. In Madrid the envoy of the duke of Parma, Giulio Alberoni, explained to ministers and to the princess of Ursins that Elizabeth would make an ideal wife, quiet and docile, 'accustomed only to discourses of sewing and embroidery'.[64] To Ursins this appeared to be a candidate who would suit her plans admirably and she accordingly recommended the princess to Philip and to the French court. Louis XIV gave his approval. The proxy marriage was celebrated in Parma and in Spain on the same day, 16 September 1714; in Parma the duke acted as proxy for the king of Spain and the mass was celebrated in the cathedral by the papal legate.

Even before the death of Marie Louise and the accession of Elizabeth Farnese, there was a strong popular reaction in Spain against French influence. While the anti-French attitude of the provinces of the Crown of Aragon hardly needs explaining, in Castile as well there was strong hostility to the Utrecht peace terms, to the remaining French ministers and to the new taxes made necessary by war expenses. 'These last few days', ambassador Brancas reported at the end of January 1714, 'they have found posters set up in all the corners of the city ordering all the French nation, in the name of the people, to leave Madrid immediately.'[65] In November Torcy was informed that 'a pamphlet has been circulating through the main cities of Andalucia threatening all the French'.[66] By contrast, Italian influence was already on the increase from 1711. The new Inquisitor General, Cardinal Giudice,[67] and the viceroy of Peru, appointed in 1711, were Italians. One of the most distinguished generals of the monarchy was the duke of Popoli, a grandee of Spain. In February 1714, despite Spanish complaints, a Milanese, the Príncipe Pío, marquis of Castelrodrigo, was appointed governor of Madrid.

When the new queen arrived, therefore, she coincided with a tide in favour of Italy. Elizabeth passed through France on her way to Spain, stopping in Bayonne, where she stayed for ten days with her aunt Mariana of Neuburg. When she arrived in Pamplona on 11 December, she was joined by Alberoni. Philip, encouraged by verbal reports from Alberoni, was torn between impatience and excitement at meeting his new bride, and sent her anxious letters every two or three days.

I cannot wait any longer, Madame [he wrote to her on 15 August, exactly four weeks before the proxy wedding], to express to you my joy at the marriage that is going to unite us, and my impatience to be able to tell you myself. I shall for my part do all I can to contribute

to your happiness, and establish with you a firm union that will be
the joy of my life. I am writing to you without formality, for I do not
wish that there be any between us; and in French, for I learn with
great pleasure that you understand this language.[68]

Philip's subsequent letters, to which Elizabeth replied in the same
style (but in Italian), were veritable love letters. On 19 November, he
wrote that 'though I have the unhappiness to be still separated from
you, it is too agreeable to write to you for me to miss the opportunity
of doing so. You can count on receiving letters from me as often as it
is possible, until I can tell you personally all that I feel for you.' A week
later he wrote: 'I count the moments that separate me from you'. On
11 December he claimed that 'the moments are for me like centuries'.
On 23 December he wrote: 'I shall be without fail tomorrow at Guadalajara, at about three or four in the afternoon. It is impossible for me to
express the joy that I feel'.

On the night of 23 December Elizabeth reached Jadraque, just north
of Guadalajara, where she was met by the princess of Ursins, who was
anxious to assert her authority over her new mistress. Ursins was to
receive a rude shock. Instead of an impressionable young girl, she
encountered a commanding young woman of twenty-two years, who
refused to brook the *camarera mayor*'s superior attitude. Their meeting
resulted in a quarrel that caused Farnese in a rage to order her guards
to take 'that mad woman' away. Ursins's own report was that 'the queen
told me that I was insolent and impertinent, shouted for the captain of
her guard and ordered him to conduct me to my room, prepare a coach,
and have fifty guards escort me to the frontier with France'. She was
given no time even to collect her personal effects. 'I left at eleven in the
night', the 72-year-old princess complained later, 'despite the frightful
snow, wind and cold.' The coach-driver drove all night. A week later
Elizabeth wrote to Louis XIV, 'I hope that Your Majesty is not offended
by the decision I took'. She also wrote at once to the king, in a note
taken specially by Alberoni, expressing her 'horrible consternation and
deep affliction' at the conduct of Ursins.

Philip replied immediately, reassuring Elizabeth that the departure
of Ursins did not affect his 'tenderness, and desire to live with you',

and that 'the princess's lack of respect deserved the punishment that you have inflicted'. As he promised, he was waiting for his bride. On 24 December the ceremony confirming the wedding was celebrated in Guadalajara, and the royal pair entered Madrid three days later through the Puerta de Alcalá. They went first to attend a *Te Deum* at Atocha, then took up residence in the Alcázar.

The fall of Ursins came as a thunderbolt to everyone, and in fact it signalled the end of the French role in Spain's government. The *abbé* Alberoni, seen by many as the new 'strong man' behind Farnese, had meetings with other members of the Italian circle at court which resulted in a royal decree of 7 February 1715 dismissing the two ministers most associated with the French, Orry and Macanaz. Philip's confessor Pierre Robinet, who had always worked closely with Orry and Macanaz, was replaced by another French Jesuit, Guillaume Daubenton, who had been the royal confessor at the very beginning of the reign until replaced by Robinet in 1705. Several other major changes were made in the administration. A decree of 9 June abolished all the reforms that Macanaz and Orry had instituted in November 1713, and restored the system of councils to its previous state; subsequent decrees modified other aspects of the administration. Italians were given important posts: Cardinal Giudice was restored to favour and made governor of the prince of Asturias, and his brother the prince of Cellamare was appointed ambassador to France. 'The court of Spain', wrote the French *chargé d'affaires* in Madrid in December, 'is totally different from what it was ten days ago. It is a completely new court and a completely new system.'[69] It was also the end of an era of Bourbon history, for on 1 September 1715, Louis XIV, Philip's grandfather and the single greatest influence on his education and formation, passed away.

* * *

The disappearance of French control marked an important change in political life, but did little to interrupt the development of French influences in Spanish culture. Philip and Marie Louise always had a poor opinion of peninsular styles and art, and from the beginning of the reign encouraged the entry of foreign artists. 'If we had good painters in Spain', Marie Louise wrote to her family in Savoy in September 1712, 'I would not have waited for you to ask me to send you portraits of ourselves; the ones that have been done till now are all so bad that I could not reach a decision. As soon as we return to more tranquil times, we shall bring a painter from France.' Perhaps the most significant artist in residence in Madrid had been Luca Giordano, but he returned to Italy in 1702. The artist whom Philip really wished to have with him was the great French portrait painter Hyacinthe Rigaud, but he resisted all invitations, merely recommending other painters he knew, who came to Spain after the war. Of these, the first significant French arrival was Michel-Ange Houasse, who came to Madrid in 1715 (at the invitation of Jean Orry) expressly to do a routine portrait of Philip. He stayed till his death in 1730, but did not achieve continuous royal patronage despite his excellent portraits, spending his time instead painting scenes from rural life, a fresh and original departure from court and Church painting. Six years later, in 1722, Jean Ranc came to work for the court and he too produced meticulous official portraits of the royal family. Only very much later, in 1737, did Louis-Michel Van Loo complete the list of prominent foreign artists who served Philip V.

Many French advisers and soldiers stayed on in Spain and continued to serve the king. In this, Philip was the key factor, for he continued always to speak French, conversing and corresponding with his wives and his children exclusively in that tongue. In the domestic sphere, his private household continued to be exclusively French in personnel, and his confessors were, until 1723, French. Father Bermúdez, who took over as confessor that year, was Spanish but fluent in French and translated into Spanish the works of Philip's favourite French preacher, the Jesuit Bourdaloue. Philip also had the good fortune that even after the war his chief ministers and generals tended to be foreigners and could all speak French to him. Foreign nobles and soldiers (such as the marquis of Bay, the marquis of Lède and the duke of Popoli) who had made their careers in the war in the peninsula, stayed on to serve the Bourbon king. Of the other professionals, one of the most important commercial agents of the crown, Antoine de Sartine, was a Frenchman who became a distinguished military administrator, while the king's own personal physician from 1717 to 1729 was an Irishman formerly resident in France, Dr John Higgins.

The continuation of French influence can also be seen in the two most innovative cultural measures of the war years, the formation of a Spanish Academy and the establishment of a Royal Library. The Academy, which is touched on below (Chapter 8), was created as a result of the private initiative of the marquis of Villena, but with the active patronage of the king. The Royal Library, by contrast, was more directly linked with the king's own interests. One of Philip's hobbies was the collecting of books and when he became king he brought with him from France a magnificent collection of several thousand volumes. In the final period of the war it was suggested to Philip by his confessor Robinet that a practical use might be made of the many valuable books that featured among the confiscations made of rebel property. Robinet's idea was to establish a collection,[70] using as its basis the volumes confiscated from the rebel archbishop of Valencia in 1710. To this end, Macanaz arranged for the transport of the archbishop's library to Madrid, where in 1713 Father Robinet became the first director of the Royal Library. Among the works incorporated into it were the king's own collection (some 3,000 volumes), as well as other items confiscated from rebels. Throughout his reign Philip would continue to show a personal interest in the Library: in 1716 he imported from France books on history, science and literature for the collections.[71]

*   *   *

A military conflict that preyed over the same land for over a decade, with several major battles, innumerable sieges and extensive occupations of territory, was bound to have a profound impact on the people of Spain. Indeed, a historian of Aragon claimed in the eighteenth century that 'the most fatal blow, that profoundly hurt our industry and population, came from the years of the War of Succession',[72] yet the evidence suggests on the contrary that, despite the inevitable sum of human misery caused by the war, the consequences were less far reaching than many have thought.

Wars and battles always cost the lives of soldiers, but in this case possibly the majority of soldiers fighting in the peninsula were foreigners. With the exception of Catalan auxiliaries, nearly all the allied troops were non-Spaniards, and a high proportion of the Bourbon troops was French. Hence, the direct victims of battles were consequently more likely to be foreign, which was one of the reasons why the generals showed impatience with the resistance of towns, such as Xàtiva, where the siege cost unnecessary loss of life among their soldiers. There were few civil victims; it was a war conducted through battles, not through attacks on the civilian population. The armies were in principle not seeking riches or land; they wished only to gain the support of the people. As the archbishop of Saragossa observed in 1705, at the start of the conflict: 'the population do not look on this war as one waged with fire and blood. The actions of the rebels do not touch their lives or their property'.[73] In the main, there seem to have been few atrocities like that which occurred in the Aragonese village of Arén, where the Catalan commander ordered the execution of ninety-one villagers for resisting his troops.[74]

The conflict, of course, aggravated other problems. It provoked epidemics: in Orihuela in 1707 there was a steep rise in deaths due to the unhygienic conditions during the siege that year. Comparable outbreaks occurred at the same time in Murcia and Cartagena. There was an epidemic too in Seville in 1709, and in Santiago de Compostela in 1710. But the rise in mortality in the centre of Castile between 1706 and 1710, observed clearly in the parish records,[75] was due more to drought and bad harvests than to the direct impact of war. In Extremadura, between 1707 and 1710, drought and a plague of locusts caused the crisis in the countryside.[76] It is, of course, true that the harvests would also have suffered from the war conditions, when the soldiers seized mules for transport, or young men were pressed into the armies. Many villages must have suffered like that in Toledo province which complained that 'with the coming of the troops this year, and the heavy tribute they levied both in cash and in grain, most of the residents have been left with nothing with which to maintain their herds'.[77] Law and order collapsed in several parts of Spain as a consequence of the war. In the years after Utrecht, there was a general increase in banditry and piracy, which may be attributed in good part to anti-Bourbon resistance in the east of the peninsula, where the authorities in 1716 reported that Catalan and Mallorcan pirates were active.[78] But in those years the highways of Old Castile were also infested by robbers.

As in all wars, there were movements of population. Peasants and villagers fled from unfriendly armies and from military tax-collectors. The dominant trend was for refugees to migrate from the rural areas to the towns. In Cáceres there was a rise in requests for residential status from people who had lived in the countryside, a phenomenon which Philip V tried to control during the difficult year 1709 through an order of 3 July, which stated that 'many and diverse people, with the excuse of poor harvests and in order to be free of taxes and royal contributions, have left the villages where they had their homes and introduced themselves into the larger cities and towns of the kingdom'.[79] In Madrid in 1714 the city police, the Sala de Alcaldes de Corte, ordered measures to be taken against 'the many vagabonds and thieves and disreputable people who have come to the capital'.[80] Otherwise, apart from temporary emigration, the war seems not to have caused a significant fall in population levels in Spain.

In strictly economic terms, the impact of the war was moderate. If we look at the movement of prices in the peninsula, a picture emerges that is far from disastrous. The Spain inherited by Philip V was, as we have already observed, on the first steps towards recovery. A historian has rightly referred to 'monetary stability and a movement of prices that made the worst military and political events coincide with a time of calm and economic recovery'.[81] It is true that the worst material conditions were to be found in Catalonia during the final years of the war, but even in these circumstances, in Barcelona 'the presence of the (archducal) court and of troops, the influx of money, the rise in prices, were more than ever before a stimulant to the economy'.[82]

When they looked back to the early years of the reign of Philip V, the Spanish statesmen of the later eighteenth century retained a positive impression of the war period. Jovellanos commented that 'though otherwise calamitous, the War of Succession not only conserved at home the money and men that would have disappeared abroad, but also attracted the same from foreign lands and set them to work among us'.[83] Campomanes observed that 'few would have believed in 1703 that those unjust invasions would turn to the real benefit of Spain. It is from then that the recovery of the country must be dated. This was the first benefit obtained by Spain in the glorious reign of Philip V'.[84] The long years of war and suffering gave Philip the leadership of a kingdom that, far from being left in ruins, returned once more to the forefront of European politics.

CHAPTER FOUR

Elizabeth Farnese, 1715–1723

'HIS MAJESTY IS SO PERPLEXED AND UNDECIDED, THAT DESPITE
THE INFLUENCE WHICH THE QUEEN EXERCISES OVER HIM,
NOBODY HAS ANY IDEA OF HOW DIFFICULT IT IS TO PRESS HIM TO
TAKE ENERGETIC MEASURES.'

GIULIO ALBERONI, JULY 1716

The new queen of Spain was twenty-two years old when she married
Philip. She was notably pretty in her early portraits, though this
soon faded. Above all, she was lively, intelligent, independent and
cultured, fluent in French and German (her mother was German)
as well as her native Italian. A description of her by the prince of
Monaco, who met her when she was on her way to Spain, says that
she was 'of medium height and a good figure; the face long, much
marked with smallpox; she has blue eyes which are as sparkling as
can be; she can say everything with them. Her conversation is gracious.
She is passionately fond of music, and can ride and hunt; Spanish is
the only language which she does not know; her will is extremely
strong.'[1] Her immediate dismissal of Ursins demonstrated that
she wished to be her own mistress, and she did not delay in imposing
her tastes on the court. Philip seems to have accepted without
complaint the removal of Ursins. '*Eh bien*, my queen,' he said to

Elizabeth after a satisfying supper in January 1715, 'if the lady had been here we could not have enjoyed these happy moments!'[2] So substantial were the changes she introduced that the rest of the reign became thoroughly influenced by the culture and politics of Italy.

Like her predecessor as queen, Elizabeth retained all her personal tastes and continued the preference at court for Italian and French style in dress. Unaccustomed to Spanish food, she had Italian wines, cheese and ham (notably that of Parma) specially imported for herself.[3] All her clothes were made in Italy (later she also had them made in Paris), and even her Italian horses were imported. She was a great lover of the theatre but found the theatre in Madrid (performed moreover in a language she did not understand) unsatisfactory, and imported a troupe of Italian actors in 1718 to perform three times a week at the Pardo. All her innovations were an important step forward in bringing more sophistication to the court for like other foreigners who visited the peninsula in these years, she found Spain very provincial and restricted in its culture.[4] Brought up in one of the greatest noble families of Italy, which had made Parma famous for its architecture and in Rome had constructed the superb Palazzo Farnese, she tried, within the limits of her resources, to update Spanish culture. As her adviser Alberoni assured her, 'God had placed her on this earth not to entertain herself with trifles but to display her talents'.[5] And Elizabeth had very many talents.

Unlike the previous queen, she was a fully mature and creative woman. The French ambassador in 1716 described her as 'vigorous, and with great capacities'. In accepting her new position as queen, she also accepted a role that she fulfilled with great fidelity: an absolute dedication to the interests of her husband. Twelve months after her arrival in Spain, she gave birth to her first son, Charles (the future Charles III of Spain), who was born on 16 January 1716. However, he had no inheritance awaiting him, since Marie Louise's two sons preceded him in their right to the Spanish throne. The situation made Philip look with favour on schemes to secure some territory for his new son, and he turned to Italy, the traditional hunting ground for Spanish military adventurers. He had the obvious support of Elizabeth, whose own schemes for her sons would continue to engage the government for the rest of the reign.

Her relationship with Philip determined the remaining years of their lives, and it is consequently important to clarify what that was. Though portrayed both by contemporaries and by historians as a powerful scheming woman who dominated a weak and helpless husband, her true role was somewhat different from what has been supposed. The king, as Alberoni realised, was by no means a weak person, and Elizabeth had constantly to use her charms to gain his confidence. 'Though she had won her husband,' Alberoni reported, 'she treated him as though he were still to win, which threw the poor king into ecstasies of delight.' Philip told Alberoni that 'it was God who had made him the precious gift of so lovable a queen'. Everything she did was conditioned by the character of the king, to which we must now turn.

As we have indicated, Philip suffered from a serious neurobiological disorder,[6] which must in part have been hereditary, since he passed the problem on to his children. There is a possibility in his case that he inherited it through his mother, in whose family, the Wittelsbachs of Bavaria, the malady surfaced from time to time.[7] It had evidently developed in his early teens, the period when it normally shows itself, and by the time he became king at seventeen he was already suffering from it. The description of his character given by Madame de Maintenon and others at the French court confirms that he had the relevant symptoms; it was, in all respects, an illness, and not simply (as they supposed) a result of defects in Philip's personality. The king, for example, was not necessarily lazy or weak; when he showed these characteristics, it was because he was suffering the consequences of his psychiatric situation. His condition developed into a bipolar disorder or manic depression, alternating between poles of depression ('lows') and elation ('highs'). It was signalled during his earlier years solely by episodes of depression, such as he had in Madrid in 1701 or in Naples in 1702. These attacks were episodic; they would come and go, often not repeating themselves for months or even years. A new phase in his illness began during the visit to Milan, when his 'lows' were succeeded by an extended 'high', provoked by his excitement over the challenge of war and battle. This bipolarity between 'lows' and 'highs' brought Philip into the full range of his disorder. During the 'lows' he would experience depression, the urge to isolate himself, headaches and a feeling of complete incapacity (with the passage of years, as we shall see, there were even graver symptoms). During the 'highs', by contrast, he would experience euphoria, excitement, hyperactivity and even a feeling of invincibility (hence the risks that he deliberately took in battle).

During his depressive phases, Philip looked desperately outside himself for support. In Madrid shortly after he became king, and during his visit to Naples, there was nobody who could offer him the psychotherapy that he needed. By contrast his marriages first to Marie Louise and then to Elizabeth supplied him with immediate and personal help. He clung to his wives and disliked being separated from them. Observers at court, who claimed that the king had an inordinate sexual appetite, had not the slightest understanding of the way in which his wives were in fact saving the king's mental health. It is significant that after his union with Marie Louise in 1703 and during the early years of the reign, there appear to be no reports of Philip's illness. In all likelihood he continued to have occasional attacks, but the supportive role of his wife and the excitement of the war always came to his rescue. During the years when no attacks of depression were reported, the campaigns of the War of Succession were the supreme therapy. They did not cure his depressions, but they led him to the other extreme of bipolarity. While he may have felt that his health was improving, because the highs balanced the lows and gave him a feeling of buoyancy and success, in fact it was getting worse. After 1715, Elizabeth's support came to be the most crucial of all; it was far more powerful, for instance, than the comfort that Philip undoubtedly gained from religion. Though religion certainly gave him some assurance and comfort, it was only secondary to the essential personal support that he received from Elizabeth, on whom he became as totally dependent as he had been on Marie Louise. The miracle, for him, was that Elizabeth's dedication to him was also total.

Both Philip and Elizabeth came from elite ruling houses that had a specific and highly restricted vision of the art of government. Philip's view of his role reflected exactly what he had been taught in Versailles. He had been appointed by God, but his duties were to 'his people', an anonymous entity with which he seldom bothered to get in contact. The people were expected to pay their taxes and behave in an orderly way. They could not rebel against a legitimate ruler: Philip's verbal judgments on rebels were always harsh, and he always supported the hard line against them, insisting for example that the Catalans must be treated severely. In practice, these verbal assaults seldom took the form of action; after ten years of war, when scores of his nobility committed open treason against him, those severely punished could almost be counted on the fingers of one hand.

He probably knew little of how Spaniards lived, for he did not habitually speak their language, nor does he appear to have been in contact with popular opinion, unlike Habsburg rulers who had made a habit of accepting personal petitions and listening to grievances. All government paperwork went to his ministers; his only task was to meet the ministers regularly, debate policy with them, sign correspondence and make his own opinions known. He believed that war and foreign policy were his direct personal responsibility, and conducted both as though they affected his personal honour. He enjoyed travelling; it matured his mind and at the same time enabled him to escape from the solitude of his depressions. By 1715 he had been through much of France, Naples and Milan, and had direct experience of sailing the Mediterranean. During the War of Succession, his campaigns gave him extensive knowledge of the greater part of the peninsula.

* * *

The rising political star in 1715 was Elizabeth Farnese's adviser, Alberoni. Giulio Alberoni, aged fifty-one at the time of Philip's marriage to Farnese, was born in Piacenza of humble origins, became a priest, and made the acquaintance of the duke of Vendôme during the French military campaigns in Parma. He entered Vendôme's service and returned with him to France and then to Spain (1711), where he succeeded in being appointed agent of the duke of Parma in Madrid. Alberoni negotiated the marriage of Parma's niece Elizabeth to Philip, and profited from the new queen's favour to establish his own influence. Short, slightly corpulent, with penetrating eyes and a soft voice, he was highly cultured and a competent author.

Effective chief minister from the end of 1715, Alberoni in fact had no official post in the administration and operated exclusively as a minister for the king and especially for the queen, who gave him his orders. His position of 'favourite' had been a traditional one under the Habsburgs, but had always attracted the hostility of the ruling elite; in his case hostility was aggravated by the fact that he was a foreigner. He was able to direct many aspects of government policy, but inevitably had to cope with obstruction from officials and ministers. The situation was described perfectly by the British minister in Spain, George Bubb, in 1717: 'There is very little trust between these gentlemen [in the administration] and Alberoni, for he does not permit them to do what they wish, yet what he does has to pass through their hands, so that everything assumes a marvellous aspect of confusion and disorder'.[8]

Alberoni's situation throws a good deal of light on the system of government practised by Philip V. The traditional objection to the old system of councils was that they despatched business too slowly. Alberoni's objection was to the fact that they despatched business at all. Although a number of changes in the conciliar system were attempted in 1715, it was not until the royal decree of 2 April 1717 that a fundamental transformation was made that established the basis of the Bourbon system of government in Spain. By this decree, state business was directed through three ministries – of War and the Navy, of State, and of Justice and Finance. The secretary of each of the ministries, termed 'secretary of the Despacho', directed all business and was in fact minister of that department. While these were truly innovative measures and began the creation of modern departments and ministerial posts, at that stage the process was only in its infancy; the real novelty of the system established in 1717 lay in something that did not appear in the decree. Concentrating power in the hands of the ministers allowed them to make decisions without referring to the councils; they could issue orders merely by consulting with the king or with another minister. This procedure, known as the *via reservada*,[9] made it possible for Alberoni to take part directly in decision-making, by acting through the 'secretaries of the Despacho'. It also enabled the king to make decisions after consulting with a minister and nobody else.

With the help of the queen, Alberoni encouraged a small team of sympathetic ministers – some of Italian origin, such as the brothers Patiño[10] – to support his efforts. The collaboration was an uneasy one, José Patiño himself objecting to Alberoni that it was unconstitutional for a minister to 'be responsible directly to one sole person without passing through the channel of the secretariat of the Despacho'.[11] In the end, Alberoni always had to rely on the king and queen. Nevertheless, for four short years, he instilled some vigour into aspects of the administration; José Patiño said later that Alberoni 'turned impossibilities into mere difficulties'. But Alberoni was never in adequate control of the government. Bubb's experience was that 'I cannot get much done with him, but without him it is quite impossible to do anything. Alberoni swears to me that there are things he does not do because it is not in his power to do them, and that these gentlemen of the Council manage everything, with the sole aim of destroying the plans of Alberoni; and in this I believe him'.[12] His tasks were limited to diplomacy – he was fluent in French and Italian – and raising money for the purposes of royal policy. Though some historians have thought differently, his intentions seem to have been directed solely towards peace. He once told Philip V: 'If Your Majesty is willing to conserve your kingdom in peace for five years, I can make Spain the most powerful monarchy in Europe'.[13]

Since the advent of Elizabeth Farnese, court groups had been divided into two main factions (in the view of Bubb).[14] They were the 'Spanish party', a name given by Bubb to the traditionalists at court, mainly the higher nobility in the councils, and the 'French party', or those who had some links with France and were opposed to Farnese's foreign policy. Both these groups were hostile to the so-called 'party of the favourites', which was in effect the group of Italians in charge of policy. The existence of a 'French party' was of special importance. Ironically, the government of Philip V was now suspicious of France. With the death of Louis XIV on 1 September 1715, a historic reign that had lasted sixty-five years and made France the supreme power in Europe was brought to an end. The new king, Louis XV, was Philip's nephew and only six years old. The regency council made Philip's old antagonist the duke of Orléans regent of France and it was he who supported and financed a sympathetic group among the ministers of Philip. Philip for his part was opposed to the French government not only because of Orléans's apparent interest in the Spanish throne, but also because France had granted to the emperor, in the treaty of Rastatt, all Spain's territories in Italy.

It should be remembered that there had been no peace treaty between Spain and Austria at the end of the War of Succession. For Philip, Spain's principal enemy continued to be the emperor, and every power that made agreements with the emperor also became Spain's enemy. His views coincided with those of Alberoni, who felt that the best way forward for Spain was in alliance with Great Britain, which was also looking for friends. A new king, George I, had just ascended the throne in 1714, but his regime was threatened by the invasion of Scotland in 1715 by the forces of the Old Pretender, James III,[15] who had the implicit support of France. The invasion collapsed, but for the next half-century the British chose their friends only from among those countries that denied support to the Jacobites, as the supporters of the Stuart cause were called.[16]

Philip was never happy with the British alliance, on which he was forced to rely time and again throughout his reign. It seemed illogical to be friends with a power that was occupying Spanish territory. For him the only natural alliance was with France, impossible at that moment because of the policies of the regent Orléans. His hostility to the emperor was because, as Alberoni explained to a diplomat, 'the king seeks a balance of power in Europe, and considers that the emperor's power in Italy is incompatible with this'.[17] From 1716, however, the king found that Spain was being driven into isolation because the other European powers sought to confirm their own positions. In that year Great Britain reached agreements with Austria and France, with the primary purpose of protecting the succession of the house of Hanover against the pretensions of the

Jacobites. Philip's angry reaction demonstrates that it was he personally, rather than his wife or Alberoni, who really decided the direction
of foreign policy.

In the 1716 treaty between London and Vienna, the British guaranteed the possessions of the Empire in Italy, for which Alberoni had
to suffer the full force of the king's indignation. 'So much for
your English whose friendship and good faith you praise so greatly!',
Philip berated his minister. 'What do you say now to defend
them, when they enter into new alliances with our greatest enemies?
Because of your advice, I have abandoned my former friends! To what
straits am I reduced!' However, there was in reality no contradiction
between the Viennese treaty and British efforts to obtain an understanding with Spain. But the king refused to make any favourable
moves towards Great Britain, and Alberoni was obliged to explain
apologetically to Bubb that 'His Majesty is so perplexed and undecided,
that despite the influence which the queen exercises over him,
nobody has any idea of how difficult it is to press him to take energetic
measures'.[18] Whenever the English minister tried to see the king,
Philip was out of the palace, on (Bubb reported) 'endless hunts and
continuous excursions'. Bubb tried to obtain some sort of a resolution
out of ministers, but all claimed that they did not have the power to
make decisions.

Philip's anger with Great Britain intensified later in 1716 when
news came through of an understanding between the English and
the regent of France, for he felt that any guarantees given to the regent
over the succession to the French throne threatened his own just rights
to the French succession. His indignation grew when he learned of a
secret clause supporting the emperor's claims to territory in Italy.
'Those islanders', he raged, 'are the eternal enemies of the house of
Bourbon, since they dare to anticipate a decision on the French succession.'[19] The king's anger was not, in fact, wholly justified. The active
diplomacy of Great Britain in Vienna and Paris had as one of its aims
the securing of peace in the Mediterranean, and the protection of
Spanish territory against Imperial claims. Both the earl of Stanhope
(the former general, now secretary for foreign affairs in Great Britain)
and George I were willing in 1716 to return Gibraltar, which was viewed

as expensive to maintain and of little strategic importance compared with Minorca.[20]

*   *   *

Alberoni's ministry coincided with the first stages of the implementation of the new post-*fuero* regime in the Crown of Aragon and more particularly in Catalonia. The domestic policy of the government in Madrid was profoundly influenced by the revolutionary alterations brought in by the War of Succession, changes which were principally in two areas: more centralisation of administration after the abolition of the provincial *fueros*, and centralised control of state finance. Such an attempt to increase central control was in line with policy in all European states, where moves towards a common government and a common market within national territory were seen as progressive. In respect of the latter, the customs barriers between the different kingdoms of the peninsula were an obvious hindrance to commercial advance. After the abolition of the *fueros*, in January 1708 the king decreed the abolition of the so-called *puertos secos* (dry ports), customs dues payable on Valencia's border with Castile and Aragon, and declared that all commerce should be regulated on an equal and free basis. When the war was over the king re-issued the decree, on 19 November 1714, resolving that 'the *puertos secos* between Castile, Aragon, Valencia and Catalonia be totally abolished, with trade continuing between them freely and without any impediment'.[21] Writing towards the end of the reign, the *arbitrista* Bernardo de Ulloa saw in this decree a measure that signally benefited the industry and trade of Valencia.[22] But a subsequent attempt in 1717 to unify the Spanish market by abolishing the customs barriers between Castile and the Basque provinces failed because of opposition by the small producers in the north. The other significant measure of centralisation was the issue of new coinage in 1718, to circulate freely in Castile and the eastern realms of the peninsula.

The steps towards unity, however, were a painful experience for the provinces of the Crown of Aragon. Subsequent generations there lamented the impact of the changes, which destroyed the political autonomy of each realm and united them all into the Spanish state. In February 1714 we find the new governor of Valencia reporting to the government that 'the obstinate demand of the Catalans for the restoration of their *fueros* finds acceptance in the kingdom of Valencia, whose people clamour with equal persistence for their privileges'.[23] Catalonia, the last realm to be subjected, suffered the most directly. The Diputació and the Consell de Cent were abolished, as we have seen, in 1714. Nevertheless, the government had no clear idea of what to put in their place. The idea of imposing Castilian institutions, taken from Macanaz and enshrined in the decrees of 1707, seemed clear in theory but did not work easily in practice, and would have to be modified in the light of existing structures. The only point on which there was agreement was that all the municipal institutions had to be abolished.[24] However, the difficulty of making immediate changes was the reason why it was two years before a formal proposal for the government of the principality, the 'Nueva Planta' or 'new form', was issued on 16 January 1716. The Planta profited from the experience of the previous nine years, in not imitating the sweeping abolition of laws decreed in Valencia. Instead, it followed the lines of the new government given to Aragon in 1711, and preserved existing civil law in the province. Further details of government were clarified in subsequent decrees of July 1717 and October 1718.

Catalonia also remained, more than any province in Spain, under martial law. The continued Castilian military presence in all the eastern realms was, indeed, the most hated aspect of the new regime. Perhaps its most symbolic act was the construction (1715–18) in Barcelona of a large new citadel, designed by the Flemish engineer Georg Prosper Verboom, for which part of a residential district, the Ribera, was demolished, with the eviction from their homes of 4,000 people. Many were never compensated for the loss of their houses, despite the express instructions of the king that they be paid. Philip had been opposed to the building of the citadel: it was, for him, an important issue 'on which it seems to me the duke of Berwick does not think as I do'.[25] He felt that if the citizens really wanted to rebel again, the citadel would not stop them. At the same time, possible centres of resistance in the principality were eliminated. Forty castles in the area of Girona were demolished, as well as two in Manresa, eight in Camprodón, three in Berga and eleven in Vic.[26] In the same period the six traditional Catalan universities were suppressed, and replaced by a new one established at Cervera (1717). The military presence also affected the population of the countryside. In the summer of 1716, there were 49 battalions of cavalry in the province and 52 units of dragoons, as well as garrisons in 13 fortresses.[27] In October 1715 the intendant of Catalonia reported that people were fleeing from the principality towards the Catalan regions of France, and 'the cause is attributed by the people to the impossibility of paying the heavy taxes, and because they have lost this year's harvest through lack of rain. To this is added the [ill-]treatment they claim to have received from the troops.'[28]

For several years to come, residents of Catalonia continued to complain of their economic difficulties and of the heavy cost of paying for an army of occupation, whose expenses kept rising. Catalonia, as we can see clearly from Diagram 5, remained Spain's main military and naval centre for the rest of the reign. In 1715 José Patiño reported that the annual cost of the army in the province was 4 million escudos, and of the navy 2.5 millions.[29] By 1717, the costs of the army there were put at 4.2 million escudos a year,[30] only part of which was actually borne by the Catalans. That year, for example, the income from the new taxes (the Catastro and other sources) in Catalonia came to 1.8 million escudos, which covered less than half of military costs. However, there was no doubting the resentment of the military presence. In May 1718 Baltasar Patiño described the population of Barcelona as being 'very restless'.[31] Nor was the presence of an army and a navy by any means motivated exclusively by a policy of repression. The international situation had in fact converted Catalonia into the base for Spain's Italian policies. In 1725 military expenses in Catalonia represented 30 per cent of the entire military budget of Spain.[32]

The onerous new regime on the Mediterranean coast of Spain affected politics and taxation, but not culture. Some writers of a later generation claimed that the regime of Philip V had prohibited and undermined the majority language of Catalonia and Valencia, a view which is both exaggerated and untenable.[33] The Nueva Planta began, two hundred years after similar laws had been decreed in England and

France, the practice of using a single official administrative language, namely Castilian; the change was inevitable, since the various military administrators in the province – Castilians, French and Italians – shared in common only a knowledge of the Castilian tongue. (The Inquisition, which felt the same need to use a language its administrators could understand, had made Castilian obligatory in the Crown of Aragon one and a half centuries before.) The impact was slow and complex. The use of Latin in the courts, for example, continued to 1778. Castilian was used in official paperwork. For all practical purposes, however, Catalan continued to be the principal and commonly the only spoken and written tongue among the people in Catalonia and Valencia. It continued also as the official language of the Church. Three generations after the abolition of the *fueros*, when virtually all the official written business of the principality was being conducted in Castilian, the bishops were using Catalan as their main administrative language.[34] Throughout Catalan society, the Catalan language remained alive and vibrant in every branch of human expression.[35]

The new regime, of course, contributed to the *undermining* of the regional language, but this was a small part of a long process that intensified in subsequent generations. For over a century before 1700 the Catalan lands had been subjected to the steady infiltration of Castilian language and culture and the preference given to Castilian by the Nueva Planta strengthened yet further a tendency that many Catalans had long encouraged. Since at least the sixteenth century, sectors of the local elite had used Castilian as their preferred medium of literary expression.[36] Increasingly after 1600, the majority of books published in the province by publishers were in Castilian. Hence, the cultural status of Catalan was already gravely undermined a century before the War of Succession; the new post-*fuero* regime only served to accentuate the process. Further measures by the state, especially under Charles III, confirmed the undermining of the regional languages.

The changes decreed in Aragon, Catalonia, Mallorca and Valencia appeared radical in political terms, not only because of the disappearance of traditional institutions but also because of the theoretical abolition of the laws of the realms and their substitution by others based on those of Castile. In practice, it was impossible to change everything:

previous local, municipal and Church laws were confirmed, and in Aragon and Catalonia the civil law was also reaffirmed. Moreover, everywhere the ruling elites were left unmolested in their control of political life. The perceived impact of the new regime was, however, deeply negative; the presence of Castilian officials and troops gave the provinces of the Crown of Aragon the ineradicable feeling that they were an occupied people.

The integration of the eastern provinces into a national state gave Spain's government, for the first time in its history, the material resources to pursue the belligerent policies favoured by Philip and his advisers. Three main areas were affected: treasury receipts increased, administrative control was established and a new army and navy were created; all were reforms that had their origin in French policies first implemented during the War of Succession. On the basis of these reforms, Alberoni and his successors, with the active encouragement of Philip, dreamed of restoring Spain's power on the international scene, something which became possible only because of the financial resources tapped by Alberoni and Patiño. In 1715 Bubb was of the opinion that 'the revenues of Philip V exceed by one third those of his predecessors, and his expenses do not come to one half'. The government's own confidential figures, as we shall now see, suggest that this assessment was correct.

One of the more remarkable consequences of the reign was the continuous increase in government income. Although there is no way of calculating state income with accuracy, we can take as a guide the quantity of money entering the main state agency, the treasury (Tesorería Mayor). In 1702 the government received an annual tax income of only 9.6 million escudos. At the end of the War of Succession, in 1713, income reaching the treasury had increased to an average annual 22.9 million escudos; by 1746 the income was an average 36.9 million. In other words, government income from all sources increased by 238 per cent between 1702 and 1713, and by 384 per cent between 1702 and 1746. When we bear in mind that the government no longer had the problem of inflation to deal with, these increases can be seen as very substantial. They were the consequence not of higher taxation, but of increased efficiency in administration. A good example is the great increase in revenue from the tax on tobacco, which had been a state monopoly since 1636. Thanks to a more systematic control of the monopoly, and its extension to the Crown of Aragon after 1707, government income from this source increased at least 400 per cent between 1702 and 1722,[37] and continued to do so for the rest of the reign (see Diagram 7). Indeed, from this early date, Spaniards demonstrated that they were the most addicted consumers of tobacco in Europe.

An important part in the growth of income was played by the new taxes in the Crown of Aragon. Before the abolition of the *fueros* in 1707 no effective income came to the government from the provinces of Aragon, but after 1713 (see Diagram 4) income from there continued to rise impressively. The change, a fundamental one, can be seen through the case of Valencia. Immediately after the abolition of the *fueros*, royal officials took over control of all tax revenue with the result that royal tax income in Valencia rose in 1712 to five times its value in 1707. From 1715, a new tax was created, the *equivalente*, so-called because it was meant to replace existing taxes while bringing in the same value as they had. In practice, many other taxes also continued to operate, and the *equivalente* came to represent less than half the total of taxes paid to the government.

Apart from the major changes that took place within the central government, perhaps the most important administrative reform of the reign was the establishment of intendants.[38] Officials with this name had long existed in France, and it was inevitable that advisers of Philip V should suggest that they be introduced into Spain. Jean Orry was the first person to make such a proposal; a memoir of his dated 1703 suggested establishing seventeen intendants.[39] However, the real founder of the post was the Flemish count of Bergeyck, who for a few months in 1711 was Philip's chief minister. At the end of 1711 Bergeyck's proposals were approved by the Despacho, and in December intendants were nominated to all the provinces of Spain. Their functions were chiefly military, and they soon ceased to exist in provinces where there were few military duties. In 1718 Alberoni and Patiño re-introduced the intendancies on a more systematic basis: twenty-one intendants were appointed throughout the country.

The Council of Castile, which tended to oppose anything proposed by Alberoni, vigorously resisted the new system and succeeded in obtaining in 1721 the abolition of all intendants in provinces where they had no military role. This apparently negative move was of limited importance. For the rest of the reign there were intendants in the ten largest cities of the peninsula, where they were in charge of military and naval activity and also played a significant part in administration. The intendancies, moreover, were the training ground of Philip V's most important administrators. Both José Patiño and his brother Baltasar rose to prominence through their work in the intendancies, as did José del Campillo, Rodrigo Caballero, Antoine Sartine and many other distinguished figures. The intendancies were the key component of the new Bourbon administration.

The most impressive achievement of the government in the years after Utrecht was the creation of a new army and navy. Spain, for the first time in its history, began to maintain a powerful standing army. Under the Habsburgs, the state had recruited armies only when required. The new Bourbon army, recruited with great difficulty because of the objections everywhere (especially in the Crown of Aragon) to military service, inevitably involved important administrative and fiscal reforms. The annual cost of the army in 1725 was 5,352,000 escudos, a massive sum that had no precedent in the history of the Spanish treasury,[40] and of which three-fifths went to finance the army in Catalonia.

The navy owed its existence mainly to José Patiño. As we have seen, at the beginning of the century the naval resources of the Spanish crown were limited. During the War of Succession, the country was totally dependent in naval matters on the protecting hand of France, and Spanish failures against the allies can be explained largely in terms of the naval supremacy of the latter. Bergeyck was the first government minister to be seriously concerned with naval recovery, and his correspondence with the French navy minister Pontchartrain refers to an ambitious plan that drew extensively on French experience. It was a subject in which Philip took a close interest. 'I have revealed the plan only to the king', wrote Bergeyck in 1713. 'It has been necessary to keep it secret because of the jealous attitude of the English ministry.'[41] In

February 1714 Philip created a new naval officer corps, and abolished all the old profusion of titles by which commanders of the various fleets were known, instituting in their place a standard superior rank of 'Captain General of the Sea'.

The real creation of the navy may be dated to Patiño's appointment as intendant of Cadiz in 1717. From that period, the amount of money set aside by the government for the navy rose spectacularly (see Diagrams 1 and 9). In 1705 only 79,000 escudos was spent on the navy, by 1713 the figure had risen eighteen times, to 1,485,000 escudos. And the cost kept rising. In his first year in charge of the navy, 1717, Patiño spent three times more than had been disbursed in 1713. He also held the posts of president of the House of Trade (the Casa de la Contratación) of Seville, and intendant of the area, so he had virtually total powers over policy, powers which he used wisely, to found dockyards and promote shipbuilding. Despite these reforms, it should be noted that the navies made available for the Mediterranean expeditions in 1717 and 1718 were not for the most part constructed in Spain. Though vessels were being built in Catalonia, Andalucia and Vizcaya, most of the ships used in expeditions were largely purchased from France or hired from private owners. Thanks to the contracts that the government made with French captains,[42] Spain was able to convert itself into a major naval power.

* * *

The island of Sardinia had been occupied in August 1708, during the War of Succession, by allied troops transported by Admiral Leake. One of the nobles who fled from the island at that time was the marquis of San Felipe, who thereafter did not cease to urge on the king the need to recover Sardinia. The cession of the island to Austria in 1714 did not change the internal politics that prevailed among the elite there, a bitter conflict between supporters of Spain and those who supported the house of Austria. Spain's intervention three years after Utrecht owed a great deal to the concern, shared by Philip, Elizabeth and Alberoni, over Spain's weakness in Italy, where Austria appeared to be threatening Spanish interests in the duchy of Parma, ruled by Elizabeth's uncle.

An occasion for conflict occurred in May 1717, when the Imperial officials in Milan detained the Spanish Inquisitor General José Molines as he was travelling from Rome to Spain. Molines was very old, and died during his confinement.

Philip V favoured a gesture of force against Imperial interests. Alberoni advised against it, but the king went on to consult the duke of Popoli, who was of the opinion that Spain had the resources for it. Dismayed by this advice from one of Spain's leading generals, Alberoni wrote to him immediately (in Italian) in protest. 'The king my master has passed to me', he wrote, 'Your Excellency's letter dealing with a matter that has filled me with horror and consternation. I do not flatter myself that my reasons are always the most weighty, but I believe that in this case they are strong enough to demonstrate that your project would be the ruin of this poor country. . . . Let us be frank', he went on, 'it would lead the whole of Europe to say and believe that a handful of mad Italians have driven the king to bring about the desolation and total ruin of Spain.'[43] The letter is revealing not only of Alberoni's opinions at this stage of his career, but also of the role that Italians such as he and Popoli were playing in the formation of policy towards Italy. Despite royal support, Alberoni's position continued at all times to be precarious. 'I am not yet master here', he told Bubb in January 1717, 'nor have the queen and myself a single person on whom we can depend. The queen is forced to proceed gradually, and I cannot always induce her to apply herself as much as I would wish.'[44]

Early in 1717 preparations were being made in Barcelona for a naval expedition which Alberoni claimed was being directed against the Turks. Patiño, who was in charge of the military preparations, strongly advised the king that no action against a distant objective such as Naples was recommended, but against his advice, in July 1717, Philip and Elizabeth signed instructions for the fleet to set out for the occupation of Sardinia.[45] The plans were unknown to the pope, who that month elevated Alberoni to the rank of cardinal. There was no doubting the strength of the force that sailed: about 100 vessels, among them nine ships of the line and six frigates, transported 8,500 infantry and 500 cavalry under the command of the marquis of Lède,

Miguel Meléndez, *Marie Louise Gabrielle of Savoy* (1712).

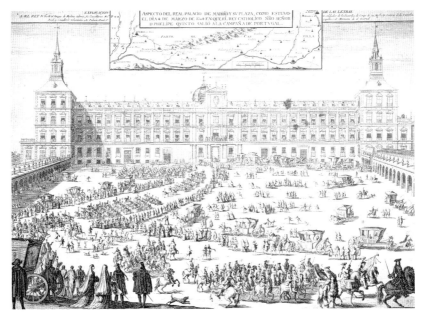

Nicolas Guérard, *Plaza de la Armería, 4 March 1704.*

La Granja de San Ildefonso.

Jean Ranc, *Philip V on Horseback* (1723).

Buenaventura de Libir, *The Battle of Almansa, 1707.*

I. Rigaud, *Assault on Barcelona.*

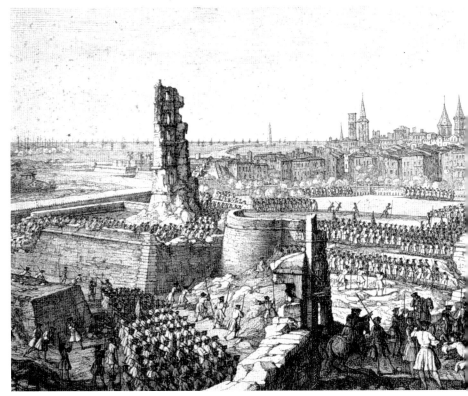

Nous nous promettons l'un à l'autre de quitter la Couronne et de nous retirer du monde pour penser uniquement a nostre salut et a servir Dieu infailliblement avant la Toussaints de l'année 1723. au plus tard. A l'Escurial ce 27.e Juillet 1720.

Philippe Elisabeth

Nous avons fait voeu ce matin a Dieu aussitost après avoir Communié sous les auspices de la Sainte Vierge d'accomplir ce que

From the secret oath of Philip V and Elizabeth Farnese, 27 July 1720.

Pedro Tortolero, *Philip V's Entry into Seville, 1729.*

(*above*) Michel-Ange Houasse, *Luis I of Spain* (1717).

Louis-Michel Van Loo, *The Family of Philip V* (1743).

a Belgian general who in subsequent years also commanded many of Spain's expeditionary forces. The vessels sailed in detachments from mid-August. By the end of September, the island was under Spanish control.

The success of the venture seems to have converted Alberoni to the selective use of force. Spain, thanks to the work of Alberoni and Patiño over the past few years, now had at its disposition a valuable instrument which the emperor lacked totally: naval power. In June 1718 the cardinal wrote to a correspondent in Italy that 'there can be no system of security in Italy without tranquillity. A good war is necessary, until the last German has been driven out.'[46] No sooner had the European powers recovered from the surprise of the Sardinia expedition than yet another fleet was launched from Barcelona, in June 1718. Over 350 vessels, among them a large number of warships, transported 30,000 men and 8,000 cavalry across to Sardinia, where provisions were taken on board. The fleet then made for Sicily, where the forces landed near Palermo on 1 July.

During these months, Philip was not always in control of decision-making. His condition was aggravated during the summer of 1717 by a recurrence of the depressive illness that he had suffered in earlier years, the problem in all likelihood having remained under control for some time because of Elizabeth's attention to her husband. Now, however, it took on new and more intense characteristics. The court was aware of the problem, for the king's absence from official duties affected all protocol. Attacks were episodic rather than continuous. There were days when he was normal, and days when he was unable to do anything at all and simply retired to bed. Some of the symptoms of his illness include, as we know,[47] sleep and eating disturbances, a loss of energy, feelings of worthlessness and helplessness, difficulty in concentrating, suicidal thoughts, and a loss of a sense of pleasure and interest in life. All these could be observed in the illness as it developed in 1717. In September the royal family were in the Escorial, where Elizabeth summoned a company of Italian theatre actors to perform for them; but it appears not to have helped at all. In October the king began to lose weight dramatically, and suffered lapses of memory. When unwell, he would remain shut up in his bedroom and refuse to see more than a few essential persons. The symptoms came and went, so that they did not necessarily affect him for long periods. In mid-October, for example, he was present at the *Te Deum* sung in the Escorial to celebrate the successful occupation of Sardinia. He would sometimes relapse into complete silence for a day, refusing even to speak to Elizabeth. In these circumstances, it was difficult to encourage him even to change his clothes. The illness, which appears to have continued in one form or another for several months and through a good part of 1718, provoked alarm on all sides. The queen attended him faithfully, though she was pregnant in the latter part of 1717 (she gave birth on 31 March 1718 to María Ana Victoria). In addition, Elizabeth's nurse, Laura Piscatori, who had accompanied her from Parma and continued to play a background role in palace politics, spent days and nights at the king's bedside.

One night in October 1717, while he was staying at the Escorial, the king had a particularly severe attack, and became convinced that he was going to die. His confessor was called and Philip drew up a testament, appointing Elizabeth and Alberoni to a regency government.[48] News of the testament got out and spurred the political opposition into action. The king's illness left decisions completely in the hands of Alberoni, and many court nobles feared that Philip's death would be followed by a regency period completely dominated by Italians. 'We well believe', the British ambassador commented with good reason, 'that the intrigues have commenced.'[49] Moreover, the wildest rumours, evidently fed by malicious tongues, began circulating in Madrid. It was said, for example, that the Italians were secretly poisoning the king.

'For the last eight months', Alberoni wrote in December 1717 to the grand duke of Parma, 'this poor gentleman [Philip] has been showing signs of insanity, his imagination inducing him to believe that he is destined to die immediately, fancying himself attacked by all sorts of diseases.' Philip believed, for instance, that the sun had struck his shoulder and had penetrated his inner organs. Alberoni watched with concern the progression of Philip's condition, in January 1718 commenting with insight on Elizabeth's complete dedication to the king during the worst phases of the illness. 'She loves him tenderly, and suffers with a courage that the greatest martyr has never shown.'[50] During 1718, too, Philip appears to have had his first phases of bulimia. He was constantly eating, according to Alberoni, but could never retain the quantities of food that he consumed. The queen's self-sacrifice during these difficult periods was observed by the cardinal, who commented disapprovingly in November 1718 that 'she has so vehement a passion for him that it has reduced her to a blind subjection and to complete loss of will'.

The possibility of a regency under Alberoni alarmed the political class in Madrid and sparked off a number of conspiracies in the course of 1718. Some of the plotters were actively encouraged by the duke of Orléans, regent of France, who wished to have a friendly Spain supporting him and therefore backed some of the Castilian grandees from the 'Spanish party'. These were the people identified by the French ambassador Bonnac in 1715 and by Bubb in 1716 as forming a sort of 'French party'. The sympathisers of this Spanish but pro-French 'party'[51] now in 1718 plotted in Madrid with the French ambassador, Saint-Aignan, and directed a quantity of letters and memorials to the regent, one memorial writer even referring to himself as 'un español *bon français*' ('a Spaniard faithful to France').[52] One group of plotters, led by the duke of Veragua and the count of Aguilar, planned to seize power in the event of Philip's death; another group hoped to set up the king's heir, the prince of Asturias, as ruler. However, none of these schemes seems to have been taken seriously by the Spanish government; plotting was (and would continue to be) standard fare in the politics of Madrid. On the other hand, the French took very seriously the only plot to which the Spanish government gave support. This was the Cellamare conspiracy.

The prince of Cellamare,[53] an Italian noble, was Spanish ambassador in Versailles, where he was encouraged by Alberoni to make overtures to opponents of the regent Orléans. His contacts blossomed into a conspiracy that should really, it has been pointed out, be called 'the conspiracy of the duchess of Maine',[54] for the ambassador played only a passive part in the events that followed. The Madrid government expelled the French ambassador Saint-Aignan for his intrigues, but instructed Cellamare to remain in Paris and continue making his contacts. As elaborated by the duchess of Maine, the Paris conspiracy had three main components: to seize the person of the regent, to stage a rising in Brittany, and to summon the Estates General of France. Agents of the regent's chief minister, Dubois, learnt of the plot after seizing the papers of two Spanish diplomats carrying information from Cellamare to Alberoni. The conspiracy had really been an attempt by leading French aristocrats to gain control of the regime: among those arrested were the duke of Maine, Cardinal Polignac, the marquis of Pompadour and the duke of Richelieu. Cellamare was expelled from the country, and war became inevitable.

* * *

The war, of course, had not been provoked simply by conspiracies. The naked Spanish aggression in Sardinia and Sicily in 1718 greatly alarmed the European powers that had agreed upon, and now wished to preserve, the conditions of the treaty of Utrecht. Accordingly, in August 1718 Britain, France, the Empire and Savoy formed the Quadruple Alliance against Spain. A British fleet commanded by Admiral Byng was sent to Naples to protect the interests of the emperor against the Spanish naval expedition and on 11 August it located the Spanish fleet off Cape Passaro, in Sicily, and destroyed or captured all its vessels save four warships. Declarations of war followed, by Britain in December and France in January 1719. The conspiracies fomented in Madrid by the duke of Orléans turned now into a real attempt to destabilise the government of Alberoni through military intervention.

The duke of Berwick headed an army of 20,000 men that crossed the Basque frontier in April 1719 in a move that took Philip completely by surprise. On the 26th of the month, he had left Madrid in order to carry out an official visit to Valencia. Accompanied by the queen and the prince of Asturias, he arrived in Valencia city on 5 May, and was greeted by the customary celebrations. Elizabeth Farnese in later years had happy memories of the wildfowl that she and the king hunted at the lake of La Albufera. However, the news from the frontier forced Philip to change his plans, and he headed northwards. Appointed to lead the Spanish forces was the Italian general the Príncipe Pio, marquis of Castelrodrigo, who was summoned from his post in Barcelona. The bulk of the Spanish forces was concentrated in Pamplona, while the king and the Príncipe Pio headed a detachment that attempted to relieve the besieged fortress of Fuenterrabía. With very little effort, the French occupied Fuenterrabía (18 June) and San Sebastián (17 August), and by the end of August were in possession of the whole of Vizcaya, Guipúzcoa and Álava. The English meanwhile in August made an expedition by sea to the shipyards at Santoña, where they took pains to destroy all the vessels under construction. The Basque provinces made a formal recognition of the occupation, stating that they were willing to accept French rule provided that their *fueros* were recognised. On 5 August the province of Guipúzcoa recognised French rule, followed by the province of Álava on 29 August.[55] These historic capitulations, had they been acted upon, would of course have meant the integration of the Basque provinces into France. The reaction of Berwick, who had announced the end of the Catalan *fueros* in 1714, is not documented; in effect, he was uninterested in the question, and no real risk existed to Basque liberties or to the continued existence of the Basque provinces within Spain. This was fortunate, for very shortly before, in the year 1718, a crisis had arisen between the Alberoni government and these provinces. The occasion was a Madrid proposal to move the customs border from its inland position to the seaports, principally Bilbao, in order to convert the whole of mainland Spain into an area without internal customs duties. There were popular uprisings (known as the *matxinada*) in about thirty towns; the decree had to be revoked in 1719, a decision that was officially confirmed in December 1722 after the war, and in 1726 Philip V issued a general pardon for offences committed during the uprisings.

Though the war with France produced many casualties in terms of lives and property, it was conducted on very informal lines. Berwick had been most reluctant to fight against Spain, and d'Asfeld refused absolutely to do so when the regent urged him. One of the soldiers on Philip's side was Berwick's own son, the duke of Liria, to whom his father wrote: 'Whatever happens remember what I have told you many times. You are a Spaniard, obliged by honour to remain faithful to the king of Spain.' Berwick made a rule during the campaign of setting all Spanish prisoners free and letting them return to their bases. In September he decided to avoid the Spanish forces in Pamplona, and instead directed an invasion of Catalonia from across the Pyrenees.

The French invasion of Spain made Philip desperate. The French were his own people, and Berwick was his personal friend. Berwick's instructions to his troops reflect the personal ties. 'If the Spaniards are defeated,' he ordered, 'do not take the king prisoner, but do your best to get hold of Alberoni.'[56] The king attempted to go and speak personally to Berwick, but was persuaded by Alberoni to desist. Alberoni reported that Philip and Elizabeth 'believe that when they are in the presence of the French army the whole of it will pass over to their service'.[57] Convinced that he was the lawful heir to the French throne, and that Orléans was an upstart, Philip also initiated a curious attempt at propaganda. He arranged for thousands of leaflets, whose text he himself had drawn up as early as December 1718, to be printed in French, asserting his rights to the crown. If the French were to invade, he wrote, 'I shall receive them with open arms, as good friends and good allies; I shall give employment to the officers and incorporate the soldiers into my troops'.[58] One of the men distributing the leaflets was captured and hanged in Berwick's camp; the propaganda effort failed dismally. Philip subsequently suffered another brief attack of his depressive illness, severe enough for him to withdraw from the campaign and retire to bed in Madrid. His place in the army was gallantly taken by Elizabeth, who inspected the troops in the king's name, on horseback and wearing a set of pistols. The French respected her endeavours, allowing clothes that she had ordered from Paris to pass through their lines.

The British, meanwhile, invaded Galicia in a campaign that was clearly punitive – like the French invasions – with no intention of conquest. At the end of September they captured the port of Ribadeo, landed 5,000 men and went on to occupy Vigo, Pontevedra and other towns.[59] They stayed only four days in Ribadeo, but remained in Vigo for four weeks. A defenceless Galicia suffered severe damage to property and crops, nor was any attempt made by English officers to prevent looting. The only serious diversion on the part of Spain, orchestrated by Alberoni earlier in the year, failed miserably. The cardinal arranged for a small naval expedition of two warships, one frigate and several transport vessels with 5,000 men to sail from Cadiz in mid-March 1719. The fleet was to head for La Coruña, where it had to pick up the duke of Ormond (who since 1715 had become a leading supporter of the Jacobite cause), and set out to invade Scotland in the name of James III. However, storms off Galicia in early April shattered the fleet even before it could enter the harbour at La Coruña, where Ormond and James gloomily watched the survivors come ashore. Of the 5,000 Spanish soldiers, reported a Galician official, 'many fell ill, not a few died, and the greater part deserted'.[60] James wrote to Philip V that 'the ill fortune that we have suffered affects me dreadfully'.[61] Still optimistic, Ormond accepted an offer from Alberoni to send to Scotland a small invasion force of two frigates and 300 Castilian infantry.[62] The enterprise was a disaster. The Spaniards reached Inverness, where they were supported by local Jacobites including the famous brigand Rob Roy, but were outnumbered and forced to surrender to the British troops in an area that is still today known as 'the Spaniard's Pass'.

The failures in Scotland and in the peninsula itself were made worse by the situation of the Spanish troops in Sicily. The destruction of the fleet at Passaro left the soldiers cut off from outside help, with no hope of withdrawal. They also had to cope with the arrival of Austrian troops transported by the British navy. The combination of military disasters could be avoided only by a complete reversal of Spanish policy, which is what the king now accepted. Never in his reign had such a total collapse taken place, and the culprit in everybody's eyes was Alberoni. All too aware of his profound unpopularity, the cardinal tried to protect his position by controlling all government business, and cutting off contact between the councils and the king. The tactic had little chance of succeeding for very long. On 5 December 1719 the king and queen departed for the Escorial, but left a signed decree with the secretary of the Despacho, Miguel Fernández Durán, marquis of Tolosa, dismissing Alberoni immediately from all his posts and instructing him to leave Madrid within a week without seeing the king. The cardinal followed the instructions faithfully. He left on 11 December, angry and

embittered, travelling overland through Catalonia and France, en route
for Italy.[63]

Philip was left to pick up the pieces. He was grievously hurt by the
war with France,[64] which he perceived as unnatural, in effect a war by
himself against himself and the conflict left psychological wounds that
were never to heal. The grandee elite in Madrid, however, was overjoyed by the cardinal's dismissal, their dislike of foreigners and of the
cardinal's political role finding expression in a number of satires which
they sponsored.

> ¿Qué juicio se podrá hacer
> del año de diez y nueve
> pues vemos la novedad
> de caer *Julio* en diciembre?[65]

(What conclusion can we draw of the year 1719, which had the
novelty of July – that is, Giulio – falling in December?)

On the other hand many, like the marquis of San Felipe, felt that
Alberoni's fall had been the consequence of a manoeuvre by 'the
three enemies of Spain, who at that time were the emperor, the
duke of Orléans and England', and that 'the monarchy of Spain lost
much, while the king lost a minister who thought only of serving
his king'.[66]

* * *

In the spring, on 15 May 1720, Elizabeth gave birth to the Infante Philip.
The event was welcome to the king, since his son Philip by
Marie Louise had died on 19 December at the age of seven, and been
buried on New Year's Day in the pantheon of the Infantes in the
Escorial. In accord with his deeply emotional nature, Philip was as
closely attached to all his children as he was to his wives, evidence of
which can be seen in his correspondence with the Infante Charles.[67]
During their periods of residence at Valsaín the king and queen
were separated from Charles, who was brought up in the care of his
tutors and sent little written notes to his parents. In October 1720,

when Charles was four and a half years old, Philip replied to him: 'Be a very good boy and follow the advice that your mother gave you, and be sure that I love you deeply and I embrace you with all my heart'. In July 1722 one of the king's letters went: 'My love for you, my dearest son, makes me very happy to receive your letter of yesterday. I embrace you with all my heart and love you in the same way, and I have no doubt that you deserve these feelings because of your good behaviour and your application to your studies.' 'I was very pleased, my dearest son,' he wrote in October 1722, 'that you made your first confession the day before yesterday, as you wrote in your letter. The more graces that God gives you, the more you should give thanks for them through your application to all your duties. I hope that you are attentive to your studies, it is the greatest pleasure that you can give a father who loves you.'

*   *   *

The only political comfort the king gained in this period was through more military action. No sooner had his forces begun their withdrawal from Sicily in the summer of 1720, than Philip used other available forces from the peninsula to mount another rapid expedition. The objective this time was the north African fortress of Ceuta, Spanish territory that had been besieged over a long period by the sultan of Morocco, Muley Ismael. Ceuta was of particular symbolic value as the only territory still held by Spain in north Africa (Orán had been lost during the War of Succession). It also had a very substantial material value, for without Ceuta the crown would (technically) cease to be able to collect the income from the famous 'bull of the Crusade', one of its biggest sources of revenue.[68] A force of 16,000 men, commanded once again by the marquis of Lède, was organised by Patiño to sail from Cadiz. It landed near Ceuta early in November, and there began military operations designed to drive back the sultan's forces. The Ceuta garrison was strengthened, and the men returned safely to Spain. Philip considered the expedition to have been a personal success for himself. He attended a *Te Deum* in Atocha at which the standards captured from the Muslims were hung in the church. He also, for the first time in his life, decided that he would attend an *auto de fe*.[69]

At the beginning of his reign, in 1701, the Inquisition had invited him to attend an *auto de fe*, but Philip had declined on the firm direction of his tutor, the marquis of Louville.[70] The event was always a disagreeable phenomenon in the eyes of foreigners. However, the king appears, in his enthusiasm after the Ceuta campaign, to have decided to make an exception. Very little is known of the activity of the Inquisition in these years, but it is possible that the king attended the *auto* held in Madrid on the second Sunday of May 1721, when one man and one woman were burnt alive, and sixteen others were also sentenced to various punishments.[71] The burnings were not part of the main ceremony, took place outside the city, and would not have been seen by the king. In general, in those years the Inquisition of Madrid limited such *autos* to small ceremonies in the convent of San Domingo el Real. However, from about 1720 an inexplicable new wave of persecution had been directed against the *conversos* of Jewish origin, mainly in the southern cities of Granada, Seville, Córdoba and Toledo.[72] The impact of the persecution was dramatic. More Spaniards were burnt at the stake in the five years between 1720 and 1725 – a total of over ninety victims – than in any comparable period in the preceding two centuries. In subsequent years another persecution was launched, in Granada, against the richest Morisco families of the province, which were accused of 'complicity' in the Islamic faith.[73] Since the reign of Philip V was not one of continuous Inquisitorial activity, and the king himself never showed any interest in the workings of the tribunal, this upsurge of persecution in the third decade of the century raises questions that remain to be answered.

* * *

By the failure of his anti-French policies, Alberoni had lost for Spain whatever advantage it may have possessed in international politics. The invasions of the peninsula in 1719 were followed by a very long period of peace-making between the western powers, when the British and the French, who had both signed a temporary peace with

Spain in June 1721, attempted to keep Philip V happy. It was in this period that for the first time, in July 1720, the earl of Stanhope sent to his government a proposal that Gibraltar should be returned to Spain. George I, who on 12 June 1720 wrote to Philip V the famous letter in which he promised to obtain the return of the Rock, supported the move, which was also privately backed by Britain's other chief minister the duke of Newcastle.[74] However, the majority in Parliament was hostile to any return of the fortress, and the matter proceeded no further.

Lengthy negotiations were now begun with the other powers. Spain was forced to join the Quadruple Alliance in February 1720 and take part in the peace talks that started informally at Cambrai in 1722 but did not officially begin until 1724. In August 1722 Fuenterrabía and San Sebastián were formally returned by France to Spain. The arrangement laid down by the Alliance at Cambrai (1724) was intended to bring peace to the Mediterranean. Philip was to return Sardinia and renounce the conquest of former Spanish territories, the emperor was to abandon his claim to the Spanish crown, and the Infante Charles's rights in Parma and Tuscany would be recognised; all this would be discussed at the talks. As a result of the military failure, the king never retained good memories of Alberoni. 'He became our master, an insupportable master', Elizabeth commented many years later,[75] but at the same time she was willing to acknowledge his outstanding qualities: 'We must be just to him, he was a great minister, but the king couldn't stand him.' The king nodded when he heard these words, and hissed, 'He was a ferocious beast!' Philip's reaction was understandable, but also unjust; at least until the beginning of 1718 Alberoni had simply been an instrument of the royal will and had never approved the king's move to a policy of aggression.

The queen still needed her nominees in positions of power, and so now gave her confidence to another Italian, Annibale Scotti. He was a native of Piacenza who had first come to Spain in 1716 but returned in 1719 as plenipotentiary of the duke of Parma and quickly occupied the place vacated by Alberoni. The cardinal's fall helped the pro-French ministers into power in the Spanish government and also made possible some changes in the administration. The three ministries created in 1717 were converted in 1720 into four and then in 1721 into five. Chief among the ministers was José de Grimaldo, who was officially the head of the Council of State but also despatched all official business with the king.

Spain reverted to its alliance with France, and in March 1721 Grimaldo signed on behalf of Spain a friendship treaty that provided for a dynastic marriage between the two branches of the Bourbon family. The prince of Asturias, Luis, was to marry Louise Elizabeth, third daughter of the duke of Orléans, known by the French as Mlle de Montpensier and aged twelve. Louis XV, then also aged twelve, was to wed the Infanta María Ana Victoria, aged five. The new ambassador sent by France was the duke of Saint-Simon, Louis de Rouvroy, a noted man of letters whose reports on the Spanish court provide one of our most valuable sources of information for the period. Saint-Simon arrived in Madrid on 21 November and was formally received by the king on the 25th. Two days later he and all the court left in order to go to the town of Lerma, at which they took leave of the infant princess and new queen of France while the court stayed on in Lerma to await the arrival of the new princess of Asturias. The exchange of princesses was carried out on the Basque frontier between the two countries, on the Isle of Pheasants, on 9 January 1722; the prince of Rohan accompanied Louise Elizabeth, and the marquis of Santa Cruz the Infanta. When the latter was handed over, she burst into tears and refused to go. At least in the Spanish court, there were many who criticised the inopportune arrangement involving such young children. Louise Elizabeth arrived at Lerma on 20 January, and was married there to the prince of Asturias by Cardinal Borja, in a brilliant ceremony attended by the whole court, the papal nuncio, grandees and ambassadors. A few days later they all returned to Madrid.

*   *   *

After the dismissal of Alberoni and his own return to apparently normal health, Philip seems to have confided more and more in his spiritual advisers. Through these years his private confessor was Father

THE HOUSE OF THE BOURBONS OF FRANCE AND SPAIN

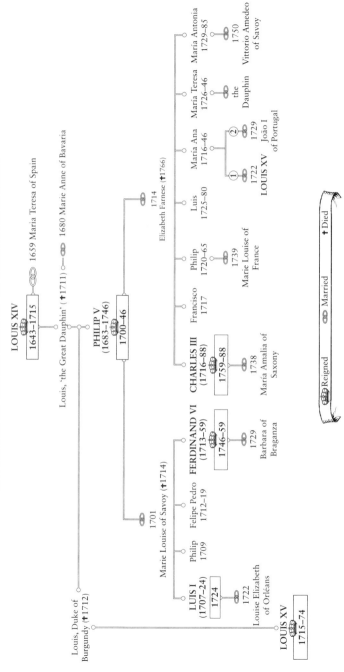

Daubenton, the French Jesuit who had been appointed to succeed Father Robinet in 1715. Schooled in France by Jesuits, Philip would admit no other order to take care of his conscience. When Daubenton died in August 1723 he was replaced by Father Bermúdez, 'who besides being a Spaniard has the universal character of extraordinary capacity, learning and piety' (according to the British ambassador).[76]

Philip's normal routine around the year 1720, as described in detail by both Alberoni and Saint-Simon,[77] was that of a king who fulfilled his role adequately. He and Elizabeth were woken every morning by their valet at 8 a.m. and breakfasted together. Still in bed, Philip then began to study his official papers for the day. At 10 a.m. the marquis of Grimaldo was summoned and positioned himself at the foot of the bed, from where he addressed the king and discussed state business while the queen attended to her needlework. On occasion Philip might choose to be dressed rather than stay in bed, and deal with business not in his chambers but in his office. Towards midday, 12 noon, he would be back with his wife, who by now had risen and begun to dress. While she prepared herself, the king issued his daily orders concerning the household, his agenda and matters of state. By this time, the major part of the royal household, including members of the royal family, were in attendance outside their apartments. The king and queen would now spend about half an hour at least with their confessor. They would also deal with any audiences that might have to be given. It is interesting that at this period of his life, when his mental state appeared to be more tranquil, the king still exhibited some signs of hyperactivity. He would, for example, be extraordinarily talkative in audiences, to the extent of leaving the queen little to say. Saint-Simon notes that in one of his audiences with them, 'the queen, who always joins in what he says and backs him up, said virtually nothing'. After audiences, both Philip and Elizabeth would attend morning mass.

Shortly after, they would have their lunch, the main meal of the day. It was a formal affair attended by several household officials, and might last a considerable time if the king was talkative. The two royal physicians never failed to be in attendance. The king ate a great deal, though the range of dishes offered to him was small and tended to be chosen from a list of about fifteen preferred items. His first course was always a substantial soup. He drank very little wine, and always old burgundy. The queen ate less, although she was a lover of good food, and drank champagne with her meals. Afterwards they would spend about an hour talking, but the main business of the afternoon was an outing or diversion, normally hunting, which they did together. It was, as we have seen, Philip's only serious recreation. The sport did not require much expertise, since the style of hunting among royalty had changed little since the days of Charles V. An area of forest was cordoned off and the beaters would frighten all the required animals into a specific area, where the king could pick them off at will. Bubb reported at the time that 'the queen devotes herself to hunting as much as her husband, whether because she is really enamoured of the sport or because she desires to please the king'.[78] Elizabeth in fact was an accomplished horsewoman, and was especially expert at shooting pigeons while on horseback. Hunting tended to last until nightfall. Then, on his return in the evening, the king would deal with his ministers and with correspondence. On feast-days there was no hunting; instead the king and queen normally went to the church of Atocha and on their way back to the palace would attend celebrations in the Plaza Mayor. At 9.30 they had a short supper, which ended around 10 p.m. They might continue with official business afterwards, retiring to bed shortly after 11 p.m.[79]

Saint-Simon was fortunate in 1722 to observe a king who was at the height of his powers, someone who still gave promise of great things. Philip had brought Spain back into the European arena, and had personally defended its interests on the battlefield. 'He loves great enterprises, troops and war.' But was he an efficient king? The ambassador had his doubts. In politics Philip was now attempting to recover from the tutelage of Alberoni, and had decided to take part personally in the process of government. 'But since he wishes to do everything by himself, things get done only with great difficulty.' It is a fair judgment in the light of the information available to us. The ambassador also had serious doubts about Philip's public role. The king, he conceded, was very just, deeply religious, free of all vices and very generous. However, 'he has little confidence either in himself or in others, and is silent to the point of embarrassment, even though he never says anything out of place. His appearance, and his difficulty in putting two words together, as well as his excessive shyness, often have a negative effect on what he says, except during audiences and solemn ceremonies.' He had only two pleasures, according to Saint-Simon: hunting and the conjugal bed; and if anything cut short his life it would be excessive eating and excessive sex with his wife. He enjoyed celebrations, particularly dancing: 'though bent and bow-legged, he dances like an expert, with majesty'. Every detail of the ambassador's report confirms (though Saint-Simon was unaware of it) the neurobiological disorder that had now overwhelmed the king, even though Philip's condition appeared to be one of relative well-being and tranquillity, with no severe illnesses or unusual bursts of euphoria.

Not all of Saint-Simon's testimony can be trusted. He wrote his account partly on the basis of notes he had made, from other ambassadors' reports, *before* he went to Madrid. During his short stay in the city, the value of his observations was limited by the fact that he did not speak Spanish. Moreover, his sketches of the king can lack perspective. The king and queen, he says, frequently spent time together in their apartments reading books, but the books were exclusively books of piety. The comment, which suggests that the king had narrow reading interests, fails to take into account Philip's well-known addiction to collecting books on all topics. In general, however, Saint-Simon presents a credible picture. His conclusion, that 'great lethargy of spirit and an even greater lack of resolution are perhaps what best describe this prince', is an exact description of the king's depressive phases. By way of contrast, the ambassador never fails to be complimentary to Elizabeth Farnese, who clearly impressed him. She had 'an air of openness, sincerity and familiarity, of being at ease with me', he says, and was 'naturally cheerful, compassionate and relaxed; infinitely alive and vibrant'.[80]

Saint-Simon's report is revealing in at least three respects. He perceptively observed the very close teamwork between the king and his queen, a phenomenon documented for no other reigning pair in Spanish history since the time of the Catholic monarchs Ferdinand

and Isabella. Spaniards at court and in the streets of Madrid tended to be hostile to the queen, believing that she dominated Philip and dictated his life as well as his government. Saint-Simon, whose *Mémoires* are often little more than high-society gossip, was able, like any good purveyor of gossip, to penetrate to the real situation. He saw that the king and queen were deeply and totally attached to each other: they shared virtually all daytime activities, including meals, audiences and hunting; and at night they shared the same bedroom, the queen keeping him company even throughout his illnesses. Elizabeth absented herself only from business meetings with the ministers, though she was usually present at policy discussions with them. Elizabeth was 'completely and tirelessly devoted to him'. She willingly sacrificed, Saint-Simon felt, all the livelier side of her character – her love of games and festivities – in order to adapt her wishes to his.[81] The picture confirms in every detail that which we have from another direct witness, Alberoni.

However, despite the health problems that increasingly beset the king, Philip did not run a gloomy court. Opportunities for celebrations were never missed. The night after the signing of the agreements for the marriage of the Infante Luis to Louise Elizabeth of Orléans in 1722, there was a big ball in the Alcázar. Saint-Simon reports that 'it lasted until two in the morning, and their Majesties seemed to enjoy it. I was surprised to see how little the king had forgotten of the French way of dancing, and how the queen danced with grace, elegance and majesty.' Ten days later, after the formal marriage ceremony in late January 1722 in the town of Lerma, there was another big ball, 'and their Majesties never looked happier'. A week or so later, when Madrid celebrated Carnival, the king and queen put on an entertainment of fireworks at the palace and took part in the festivities.[82] In June that year, on returning to Madrid from a short visit to Valsaín, 'the king and the prince took part in the Corpus [Christi] procession, accompanied by all the grandees, the papal nuncio, and all the ministers; the queen, with the princess and the Infantes, watched from the balcony of the palace'.[83] During Holy Week in 1723, the king assisted at all the public ceremonies, washed the feet of the poor according to tradition, presided at a ball on Easter Sunday, attended a musical comedy on the Monday, and then went to Aranjuez for the rest of the week in order to hunt and fish. There would be bad times in the future, but not in Philip's court as it was in 1722 and 1723.

Finally, the ambassador gives us precise information about the movements of the court in the third decade of the century.[84] For nearly fifty years, thanks to the incapacity of Charles II and later to the conflicts of the war in Spain, the monarchy had ceased to project an active royal presence. Philip V resumed the court life of the Habsburgs. Like Philip II, he established a regular pattern of movement. The court usually spent the months of December and January in the royal palace in Madrid. In February they all moved to the Buen Retiro. Easter was normally spent away from Madrid, at Aranjuez, but Corpus Christi was spent at the royal palace. In July the whole court moved to the Escorial for about six weeks, and then afterwards to the Pardo. From 1720 the Pardo visit was substituted by visits to Valsaín, which Philip used as his base so that he could supervise the building of the new palace in San Ildefonso. Early in December the court would return from Valsaín to Madrid. Pursuing the king from palace to palace was not a task relished by ambassadors. When Saint-Simon had to go and take his leave of Philip in Valsaín in the winter of early 1722 he complained bitterly that 'it is one of the most painful journeys that one can make in this country', because of the impassable snow that covered the mountain roads that year.

CHAPTER FIVE

Abdication and Second Reign,
1724–1729

'THE WHOLE COURT, ALL THE GRANDEES, NOBODY WANTS ME. I
WANT TO RETIRE.'

PHILIP V TO MARSHAL DE TESSÉ, 1724

The whole of Europe was shaken – San Felipe refers to it as 'a most extraordinary and unexpected event' – by the king's announcement, in January 1724, that he was resigning his throne.

As early as 1701, Philip's remarks to Louville show that he began his career as king with doubts about his aptitude for kingship. None of the French officials surrounding him contributed in any way to increasing his self-confidence. Louis XIV had originally urged him to act like a king, and then had gone on to make every major decision affecting Philip's government. But twenty years later Philip had matured and developed, thanks in great measure to Elizabeth Farnese, who gave him the support and dedication he needed. He was active in the politics of state, and continued to demonstrate his enthusiasm for an aggressive foreign policy. The apparently illogical resolution to leave the throne therefore requires some explanation.

For Philip himself it was not a sudden decision. The earliest concrete evidence that he might leave the throne seems to date from the year 1719, when he suffered deep personal distress after the French invasions. 'The Navarre campaign', he commented afterwards, 'first laid the foundations for our resolution.' He set the idea down for the first time on paper on 27 July 1720, in the form of a secret written vow signed by Elizabeth and himself at the Escorial, in which they both swore to leave the throne before 1723.[1] 'We promise each other', runs the text, written in French (and reproduced here in the plate section), 'to leave the throne and to retire from the world in order to think only about our salvation and to serve God, unfailingly before the day of All Saints in 1723 at the latest.' They would repeat this solemn vow in writing on the same sheet of paper, but with a different text, on four subsequent occasions: on 15 August in 1720, 1721 and 1722 at the Escorial, and 15 August 1723 at Valsaín.[2] Each text reads: 'we have again confirmed the vow noted above, this morning after taking communion, in the same terms and subject to the will of God and the favour of the Holy Virgin'. The repetition of the vow in this determined way, each time on the great feast day of the Assumption of the Virgin, indicates that it was profoundly considered. The part played in it by Elizabeth was, as in almost all other important acts involving Philip, supportive rather than approving. All Saints' Day in 1723 came and passed without incident. But in effect the resolution was now firm. Early in January 1724 Philip informed the prince of Asturias of the decision, and advised him on the responsibilities he was about to assume, in a long and interesting document of seventeen pages, on which we shall comment later. On 10 January, from San Ildefonso, he communicated his historic decision in writing to the Council of Castile. The text read:

> Having for the last four years considered, and reflected deeply and profoundly on, the miseries of this life, through the illnesses, wars and upheavals that God has seen fit to send me in the twenty-three years of my reign; and considering also that my firstborn son Don Luis, sworn Prince of Spain, is now of sufficient age, as well as married and with capacity enough to rule and govern this Monarchy with wisdom and justice; I have decided to retire totally from its government and direction, and I renounce it with all its territories, realms and lordships, in favour of the said Prince Don Luis, retiring

with the queen (in whom I have found a readiness and willingness to accompany me) to this palace and site of San Ildefonso, to serve God, free from other cares and to meditate on death and seek my salvation.[3]

With this document he sent three lists: one nominating the junta of seven who would administer government until Luis began to reign; one appointing the household of the new king; and one naming twelve individuals he wished to receive the Order of the Golden Fleece. Grimaldo took the appropriate abdication papers from San Ildefonso to the Escorial, where the prince of Asturias was residing with the other children of the royal family, on the 15th. Luis expressed a wish to go and see his father in San Ildefonso, but Philip dissuaded him. The new king arrived in Madrid four days later, to the cheers of the people.

Philip's stated motives for abdicating are clearly documented. Any other motives that may be attributed to him, such as a feeling of his inability to reign, or a wish to give up the Spanish throne in order to succeed eventually to that of France, are based on pure speculation. He was frequently conscious that he might not be able to carry out his duties as king, and he indeed nurtured a permanent desire to become king of France, but neither motive can be identified in the documents associated with his renunciation in 1724. The lack of evidence for such motives was, of course, no hindrance to the scores of satirical pamphlets that emerged when the news broke. Completely unaware of the king's illness, or of the anxieties that always haunted Philip, the public gave itself up to gossip and speculation. In their traditional manner, Spaniards disbelieved the official explanation, and invented their own. They were not alone, for opinion in the rest of Europe also refused to accept the reasons adduced by Philip. The preponderant view, that he had given up one throne in order to conserve the possibility of succeeding to another, was reflected in several satires of the day, and encouraged at least one Spanish legist[4] to pen, that same year, a treatise arguing that Philip's renunciation of the French throne was invalid.

The direct religious explanation offered by Philip for his renunciation must be accepted, for it accords with the permanent problem of his health. Other extraneous factors may have been at the back of his mind, but they were not the direct cause. Quite simply, the king had developed a deep – it would be correct to say pathological – religious obsession that he could save his soul only in an atmosphere of complete tranquillity. Several notes scribbled by him in these months, as well as his messages to his confessor, leave no doubt that his conscious intentions were exclusively religious.[5] It should be added that the confessor did not encourage Philip in his wish for self-mortification. In one scribbled note to the confessor, the king wrote: 'Father, as this evening is my day for discipline [i.e. flagellation], please let me know what I should do, if I can say a *Miserere* in its place, and if you can relieve me of the obligation'. The confessor wrote back: 'Sire, Your Majesty has no obligation to do the discipline, or to say the *Miserere*, or to do anything else in its place. I relieve you of the need to do anything.'[6] But Philip continued to be troubled by matters that lay deep within his mind, concerning the salvation of his soul.

He therefore proposed to build himself a retreat from the world, to which he would retire. He obviously drew on his own spiritual upbringing in order to arrive at the conclusion. In a letter to the pope he spoke of himself and of 'my temperament, which is naturally more inclined to seclusion than to much activity'.[7] It is possible to speculate that the mystical influence of his old tutor Fénelon, whose predilection for the spiritual and pastoral life (as seen in his work *Télémaque*, discussed below in chapter 8) appealed strongly to Philip, also played a part in his decision. Consultations with his confessor appear to have had little influence in one direction or the other. He was firmly decided, on spiritual grounds, and let the question mature in his mind for a very long time. 'We have been preparing for this for four years', Elizabeth later told the marshal de Tessé. It was symptomatic of her absolute dedication that she accepted the possibility of abdication, and at that time made no apparent effort to change the king's mind.

The religious motive for the abdication offers us, of course, only the official explanation. The real explanation, as we have seen by Philip's development over the years, was his bipolar disorder. He had been periodically unwell until the summer of 1719, and had had to withdraw from the battlefront that year because of his illness. After that date, he was apparently in good physical health, and his mental condition did not ostensibly affect his actions. In the past, when he suffered periods of depression he would doubt everything: his own capacities, his role as king, his eternal salvation. Some of this may have remained in his mind even after he had recovered, and with particular force in 1719, the year that he had been obliged to wage war against his own country, France, to whose throne he still reserved his claim.

We are in the realm of psychiatric speculation, but it seems that Philip had begun a more intense phase of his illness, in which one of the components (which later became more apparent) was a death wish, understood not literally but psychologically. Alberoni had already commented on the king's preoccupation with death. Among those who suffer from severe depression from their teens into adulthood, a tendency to suicidal thoughts can develop,[8] and Philip's radical decision to abdicate, first broached in 1719 and carried out five years later, was deliberate professional suicide. It was a typical response of someone in the grip of the euphoric phase of manic depression, in which self-destructive behaviour leaves the subject feeling comforted and relieved, with no real awareness that the decision made is inappropriate. His religious feelings did little more than confirm Philip in the conviction that the step he was taking was a perfectly correct one. 'Thank God I am no longer king,' he told a British diplomat, 'and that the remainder of my days I shall apply myself to the service of God and to solitude.' The opinion of those around him was of course quite different. 'No one can understand', Annibale Scotti wrote home to Italy, 'how the queen, with her high spirits and intelligence, could have concurred in so extravagant a proceeding, of which everyone disapproves'.[9]

* * *

La Granja de San Ildefonso is the central symbol of Philip's reign. In the tranquil years after the War of Succession, Philip and Elizabeth began hunting in the woods of Segovia, in the area of the royal palace of Valsaín. Their first visit there appears to have been in March 1716,[10] and they returned frequently. Philip II's charming palace at Valsaín had burnt down in 1686, and when Philip discovered the ruins he gave instructions in 1717 to the chief architect of the city of Madrid, Teodoro Ardemáns, to rebuild it. Only a limited restoration was carried out, sufficient to allow the king and queen to lodge there in case of need, which is what they did when they went hunting in the area. At the same time, while on a hunting expedition he chanced on a new site that encouraged him to think of an entirely new residence, and he purchased the land – a small monastery just over 3 kilometres distant from Valsaín – from the Jeronimite friars in March 1720. Soon after making his secret decision to abdicate in 1719–20, the king took steps to begin constructing the new residence. He conceived of it primarily as a spiritual retreat in the woods, in much the same way as Philip II had thought of the palace of Valsaín. The site began to be cleared and prepared during the last months of 1720. Construction of the proposed building was entrusted to Ardemáns, who directed the main part of the site in the years 1721–3 where he built a traditional four-towered palace modelled on the style of an Alcázar. In the year 1722–3 Philip and Elizabeth went often to stay in the residence at Valsaín, as a base from which to supervise details of the construction of La Granja. On one visit, Elizabeth commented on the '*beauté ravissante*' of the surrounding countryside, 'full of yellow, violet, white and blue flowers, and very many deer watching us'.[11] After Ardemáns's death in 1726, the style of the building was substantially modified. Those who took over, the Roman architects Procaccini and Subisati, continued throughout the reign to build new courtyards, adapt the layout and extend the gardens.

La Granja ended as being more European than Spanish in style, and inevitably provoked hostile reactions from Spaniards who preferred what they were familiar with. The palace remains as the principal example of European Baroque in Spain.[12] The façade of the Colegiata building, for instance, was modelled on a church in Salzburg. It has been said that in La Granja 'the nucleus is Spanish, the setting is French, and the surfaces are Italian',[13] an impressive but controlled display of European taste. There was no intention of imitating Versailles; only the gardens, carefully planned by French landscape architects, were a conscious borrowing from Philip's memories of the

Versailles he had known. The disposition of the statuary in the gardens was, in effect, a counterpoise to the explicit display of power in the Versailles of Louis XIV. The key figure among the statues was Apollo, god of the sun, who presides over three of the four main perspectives of the gardens. But this Apollo, far from being a symbol of 'the Sun King', represented rather the wisdom, the military valour and the virtue of the prince.[14] Moreover, a commanding position in the statuary was occupied by the goddess of the moon, Diana, whose power therefore complemented that of Apollo, and who as goddess of the hunt represented one of Elizabeth's interests. It was the king's first major contribution to the royal architecture of his time, but it was an unwelcome burden to the treasurers of the government, who were struggling in that period to cover their war debts.

Just as Spaniards had criticised the building of the Escorial by Philip II, so they criticised the building of La Granja. Expenses for construction and maintenance of palaces rose by 50 per cent between 1718 and 1722. The most relevant criticism, however, was that the new palace – built in the record time of two years – removed yet further from the centre of government a king who participated little in the daily business of administration and limited himself to making policy decisions. The king and queen began to live in La Granja from 10 September 1723, before the building was completed and several months before the abdication took place. In December 1723 the British ambassador William Stanhope[15] reported that he could get no decisions out of the foreign secretary in Madrid because the court was at La Granja. 'Between San Ildefonso and Madrid there is scarcely any communication, and the answers to letters written from Madrid for the Indies come back almost as quickly as those for San Ildefonso.'[16]

Our best insight into life at San Ildefonso during the months after the abdication is provided by the marshal duke of Tessé, who had reluctantly in 1724 at an advanced age (he was seventy-three, and died the year after, in 1725) accepted the post of special ambassador of France to Philip. He passed through Bayonne, where he visited the former queen mother, Mariana of Neuburg, then made his way directly to La Granja through a snow-covered landscape, arriving there on 23 February 1724. Its site seemed to him 'perhaps the most barbarous and most uncomfortable place in the world'. As his carriage drove up through the wintry woods, he could see several hundred head of deer wandering around in the vicinity of the palace. The court in La Granja had a very small number of personnel,[17] of whom the most important was the marquis of Grimaldo,[18] who had retired with the king and continued to handle all his public affairs. In view of its complete isolation, the palace offered little opportunity to vary the daily routine of the court. Philip and Elizabeth attended mass every morning in the chapel, then in the afternoon either went hunting or a little further afield and visited the churches and convents of Segovia. If the weather was very bad, they stayed indoors and played billiards. Evenings were devoted to consultations with the confessors, and business with Grimaldo.

Tessé was certain of one thing: apart from the king, nobody was entirely happy to be there: 'Everybody is desperate about having to live in this desert'. When he spoke to the king and queen, he judged by her expression that she wanted to return to civilisation. For the marshal perhaps the most telling phrase came from Grimaldo: 'The king is not dead nor am I, and I have no intention of dying,' he said to Tessé. 'That is all I can tell you.'[19] After five days in San Ildefonso, Tessé went on to visit the court in Madrid. The sentiments he had heard expressed at La Granja are amply confirmed by the queen's own letters. Her correspondence in 1724 makes frequent reference to La Granja as a 'desert', 'a desert, with deer and boar', and finally the phrase 'Don't forget those who live in the desert'. The use of the word 'desert' was not exclusively an expression of her feelings. It was common in Madrid to refer to the retreat of the king as 'that desert'.[20]

Philip, of course, doted on the palace he had created. It was literally the only residence in all Spain where he felt at home. On one occasion in 1724 when Stanhope called to see them, 'during the conversation the king remained silent, but when the queen mentioned the gardens of San Ildefonso, he asked me if I had seen those of Versailles and Marly, and compared some of their fountains with those of San Ildefonso'.[21] The success of the work encouraged Philip to proceed with other schemes. In 1715, he had commissioned a project for the restoration of the palace at Aranjuez, with drawings based on those of Juan de Herrera. Work began in 1727 under two French military engineers, Étienne Marchand and Léandre Brachelieu, assisted after 1731 by an architect from Piacenza, Giacomo Bonavia. Bonavia went on to become in fact the second creator of Aranjuez, after Herrera, and it was his designs that brought into existence the palace we see today. Among the assistants who helped Marchand at Aranjuez was Ventura Rodríguez, destined to become the great Spanish architect of the Bourbon period.

* * *

The prince of Asturias was seventeen years old when he succeeded to the throne as Luis I of Spain and was proclaimed king on 9 February 1724. The acclamation and raising of the royal standard were effected in Madrid in traditional style, in the square of the Alcázar. The *Gaceta* describes the event: 'With Their Majesties on the main balcony, and the Infantes on the one next to it, the senior King of Arms said: *Hear ye, hear ye, hear ye: Silence, silence, silence.* And the count of Altamira announced, as he shook the standard: *Castile, Castile, Castile, for the King our lord Don Luis the First, God save him.* And the people responded: *Amen, viva, viva, viva,* and this was repeated three times.'[22] The same procedure was repeated in other public places of the city.

Saint-Simon offers the following sketch of the new king during the wedding celebrations a couple of years before, in 1722: 'The prince of Asturias is like a picture: tall, slim and delicate, but in good health. He is fair, has a pretty head of hair, but an unattractive face. He is apt for everything, is active, and rides.' Apart from the detail about the face, which artists always endeavoured to re-touch, the sketch confirms the attractive appearance given to Luis in the portrait by Jean Ranc, in the Prado. Saint-Simon went on to say that 'he is still very young'. And it was the youth of both the prince and his bride that motivated Philip's decision to keep the couple separated until an appropriate time after their wedding. They were lodged separately, and were not even allowed to eat together for several months, and it was not until 25 August 1723 that they were permitted to share the same bed. There is conflicting evidence about their relations with each other; some witnesses say that they detested each other, others that they had a normal disposition. The very volatile and capricious character of the new queen may be the explanation for the differing assessments.

Predictably, the hopes of the 'Spanish party' in Madrid were concentrated in the new king. After a quarter-century of 'foreign' rule, the country at last had a Spanish-born ruler. The composition of the councils and ministries was changed, and it seemed that a new era had begun.

> Se vino a la corte
> Nuestro rey moderno,
> Y el pobre Filipo
> Yace en el desierto.[23]

(Our up-to-date king has come to town, and poor Phil is left out in the desert!)

The marquis of Miraval was now president of the Council of Castile, and foreign affairs were entrusted to Juan Bautista Orendain. However, it very soon became clear that the new court in the palace at Madrid remained under the control of the former king. Grimaldo, who in theory was head of the ex-king's cabinet and therefore outside the government, was seen by all commentators as the man who really controlled it. Sir Benjamin Keene, the diplomat who was resident for some years in Spain before he became British minister from 1727 to 1739, reported three weeks after the abdication that 'the authority still resides in Mr Grimaldo'.[24]

A verse that appeared in these months described the very palpable disappointment of those who had expected a change of regime:

> Rey y reina en el monte retirados,
> Rey y reina en la corte, ya reinantes;
> Aquellos, como siempre, dominantes,
> Estos, como siempre, dominados.[25]

(A king and queen retired in the woods, a king and queen reigning in Madrid, the former still in control, the latter still controlled.)

Decisions were made in Madrid, but were normally also confirmed in San Ildefonso. An anecdote illustrates the situation. One day the queen complained to the king because she could not get something she wanted. 'Aren't you the king, and aren't I the queen?' she asked. 'Yes,' Luis answered, 'I am the king and you are the queen, but the king my father is my master and yours.' At the end of March the king made his first visit, alone and for a couple of days, to San Ildefonso, where he walked with his father through the gardens and explained some of his problems. Pamphlets that circulated in Madrid at the time expressed the clear disappointment of the political class at the continuation of the previous regime. Bitter attacks were made on the role of Grimaldo. One pamphlet read:

> ¡Grimaldo ermitaño!
> ¡Por Dios, lindo cuento!

> (Grimaldo a hermit! That's a tall story!)

Luis and his wife visited San Ildefonso and stayed there for three days, from 26 June to 1 July. While they were there, Philip took it upon himself to have a serious talk with Louise Elizabeth. Now aged fourteen, Louise had made herself generally unbearable by her erratic behaviour. Popular rumour blamed it all on her father, the regent of France, who was reputed to be both dissolute and a debauchee; this suggests that what appeared most shocking in Madrid was Louise's sexual frivolity. She became well known at court for her indecent language and indecorous conduct; she frequently did not wear underclothes, and moved about the court clothed only in a flimsy dressing gown, which left nothing to the imagination. A court noble, the marquis of Santa Cruz, wrote to Grimaldo that 'every day is a continuous headache, enough to make us lose our health. . . . This poor king is going to be most unfortunate if this lady does not mend her ways completely'.[26] It was the reason why Philip was obliged to speak to her. Louise accepted the rebuke from her father-in-law and promised to change her conduct, but when they returned to Madrid she was the same as ever. In despair, Luis wrote on 2 July to his father that 'the only solution I see is to confine her, because she pays as little attention to what the king told her as if he were a coach-driver'.

Finally, on 4 July, Luis ordered her to be put under close arrest in the Alcázar, 'considering that the unseemly conduct of the queen is prejudicial to her health and does harm to her august person'. She was isolated for seven days, and released only when she promised to behave herself.

The domestic problems of the king were soon superseded by a more serious situation. A month later, on 14 August, Luis was suddenly taken ill and confined to bed. On the 19th the doctors diagnosed smallpox, and he was separated from the rest of his family. Ten days later he contracted a high fever and became delirious. Relics, including that of San Diego of Alcalá, were brought to his bedside in an effort to help him. Fearing the worst, Luis drew up a testament, naming his father as his universal heir. He died in the early hours of 31 August, after a short reign of seven and a half months. His body lay in state for three days, and was then transferred to the Escorial.

*   *   *

The terms of Philip's abdication had stated that if Luis were to die without an heir Ferdinand should succeed to the throne. However, Philip had never really let go of the reins of power and it was clear that Elizabeth had supported the abdication only out of loyalty, so it made sense for them to return to power. First of all the reluctance of Philip had to be overcome. He and Elizabeth returned to Madrid with all their court on 1 September, immediately after the death of Luis. Philip did not wish to resume the throne and made his views perfectly clear to marshal de Tessé: 'I don't want to go to hell, so I'm leaving. They can do what they like, as for me I'm going to save my soul.'[27] Elizabeth tried to persuade him to change his mind, but to no avail while her nurse, Laura Piscatori, scolded Philip for paying attention to the opinions of his 'scoundrel' of a confessor, Bermúdez, who had refused to instruct Philip to take up the crown. For several days there was a real battle among Philip's advisers about the problem of retracting his solemn oath to give up the crown. Various theologians were asked for an opinion, but their views were divided. Then Elizabeth persuaded Philip to consult the pope, whose personal opinion was that the oath to abdicate was not binding. Further deliberations with theologians convinced Philip that he could in all conscience return to the throne. It was also pointed out that Ferdinand was not yet of a sufficient age to be able to succeed to the crown (he was only just eleven), and that if he did so there would have to be a regency, which would logically fall on Philip. Left without any real choice, towards midnight on 6 September, just before going to bed, Philip signed a decree stating that he was resuming the crown.

A week later, orders were issued for summoning a Cortes to swear loyalty to the Infante Ferdinand as prince of Asturias. These were the first Cortes to be called after the War of Succession, and consisted in all of thirty-six delegates, among them for the first time delegates from six Catalan cities.[28] The ceremony took place on 25 November; after it, Philip and Elizabeth withdrew to San Ildefonso for a period, to avoid contracting any infection from Louise, who was also diagnosed with smallpox.

The controversy over Philip's return to power created a serious division of opinion among the political class. Those who supported the king were viewed as supporters also of Farnese and of the Italian interest; they were returned to power in the new administration, which took care to remove opponents from all key posts. Those who opposed the king's return were largely traditionalists; they came from the aristocracy and clergy, and included all those who opposed further Italian influence. Firmly Castilian in outlook, they had supported Luis I as a truly Castilian king; now backing the rights of the young prince of Asturias, they came to be known as 'the Fernandine party', an alternative name for the group otherwise described by ambassadors as 'the Spanish party'. In this way, the question of the succession to the throne, fated to play a very long role in Spanish politics, emerged centre stage. So tirelessly did the regime's opponents campaign, both through rumours and through pamphlets, against Philip's tenure of the throne, that in August 1726 the king had to issue orders calling for an investigation into 'rumours circulating in Madrid and other parts of the realm, to the effect that His Majesty is going to retire from the government of the monarchy'.[29]

The most serious consequence for Philip was that for the first time the legitimacy of his rule began to be questioned. If he had, as some still felt, no right to resume the throne after having solemnly abdicated, then he had no right to rule. Tessé gave first-hand evidence of the way in which certain clergy were manipulating the matter. 'Father Bermúdez has said that he is of the opinion that the king should resume the throne, but since the theologians were of the opposite view he would follow their opinion, that the king could not in conscience be king. I have seen all this for myself.'[30] Not surprisingly, Tessé insisted firmly to Elizabeth that the king must never again have a Spanish confessor and Bermúdez was subsequently sacked and replaced. The damage done to Philip by the moral theologians was in effect important. Until 1724, those who had questioned his throne had done so principally for dynastic reasons, since an alternative king of Spain existed in the shape of the Austrian candidate Charles III. After 1724, it became possible to question Philip's right to rule simply on moral grounds. Above all, those who had looked to the succession of Luis I as the beginning of a new, truly Spanish reign, free from the influence of Italians and other foreigners, were now obliged to witness the return to power of precisely those influences they had so long detested. It was the first serious split in sympathy between the Spanish crown and the ruling political class, and had long-term implications that would affect the Bourbon dynasty up to the beginning of the twentieth century.[31]

* * *

Philip returned to political life with a new star to guide him. This was Jan Willem Ripperda, who had represented the Dutch in the negotiations for the peace of Utrecht, and was sent to Madrid in 1715, at the age of thirty-five, as ambassador of the United Provinces. He made Spain his home, converted to Catholicism and was appointed by Alberoni director of the textile factories in Guadalajara. After Alberoni's fall he became influential in matters concerning commerce and diplomacy. In 1721 he married a Spanish lady of the court, was promoted to director of the textile industries in the kingdom, and became an adviser to the crown on the basis of several memoranda he drew up for the government on economic affairs. However, Ripperda's place in history centres not on his contribution to economic reform but on one particular scheme which he managed to sell to Philip and Elizabeth.

Despite the conditions for peace that had been agreed by the Quadruple Alliance in 1722, the emperor was reluctant to carry out his compromise and grant the investiture of Parma and Tuscany to the Infante Charles. He further antagonised the English and Dutch by allowing his Ostend Company (established in 1714, with further privileges granted in 1722) to trade with areas where their East India Companies were operating. Finally in April 1724, at the Congress of Cambrai, France (governed now by the duke of Bourbon, since Orléans had died in December 1723) and Britain attempted to take up these issues with the emperor, on behalf of Spain. But after six months of discussion, nothing substantial had been achieved.

In view of the royal concern to find an inheritance for Charles, Ripperda suggested that an alliance with the Empire, which he offered to negotiate personally (he had been educated in Germany and spoke the language perfectly), could lead to a dynastic union that might even allow Charles to become emperor. Philip was not averse to a change of alliances. He had returned to the throne still haunted by the humiliation suffered at the hands of France in 1719–20, a circumstance that (we have seen) had intensified his neurobiological disorder and directly provoked the decision to abdicate. His agitated outburst to Tessé in October 1724 reveals much about his state of mind. 'France', he protested angrily to the marshal, 'supplied the money that burnt my fleet, destroyed my naval forces, and made me give up Sicily which would still be mine had France, with its dagger at my throat, not forced me to abandon Sicily and abdicate from that kingdom!'[32] The king's animated conversations with his old friend show that he was on one of his extended highs: he appeared to be in perfect health, exceptionally clear in mind, and willing to talk interminably.

Ripperda's instructions from the court were that he seek a marriage between Charles and the emperor's daughter Maria Teresa, as well as the future election of Charles as 'King of the Romans, given his high qualities and the commendable circumstance of being married to the eldest daughter of the emperor'. A number of other objectives, largely pipe dreams of the king and queen, were also listed; the emperor was asked, for example, to help recover Minorca and Gibraltar. Ripperda went to Vienna in November 1724 and managed, to everyone's astonishment, to get the emperor to agree a few months later to the treaty of Vienna (30 April 1725).

By this remarkable accord, some important concessions were made on both sides that, effectively, brought the conflicts of the War of the Succession to an end. There were three separate agreements. By the first, Philip recognised the Pragmatic Sanction (the main objective of Imperial diplomacy), a decree whereby the emperor wished to make sure that the Imperial throne would pass without obstacles to his daughter Maria Teresa. By the second, Charles VI renounced his claims to Spain and the Indies, and Philip renounced yet again his rights to the throne of France. Philip was to pardon all nobles who had defected from the Bourbon cause during the War of Succession, allowing them to retain their titles and return to their property in the peninsula. Charles recognised the Bourbon succession in Spain, and Spain's claims in Italy as laid down by the Quadruple Alliance. By the third, Philip confirmed the rights of the Ostend Company, and conceded commercial privileges to Austria. It was a positive treaty for both sides. But through the means of deliberate filtrations of information, Ripperda hinted to the European powers that much more was being accomplished. Britain, in particular, took alarm at the information that it was receiving. At the end of 1725 the major western powers acceded to an agreement organised by Britain and known as the Alliance of Hanover (George I was also Elector of Hanover). In retaliation, Ripperda obtained a further secret agreement with Vienna, signed in that city on 5 November, in which the possibility of a marriage agreement was mentioned. The emperor also promised help 'to recover from England and return to the Spanish crown, the island of Minorca and also the city of Gibraltar'.[33] The treaty was strengthened later by the adhesion of Russia and of Prussia.

During Ripperda's absence in Vienna Philip made an important decision over his late son's wife, Louise Elizabeth. A dowager queen at the age of fifteen, she had the right to be maintained by the Spanish state in an appropriate palace and with an appropriate income. Philip considered that this would be an outrageous waste of funds, particularly so in the case of a young girl who spent money like water and behaved in a way not suitable for widows. After careful consultation with members of the Orléans family, Philip decided to send Louise back to live in Paris, a move which served as an excuse for the French government to take a reciprocal step. Louis XV's wife María Ana Victoria was only nine years old in 1724. She was too young to consummate marriage or to bear children, a situation that endangered the whole Bourbon succession in France. Accordingly, in March 1724, Philip V was informed that the French proposed returning the Infanta to Spain. On 17 May 1725, the two girls were exchanged at the frontier. Spain was still legally obliged to pay for a proportion of the costs of Louise's household, which the French government also found excessive and reduced immediately.[34]

The return of the Infanta was seen in Madrid as an open insult, and led immediately to a crisis in relations between France and Spain. The king ordered reprisals against French traders in Spain and the suspension of diplomatic negotiations with France. Anger in the royal family was profound. At dinner one night Philip was speaking of the current food shortages in France, caused by harvest failure, and commented that 'we must not let the people die of hunger', to which Elizabeth retorted sharply, 'Yes, let them all die!'[35] The dissolution of the dynastic link with France also encouraged Elizabeth Farnese and Philip to place their hopes very firmly in a dynastic link with Vienna. The proposed marriages between Elizabeth's sons and the emperor's daughters 'were always', as the marquis of la Paz observed later, 'the principal objective of the great decisions that the king has taken since the year 1724'.[36] At the same time Spain refused to have France as a spokesman at the Congress of Cambrai, and offered the role to Britain.

When Ripperda returned to Madrid in December 1725 he was showered with honours, created duke and grandee, and placed at the head of the government, in which over the next few months he came to control the secretariats of Despacho of the departments of State, and of War and the Navy. The faithful but now ageing and sick José de

Grimaldo was set aside. Baltasar Patiño, marquis of Castelar, was removed from the War department in order to make way for the favourite. The responsible secretary of the department of State, Juan Bautista Orendain, was created marquis of la Paz. Ripperda thus took control of government in a way that Alberoni had never been able to. But his rise inevitably created fierce opposition in the administration. The members of the Council of Castile made futile protests against his interference in their area of authority. A satire from the opposition went:

> Este duque solicita
> Remediarnos, y será
> Para pocos Ripper-da,
> Para muchos Ripper-quita.[37]

(The duke claims that he wishes to help us, but he will give to few and take from many.)

It was a bubble that soon burst. The secret clauses about a marriage and the recovery of Gibraltar were so vague as to be useless. Moreover, the treaty contained financial conditions that Spain could not fulfil, and it provoked a threat of war from Britain, which sent a fleet to the West Indies to prevent the passage of the silver fleet from America. Reluctantly, the government had to agree to the dismissal of Ripperda, who took refuge in the house of the British ambassador, William Stanhope, but was seized and imprisoned in the Alcázar of Segovia in May 1726. The favourite escaped fifteen months later, and continued to pursue his colourful career first in England and then in Africa.

Various ministerial changes were made as a result of Ripperda's fall. That October Stanhope, always alert to anti-British trends in the queen's policies, reported to London on 'the absolute power she exercises over the king, of which she has just given the most signal and convincing proof by obliging him to dismiss from his service the only two persons for whom he was known to have a real affection', [38] namely the minister Grimaldo and the confessor Father Bermúdez. It was yet another example not of Elizabeth's domination but of the ambassador's own bad information. Grimaldo, now sixty-four years old, had for some time (according to the marquis of San Felipe) been suffering from 'illnesses, pains and age'. He did not expect to be removed from power; like most good politicians, he felt that he was irreplaceable. But he had to give way before the rising star of José Patiño, who (it was reported) 'increases his influence every day with Their Majesties, and if he acquires full power he will keep it for a long time'.[39] Grimaldo therefore retired definitively from the ministry of State, which remained in the hands of the marquis of la Paz. Bermúdez had eliminated himself by his unpalatable advice over the return of Philip to power, and was replaced by an Irish Jesuit, Father Clarke, who spoke French with difficulty. The ministries of the Navy and the Indies, and of Finance, were entrusted to José Patiño, and that of War was given back to the marquis of Castelar.

The Ripperda episode had a substantial impact on Spanish politics. It aroused yet further opposition of the Fernandine party. If the British ambassador in Madrid is to be believed, it even elicited criticism from the heir to the throne. According to Stanhope, the prince of Asturias condemned the part of the king and queen in the matter as 'destructive to his interests and those of the Spanish monarchy, and carried on by the queen purely for the aggrandising of her own children'.[40] The wild diplomacy of Ripperda seemed to many to be the consequence of a regime directed by a mad king. Moreover, it seemed that the king had lost all real control over decisions in government, and was giving way to the whims of Elizabeth.

*   *   *

At the same time an issue of immense personal importance to Philip arose, one which obliges us to go back a few years in the narrative. At the time that he had accepted the crown of Spain, the king renounced all his rights to succeed to the throne of France. A union of the thrones of France and Spain was opposed unanimously by all the other European powers and both Louis XIV and Philip had been happy to reassure them on this point in 1701. During the War of Succession, however, one by one the heirs of Louis XIV died. His direct heir the dauphin, Philip's own father, died in 1711. The next in line, Philip's elder brother the duke of Burgundy, died in February 1712 (the duke's wife also died in the same month of the same illness). Then in March 1712 Burgundy's son the duke of Brittany died. Only Brittany's younger brother, the two-year-old duke of Anjou (the future Louis XV), interposed between Philip and the throne of France.

In the spring of 1712, consequently, Philip became the proximate heir to the French throne as well as being king of Spain. The new situation had a profound effect on him. Despite his early hesitations, he was now proud and happy to be the ruler of the Spanish people. But the possibility of succeeding to the throne of his grandfather continued to arouse deep within him all those yearnings for greatness that he had so far played out only on the battlefield. He always remained French at heart, and lived like a Frenchman. The possibility of ruling France took root in his mind in 1712, and grew in later years to become an obsession. As soon as he received news of the death of the duke of Brittany, Philip expressed 'a vehement desire to return to France in order to claim his rights', although there was still a war on.[41] The duke of Vendôme and the French ambassador Bonnac had to make great efforts to convince him that this was not advisable. In reality, there was no real obstacle to him becoming king of France. The leading French jurist of the day had given his firm opinion that the renunciations made by Philip in 1701 were invalid, and Louis XIV was also in favour of leaving the succession open to Philip. For their part, the allies were well aware of the position, and the English insisted early in 1712 that Philip should make yet another renunciation if peace terms were to be agreed. He should choose to be king of Spain, or of France, but not of both.

Accordingly, on 8 July 1712, Philip issued a decree that was accepted by the Council of Castile, affirming his decision to remain as king of Spain. He expressed his gratitude to 'the Spaniards, whose devotion and loyalty have placed the crown on my head. For the love that I bear them, I shall not only prefer Spain over all the monarchies in the world, but even rest content with the smallest part of this realm, rather than abandon so faithful a people. I declare that of my own volition I renounce my rights to the crown of France.'[42] Later, on 5 November, the official renunciation was signed by the king in his chambers, and presented that afternoon to a special session of the Cortes. Four days later the Cortes approved the document, which was decreed as law in March 1713. The renunciation was later incorporated as one of the clauses of the treaty of Utrecht.

It was possible to argue, as some did at the time, that a moral and legitimate right such as the succession could not be annulled by a renunciation. In Philip's case, the right to the French throne came to play a continuous part in his pathological illnesses. Though he had in 1712 entertained the hope that he might some day occupy the place of his famous grandfather, he did nothing about the matter, and firmly supported the succession in 1715 of his infant nephew Louis XV to the throne of France. He resumed his interest, however, whenever there were fears about the health of the new king. Later, in 1724, there were suspicions that his abdication was deliberately calculated so that he would be in a position to claim the French succession without any risk of uniting the two crowns.

The French throne became an issue again in the later months of 1726. From early June Philip suffered a sudden recurrence of his illness, which lasted for several weeks. There were long respites that allowed him, for example, to participate in the public midsummer festivities. But in July the British ambassador described the king's ill-health as a 'touch of madness'. The attack was so serious that Philip immediately drew up a new will, and signed a decree making Elizabeth governor of the realm. Without hesitation she took over direction of the government, and organised business directly with ministers, none of whom was permitted to see the king. Only the confessors were allowed into the royal chambers, to fulfil their religious duties. The prince of Asturias was for the first time admitted to sessions of the Royal Council. There was a significant improvement by July, when the king joined the royal family in order to inspect the royal guard or in attending bullfights; then from the end of the month Philip and Elizabeth were back in San Ildefonso. The alarm over Philip's health had been profound, and reinforced the absolute dedication of the king and queen to each other. In an audience that they gave to the French ambassador Rottembourg in October, Elizabeth told him quietly and intensely, in Philip's presence, that 'the king and I are never apart from each other; I do and think nothing without him'.[43]

The recovery from illness was only partial, for by the end of October Philip was struck down again, this time with serious physical symptoms. He appeared to have lost all use of his body, though his mind remained active and clear. Three assistants were required to help him get out of bed. Normally he would lie there for hours, doing nothing but staring fixedly at the ceiling and moving his lips soundlessly. Elizabeth was at his side by day and by night. Then in November news arrived from France that the king, Louis XV, was ill. The information was exactly the therapy that Philip needed. It awoke in him his profound concern for the situation in France and immediately galvanised him into hyperactivity, the other pole of his depression. He decided to reassert his rights to the French throne. In November he contacted the *abbé* de Montgon, an agent of the duke of Bourbon in Spain, and ordered him to go to France and examine what support he would have if he claimed the succession. His instructions to Montgon, dated Christmas Day 1726, stated explicitly that if the young king were to die without issue, 'since I am the closest relative, I have the right to succeed to the crown'.[44] His obsession with the French succession remained with him all his life.

*   *   *

Meanwhile the consequences of Ripperda's anti-British policy took their course. On the crest of a high, and fully recovered from his attacks of depression, Philip V in December 1726 was roused into action by the prospect of battle, and ordered his forces to proceed to Gibraltar. Some time before, Elizabeth had warned the British ambassador that 'you must choose between losing Gibraltar or suffering the ruin of your trade in America'.[45] In February 1727 the siege of the Rock began. It had little hope of success, however, against the superior naval strength of the English, who continued to supply the besieged from the sea.

The hostilities between Spain and Britain never reached the stage of open war, and were brought to an end by France. In June 1726 the duke of Bourbon was dismissed from power by Louis XV, to be succeeded by the king's former tutor Cardinal Fleury, now aged seventy-three. Fleury was firmly dedicated to peace, and negotiated an agreement signed in Paris in May 1727. The principal concession made by Spain was significant: the commercial privileges granted to Vienna were revoked, and the emperor also agreed to suspend the Ostend Company for seven years. On the other hand, the privileges previously enjoyed by Britain were confirmed, and in return Britain and France were to help Spain introduce Spanish garrisons into Parma and Tuscany. Although the siege of Gibraltar was raised in July, the Rock remained, inevitably, on the diplomatic agenda. In October 1727, during an audience with the French ambassador, the king and queen raised the subject of Gibraltar. While the king talked animatedly about it, Elizabeth went to her desk and drew out from a drawer the original of the famous letter from George I, in which he promised to give back Gibraltar as soon as it became possible. 'Help us to get back what the English have taken from us,' Elizabeth pleaded with the ambassador. 'What right do they have to come to our coasts and blockade our ports?'[46]

The agreements subsequently reached between Spain and Britain were confirmed and signed by representatives of the two countries in the Convention of the Pardo, of March 1728. The various negotiations between all parties were debated finally in a big general congress held at Soissons in France, which opened in the middle of June 1728. Thanks to the periodic illnesses of the king, Elizabeth took a larger part than usual in the formation of policy. Her dominant feeling was one of frustration with the Austrian alliance, which had brought no practical benefits to Spain or to her own dynastic pretensions. After Soissons the king and queen were in no doubt that their principal objective was in Italy, and that their principal enemy was Austria.

Impatient with French refusals to collaborate, and with the lack of sympathy from Chauvelin, the foreign minister appointed by Fleury in 1727, Elizabeth proceeded with her own policies, which centred (like those of Alberoni a few years before) on close collaboration with Britain. First an agreement for a dynastic alliance was made with the Crown of Portugal, Britain's close ally. This led to the celebration, mentioned below, of the marriage between the prince of Asturias and the princess of Portugal. Later, when the Spanish court had settled down in its new residence in the south of the peninsula, the discussions at Soissons were made the basis for a tripartite alliance between Spain, Great Britain and France. This was the treaty of Seville, signed in November 1729, a treaty that, as we shall see, converted into reality all the aspirations of Philip V and Elizabeth Farnese.

* * *

The king's illness came and went, each time assuming stranger and more severe forms. At the end of May 1727 he was taken unwell again, in Aranjuez, and could not engage in the tasks of government. The doctors bled him because he had a slight fever. Elizabeth dutifully played her part as governor (she was formally granted the powers by a decree of 2 June)[47] and also directed foreign policy, but refused to make any major decisions until the king had recovered. In the second week of June he was completely well again, or so it would seem, though his manner of demonstrating his good health was odd. Very late one night at Aranjuez he called for his carriage and asked the driver to transport him to Madrid, where he arrived at 7.15 in the morning, to the great surprise of the citizens.[48] In August Montgon returned from his mission to France, and came to court to make his report to the king. He found Philip sunk once more in a profound depression. Montgon made a verbal report, but the king gave no sign of hearing other than a gesture now and then or a fleeting smile.[49]

In early 1728 Philip was well again, and in full control of the government. However, the first signs of a major change in his mental disturbance made themselves evident. He now suffered attacks that caused him to spend several days at a time in bed, and he also began to invert the order of day and night. Sometimes he would not see his ministers for weeks. Then when he saw them he would hold the meetings in the small hours of the morning, terminating at dawn. Audiences with ambassadors were held at midnight. The most serious development came in June: he made it clear that he was going to abdicate again.

Elizabeth recognised the auto-destructive forms of the illness and was fully prepared for the crisis, which took extreme forms.[50] She attempted to talk to Philip, but he refused to listen to reason and their discussions ended up as serious, sometimes daily, quarrels. When Philip became very angry he also became violent and beat her. Elizabeth in one audience that she had alone with the French ambassador had to explain to him the very visible scratches and bruises that she had suffered. It was, she told him, 'a cruel situation'. To prevent Philip proceeding to act on his threat, she removed all paper and ink from the royal suite, and tried to keep a watch on all his movements. The king realised that the only way of carrying out his intention was to escape from the palace, which he attempted to do. One day that month of June he awoke at 5 a.m. without disturbing Elizabeth and tried to leave the palace dressed only in his nightshirt. The queen woke up, ran after him and ordered the guards to detain him. She changed the locks on all the doors frequently, and gave the guards instructions to stop the king leaving the palace. Nevertheless, he continued to make attempts to leave the palace half-naked in the early hours of the morning.

None of the security measures proved adequate. On 28 June he profited from the queen's temporary absence in another chamber, found some paper and wrote out in his own hand a decree which he slipped to his most trusted chamber servant, to be handed to the Council of Castile. The councils normally held their sessions in a hall in the main floor of the Alcázar, where the king and queen were staying, so the task was easily carried out. The decree ordered the council to publish his abdication immediately and to proclaim Ferdinand as king. When she learnt what had happened, Elizabeth immediately sent a noble to recover the document. He arrived in the council just as it was discussing the paper, which was seized and destroyed.

Philip's condition that summer became common knowledge among all who frequented the palace. His health and reason were normal, and he continued to discuss affairs of state perfectly normally and sanely with his ministers. We have ample proof of his close personal dedication to his work as king in these years, by the various notes, scribbled by him in Spanish, that he left within his state papers. His attention was centred not simply on affairs of foreign policy, as historians often assume, but on all matters, both large and small, that demanded his attention.[51] 'On distributing charity in cash instead of grain', runs one note; 'on my agreement with a decision of the Council of War', runs another. The variety of business was immense: 'on taking on a credit to pay for the damage in Guipúzcoa', 'on my agreement with a decision of the Council of Finance', 'settling the price of slaves for the galleys', 'on the matter of destroying settlements that the English have constructed inland in America', 'on sending an ambassador to Holland', 'on removing a staff sergeant from his unit and transferring him to another, because of differences with his colonel', 'on the *asiento* of negros', 'the two reports that I questioned, one allowing an appeal to the court, but the other disallowing more judicial action', 'on the construction of seagoing ships'. At the same time, there were many matters that touched him very directly: 'on my penance', 'the mediating powers want to make a peace unfavourable to me', 'what I said in my letter about the Crown of Aragon, at the time I was not thinking properly', 'the revenue from what has been sold, afterwards I had a few doubts about whether the reports said more about it', 'on why the guards at the gate of San Ildefonso were removed', 'what I forgot and failed to note down, and what I forgot seemed afterwards to be out of date'. Then there were matters of which he had to remind himself: 'tell Patiño about it', 'on telling Castelar what he didn't know', 'what the father confessor told me about the Council of War'. Within the limits of his possibilities, Philip was a conscientious king, attentive to all the responsibilities of his position, even to small matters such as 'on the cows, maybe the fault of the gardener in Madrid', no doubt a matter of a neighbour's cows straying into the royal gardens.

However, his conduct at times was wholly bizarre. He spent several days at a time in bed. He was allowed to perform most of his duties, but with unexpected results. He would sometimes give audiences to ambassadors dressed only in his nightshirt or almost naked, without trousers or shoes. He also began to develop the most extreme symptoms of manic disorder: apart from being unable to sleep, he began to suffer from terrors, delusions and hallucinations. He dwelt again on the plots against him that had been backed by Orléans. Because he was afraid of being poisoned through a shirt (it was one of the schemes of which Flotte and Regnault had been accused in 1709), he would only wear shirts that Elizabeth had worn previously, and in one ambassadorial audience presented himself wearing two shirts, Elizabeth's under his own. At certain times, he would behave quite irrationally: at night he would bite himself, or scream, or start singing. Sometimes he would urinate and evacuate in his bed. His psychotic condition led him to withdraw totally from reality. At one time in July he believed that he was a frog, at another time he believed that he was dead. On occasion, he would have attacks of bulimia, and would eat voraciously for an hour or so without stopping.[52] At every stage, when he was stable and when he suffered attacks of his illness, Elizabeth attended personally to his needs and attempted to control the impact of Philip's behaviour. In a private letter of June 1728 the marquis of la Paz expressed his admiration for the way in which she coped. 'Despite all her cares and concerns, the queen remains strong and in perfect health, and she needs all of it to stand up to this constant anxiety.'[53]

After the episode of the attempted abdication, Elizabeth made the radical decision that the king needed a complete rest. She wished to protect him as well as herself from the possibility of another abdication, and the court environment in Madrid did not seem to guarantee adequate isolation. In the last months of 1728, she took over effective decision-making. The king was technically in good health and therefore there was no need for any transferral of his powers. When documents needed the royal signature, use was made of the official seal that reproduced it. At audiences with ambassadors, which the royal couple always attended together, Philip was allowed to be present but normally said little or nothing; Elizabeth dominated the conversation and made the declarations. This was not as simple as might appear, for the king though silent was often stubborn, and if he insisted on something the queen could do nothing to change his mind. Elizabeth's high profile was not a role she chose, although ambassadors constantly misinterpreted it as proof of her control over the king. In reality, she constantly stressed that she merely obeyed the king, and had no interests that were not those of her husband, nor any ambition save the glory of Spain.⁵⁴

The king's deep and subconscious obsession with the French succession became evident in October 1728, when the court received news that Louis XV was seriously ill with smallpox. Philip's mind concentrated itself on the problem, which seemed to take on grave proportions when no further news arrived from Paris for days. Both the king and queen were alarmed. What if the absence of couriers meant that Louis XV had died? The unexpected possibility of succeeding to the throne of his grandfather drove Philip into a frenzy of excitement, and swung him back completely from a depressive phase to a mood of elation and euphoria. 'If I were in France,' he told his *valet de chambre* excitedly, 'I would feel much better, and would eat and drink without fear because there would be no danger of someone poisoning me.'⁵⁵ He went to his office and on 9 November dictated letters to France asserting his claims to the French throne. His formal letter to the Parlement of Paris stated that if it was true that Louis XV 'had just died without leaving a successor, I claim the right, given me by my birth, to succeed to the throne of France'.⁵⁶ Four days later Philip was fully recovered; it was as though he had never been ill. He ordered preparations to be made for his journey to France. Then news arrived that same day that Louis was in fact recovering; there had been an interruption in the courier service, nothing more. The English minister Benjamin Keene reported later that during those days Elizabeth had asked the king what he would do if Louis were dead. Philip replied 'that he would go to France with her and the other members of the royal family, leaving the Infante Charles in Spain. It would be a pleasure for him to reign in France, because there they despatched business in a different manner from here, they had more greatness there.'⁵⁷ They were words from which Elizabeth could deduce very clearly that the king, despite his appearance of normality, had not yet returned to the real world. She became determined that the only solution was to remove Philip for a while from the stresses put on him by the government in Madrid.

Towards the end of 1728 plans matured for the exchange of partners in the double marriage between the prince of Asturias and the princess of Portugal, Barbara of Braganza, and the Infanta María Ana Victoria (the former wife of Louis XV) to the Portuguese heir, the prince of Brazil. The agreements were signed in October 1725. The proxy marriage of the latter was carried out on 27 December 1727, and of the former on 11 January 1728, but no exchange of partners was possible for several months because of the indisposition of Philip. As a result, nothing could be planned until after October, when the king became normal again.

It was agreed that the exchange of partners would be carried out, in exact imitation of preceding royal marriages within the previous century, on the frontier between the two countries. In this case, the entire royal court of each country was going to be present. It was agreed to celebrate the rendezvous on a specially constructed bridge over the river Caya, a short distance from Badajoz. The centre of the bridge was occupied by a house-like structure where the exchanges would be made. The weather seemed at first to be a likely obstacle. It was bitterly cold, with 'abundant snow that fell in the first days of this year'.[58] But Philip was determined that the arrangements would take place, and virtually the entire court set out from Madrid on 7 January 1729, including the higher nobility and foreign diplomats, and reached Badajoz in ten days. The Portuguese court, meanwhile, based itself in Elvas. The contracts of marriage were signed in the middle of the bridge on 19 January. The only person who seemed to be displeased was the Infante Ferdinand. Keene, who was present, reports the prince's disappointment when he saw his new wife. 'I had a perfect view of the meeting of the two families and could see that the princess's appearance displeased the prince, who was looking at her like someone who feels he has been deceived. Her large mouth, thick lips, fat cheeks and tiny eyes, did not represent to him an agreeable picture.'[59] Contemporary portraits of the princess give a quite different impression, of a young and pretty girl; but they were deliberately misleading. The Infante did not like his wife, and never grew to like her.

The celebrations of the marriage lasted a week. After them, most of the nobles and diplomats returned to Madrid, together with some of the court. The royal family, their dependants and ministers of the government were, however, invited to visit Andalucia. It seems that

Elizabeth intended to take the king on a tour of the south of the kingdom, similar to those undertaken in medieval times. It was going to be a brief visit, and would not last much longer than six months, according to one testimony.[60] The court began the move southwards at the end of January, on an adventure that was to last for very much longer than anyone had anticipated.

CHAPTER SIX

Andalucian Interlude, 1729–1733

'THE KING AND I ARE NOT CHILDREN YOU CAN FRIGHTEN, WE
ARE NOT AFRAID OF GREAT ENTERPRISES.'

ELIZABETH FARNESE TO THE FRENCH AMBASSADOR, 1732

The visit to Seville had been planned for some time by Patiño and his government team,[1] but nobody appears to have had any idea how long it would last. The city authorities received no confirmation of the dates until ten days before, barely time for them to prepare an adequate welcome for the king. In the event, the expected short visit turned into a very long one. From 1729 and for the next five years the Spanish state went through the unprecedented and curious experience of having its royal court in Seville and its government in Madrid. The court and its households entered Seville, which in effect now became the capital of the monarchy, in the evening of 3 February 1729. They were received – despite the express wish of Philip that 'in no way do I wish formality and ceremony for the entry into the city'[2] – with festivities, fireworks, displays of *cañas* (a form of jousting) and bullfights, a truly Sevillan welcome. The Sevillans gaped at the seemingly unending procession – 85 carriages, over 400 conveyances, 750 horsemen and a great number of transport mules – that entered the city.[3] It was more than a century since the last king of Spain had visited and the whole city and all the bridges were decorated. Over 600 attendants and government ministers, among them Patiño and other officials, accompanied Philip. The royal family was lodged in the Alcázar, which had just received some urgent repairs and for the first time in four centuries became the seat of the ruling monarch. There was of course no reason why Seville should not be the capital, as Valladolid had been two centuries before. One of the largest cities of Spain, with a population in 1705 of around 85,000, seat of an archbishopric, of a university, of a tribunal of the Inquisition, of one of the supreme courts of Castile, and until recently the official centre of the lucrative trade to the Indies, Seville was a rich and flourishing city that housed a large business and international community. An annalist of the time records that thousands of people had died in the epidemic of 1709, but by the 1730s the city's population was growing, and by the 1760s it contained close to 100,000 people.

The stay honoured Seville, and all southern Spain. From Granada in March the civil governor sent a letter to the king thanking him for 'honouring the Andalucias with his royal presence'.[4] But the visit also caused serious problems. The city council of Seville had to raise loans to pay for all the extra expenditure on organisation, services and entertainments. Nor did the city have adequate housing for so many dignitaries, and lodging also had to be found for the hundreds of soldiers and members of the royal guard. The court stayed, moreover, on the premise that this was merely a temporal visit; it therefore exercised the medieval right to be lodged free of charge, even in private households. In the days after their arrival, members of the royal family went sightseeing, or fishing in the river; every afternoon they went hunting in the vicinity. On their second Sunday there, the central streets were shut to traffic and they were given a private tour of the cathedral and its riches.

The court did not remain fixed in Seville, but made several excursions to other parts of Andalucia. On 17 February they embarked on the Guadalquivir 'in a beautiful and spacious Gondola that the city placed at their disposal, painted in gold, with a glass enclosure at the poop, and twenty rowers dressed in crimson velvet with gold braid and velvet bonnets'. A city councillor controlled the rudder, and that afternoon they spent three hours until nightfall travelling along the river. A couple of days later news came of the impending arrival in Cadiz of the treasure-laden galleons from America. The king decided that he wished to witness the event, so on the 21st the royal family travelled down to the Isle of León, changing horses seven times, and on their arrival were lodged in a spacious country house. They were followed by their entire households as well as by government ministers and ambassadors; it was a foretaste of the travails that all these personages would have to put up with over the next few months, as they accompanied the king around Andalucia. From where they were on the Isle of León, the king and queen could see the galleons, bearing a treasure of 30 million pesos, as they sailed into the bay of Cadiz on the morning of 22 February. Five days later the king and queen made their first visit to the city of Cadiz, where they stayed six days in the midst of celebrations.

The day after returning to the Isle of León, the king arranged for a visit to the galleys of the Mediterranean fleet of Spain, which was visiting the bay of Cadiz. As part of the outing, he also took the royal family on board the Spanish warship *San Felipe*. In subsequent days further visits were made to the dockyards of Cadiz, where he assisted, together with Patiño, at the launch of a newly constructed vessel. Philip's close interest in the Atlantic galleons and the Mediterranean galleys was by no means purely formal, but demonstrated his personal commitment to the naval resurgence of Spain and he obviously shared with Patiño a belief in the importance of sea power. At the end of March the royal family left the Isle of León and went on to visit Puerto de Santa María and Sanlúcar, lodging in the latter in the palace of the duke of Medina-Sidonia. Then, on 4 April, they went to the game preserve of Doñana, where they stayed in the country house of the duke and devoted four days to hunting and fishing. Thereafter they embarked on the galleys of the Mediterranean fleet, returning by river to Seville on 10 April.

All the evidence points to the fact that the king was charmed by his new surroundings. He followed his previous custom of going out every afternoon, sometimes to visit monuments, sometimes to walk along the river or sail up the Guadalquivir; he fished frequently in the ponds in the gardens of the Alcázar. That spring one of the memorable events of Seville's history took place. On 15 May 1729 the body of the medieval saint and king, Ferdinand, was translated from its old coffin to a silver tomb prepared in the cathedral (where it remains today). Philip and Elizabeth presided over the ceremonies, and in the evening there was a procession through the city, which ended at 9 p.m. It was a magnificent occasion. As the procession entered the cathedral, we are told by the contemporary account, 'the sacred urn [of the saint] was preceded by the musicians and twelve royal chaplains, followed by the grandees and the knights of the Orders of the Golden Fleece and the Holy Spirit. From the base of the urn hung eight golden cords, which were held by members of the royal family, the front two by the Infantes Don Luis and Doña María, two and three years old respectively, those on the left by the serene Infantes Charles and Philip, those on the right by the prince of Asturias Don Ferdinand and Doña Bárbara, and the last two by Their Majesties, who were followed by the ladies and the whole court.'[5]

Away from the tasks of government in Madrid, the king was relaxed but it seems that he nevertheless began to entertain a desire to return to San Ildefonso.[6] The queen therefore took him travelling again. The royal family spent the summer of 1729 in Puerto de Santa María, where they arrived on 6 June and stayed for three months. However, they had to return to the Alcázar at the end of September, since the queen was in the advanced stages of pregnancy. The group travelled by water up the Guadalquivir to Seville, where they arrived on 27 September. The most pressing political problem was presented by the treaty of Seville (discussed below), which was signed early in November. Eight days afterwards, on 17 November, Elizabeth gave birth in the Alcázar to María Antonia (who years later in 1750 was to marry the duke of Savoy), and the appropriate celebrations followed, with a display of fireworks which the queen watched from the palace window.

*   *   *

Government in Madrid, meanwhile, was in the capable hands of Patiño. José Patiño was born in 1666 in Milan, of a Galician family.

Brought up there by the Jesuits, he spent his active career serving the Spanish government in Spain, where he began in 1711 as a military intendant in the provinces. In 1713 he became intendant in Catalonia, administering the post-*fuero* regime there, and was responsible for the new taxation imposed on the province. When Alberoni came to power he was appointed in 1717 intendant of Seville with responsibilities for the navy. In this capacity he steered through one of the most important commercial measures of the period: the transfer from Seville to Cadiz of the administration of the American trade.

Patiño turned out to be Philip's best minister and in effect the creator of the new-style Bourbon monarchy. His potential was demonstrated by the amazing success with which he managed in 1717 and 1718 to put together an army and navy for the expeditions to Sardinia. After the fall of Ripperda, he moved to the central administration in Madrid, becoming minister of the Navy in 1726. When in 1730 his brother Baltasar Patiño, marquis of Castelar, was appointed ambassador to Versailles, he took over the post of secretary of War. In 1733, when the marquis of La Paz fell ill, he also assumed the post of secretary of State, an office which he had been helping to direct well before that date. He thereby became in theory the supreme head of the government, though in practice he was merely the executive head and his capacity for action was restricted both by the dictates of the king and by the willingness of the ruling elite to co-operate. Throughout his career he combined outstanding efficiency with complete anonymity. Totally obedient to the wishes of the king and queen, he consequently gained many enemies among the bureaucratic class.

His outstanding achievement was, as we have seen, the creation of the Spanish navy. 'Ever since I returned to this country,' Benjamin Keene wrote in 1728, 'I observed with the greatest concern the progress Patiño was making towards a powerful marine. That idea is so strong in him that neither the subsidies paid to the emperor nor the misery of the Spanish troops nor the poverty of the household and tribunals can divert him from it.'[7] Patiño paid for the building of ships in Vizcaya and Cadiz, promoted support industries, and reformed naval administration.[8] At the time of his death the navy totalled 34 warships, 9 frigates and 16 smaller vessels. Without these vessels neither the great

expeditions of Alberoni nor the king's enterprise of Orán would have
been possible. There continued, of course, to be major deficiencies in
the navy. As a satire of the time observed, there were few experienced
personnel:

> Si no hay marineros,
> pilotos y pagas
> ¿de qué sirven flotas
> si no hay quien las traiga?[9]

> (If there are no sailors, pilots or wages, what use are fleets with
> nobody to serve in them?)

Keene also observed in 1731 that 'their naval officers do not deserve
that name'. It is true that the Spanish ships were excellent as transport
vessels and disastrous as a fighting force, but for the first time in its
entire history the country was now a serious military power. Spain's
naval past had been one of temporary solutions to the needs of the
moment; from Patiño's time an effort was made to create a permanent
marine fighting force controlled directly by the crown.

Reform of the army complemented the naval reforms. We have seen
that the poor condition of the Spanish forces in the War of Succession
made it necessary at every stage to have the support of foreign troops
and foreign generals. Philip had decreed a few limited reforms during
the war, mainly in order to obtain recruits. A law of November 1704,
for example, imposed selective recruitment and regulated the selection
and training of officers. But the problem of securing a good standing
army remained unresolved. Fortunately, many of the foreign soldiers
and officers who had served in the war continued their career under
the Spanish crown. As a result, in the 1720s one-third of the infantry
of Spain consisted of foreigners. The need to garrison the fortresses of
the peninsula adequately, to maintain the security of the ex-*fuero*
provinces and to contribute towards the military expeditions of the time
all served to make it essential that Spain have a permanent military
force. There is no reliable calculation of its size. Official figures suggest
that the army reached its peak in 1734, when it had 30,000 men; but
Benjamin Keene reported at around the same date that the army actu-

ally totalled 70,000 men. A few years later he put the figure even higher. 'The king of Spain', he reported, 'has upon paper and in his imagination 150,000 men, of which 30,000 are militia. His regular troops I believe may be computed at 70,000 effective men, of which about 19 battalions are in the garrisons of Orán and Ceuta.'[10]

* * *

As soon as Philip had settled down in Seville, after the wanderings round Andalucia, he and Elizabeth concentrated their minds on the Italian question, which remained to be resolved after the sessions at Soissons the previous year. On 9 November 1729 the treaty of Seville, which was in reality the idea of the British prime minister, Sir Robert Walpole, was finally signed after negotiations between the British envoy, William Stanhope,[11] and Patiño. The signatories, namely Spain, France and Britain, would each raise a small force of 8,000 infantry and 4,000 cavalry, to be used when any of the three required military help. It was also agreed that a Spanish military contingent of 6,000 men could take possession of the fortifications in Livorno, Porto Ferrayo, Parma and Piacenza, to ensure the succession of the Infante Charles to those Italian territories. The Spanish ministers signing the agreement were the marquis of La Paz and Patiño. Though the treaty seemed to contain little but promises, in reality it put an end for the moment to disputes with Britain, and also secured for some time to come the collaboration of France.

Philip was excited by the possibilities offered by the treaty, which he was anxious to put into effect. 'He desires nothing so much as war', the French ambassador observed.[12] The purpose of the treaty, in the view of both the English and the French, was to protect the peace. But Philip and Elizabeth did not see things that way. It was reported to them that Fleury was reluctant to put into effect the clauses that permitted Spain to send garrisons into Parma, and had stated that he did not wish to go to war (in Italy) 'to satisfy the caprice of a woman'. Elizabeth's reaction was an angry retort to the French ambassador: 'This woman has a husband who is a man, and who shares the same caprice as his wife'.[13] The outburst was, from our point of view, highly significant. French and English diplomats tended to assume that because Elizabeth took the lead in conversations with them, she was the real creator of policy. In practical terms, this was true. But Elizabeth always followed, both in public and in private, the ideas and wishes of her husband.

In early February 1730, after the queen had completed the customary forty days of convalescence after a birth, the court went to stay in Castilblanco for ten days, in order to devote the time exclusively to hunting. On 5 March they set out from Seville once again, but on a longer journey. The objective was to spend the spring months in Granada. They took the route through Marchena and Osuna, and had to make a stop of four days in Antequera, because the king and several members of the court were suffering an attack of influenza, which had taken on epidemic proportions in parts of Andalucia. When they finally reached Granada on the 23rd, celebrations and triumphal arches in the streets greeted them. The lodgings prepared for the royal family were in the Alhambra, which they spent the following day visiting. For Philip the most moving experience was the visit to the tombs of the Catholic Monarchs Ferdinand and Isabella, revered traditionally as the founders of the Spanish monarchy.[14] Moreover, their stay coincided with Holy Week and its ceremonies. But Philip soon tired of having to go up and down the hill. He let the Infantes continue living in the Alhambra, and moved instead with Elizabeth to a country residence in a nearby wood, the game reserve (or *soto*) of Roma, where he could hunt more easily, deal with tasks of government and receive the visits of diplomats. It takes little effort to imagine the strange situation that now turned the Soto de Roma into the centre of the Spanish monarchy. To celebrate Philip's name day on 1 May, a reception (a *besamanos*, literally a 'kissing of hands') was held in the country house in the *soto*. The *Gaceta* reports that 'the assemblage of heads of the royal households, grandees, ambassadors and foreign diplomats, as well as noble lords and ladies, was numerous and resplendent; a great number of tables was set out for them, and the festive night ended with a grand concert with singers and instruments'.[15] To be able to attend the function all these notables had followed the court across Andalucia and were lodged in dwellings around the countryside.

We should recognise the immense effort of hospitality made by the people in the towns of Andalucia, for they had to supply the transport animals, lodgings and food required for so many people, and were often not reimbursed for the sums which they had spent in the royal service. During the 1730 visit, the city of Granada tried to find lodging for about 5,000 people, but within the area controlled by the city it was able to accommodate only 1,500. A large number of notables had to be satisfied with fairly humble living quarters in nearby villages. Food also became scarce in Granada, not because it was not available, but because all the suppliers withheld their stocks in order to profit from the higher prices that would be paid. In sum, the progress of Philip's court across Andalucia may have seemed triumphal, but it was a heavy burden to the people and the town councils.[16] The citizens of Seville were the only ones to receive some benefit from the royal presence because the authorities there were forced to take measures to improve the streets and to restore public spaces; several religious institutions also took the opportunity to embellish their buildings. Upper-class Seville society was periodically invited to balls at the Alcázar, and the populace were entertained by the royal presence at public fiestas. Elizabeth took an active interest in aspects of Andalucian art, and discovered the attractions of the painter Murillo, whose work she began collecting. Philip extended his patronage to some Seville artists, but his preference was for the French painter Ranc, who spent some of his most fruitful days with the court in Seville.

On 5 June the itinerant court moved on another long journey, this time to Cazalla de la Sierra in the Sierra Morena, where Philip had first stayed on the journey to Seville from Badajoz, and where he decided it would be ideal to go hunting. The court took the route through Archidona and Ecija, crossing the Guadalquivir in order to arrive at Cazalla. It was a hot summer, made more uncomfortable by the presence of a major forest fire in the Sierra Morena. Even so, they remained in the area until 20 August, returning thereafter to Seville, where they arrived three days later. Philip continued to be impatient that the treaty of Seville was not being translated immediately into action. 'France does not wish to do anything this year,' he grumbled to that country's ambassador. 'One can have good reasons or bad reasons for doing nothing, but they should not be employed to trifle with me or to deceive me.' His special envoy in Paris, Luca Spínola, was having little success at putting pressure on Cardinal Fleury. Finally in September a special ambassador, Patiño's brother the marquis of Castelar, was sent to Versailles to make a final effort to have the treaty put into effect.

By the end of the summer, the king was once again suffering severe depressive attacks, and in September began to confine himself to bed. He refused to consult any doctors: 'all those fools,' as he put it, 'who didn't take me seriously when I said that I was ill.' He reverted to his phases of nervous bulimia, ate enormous amounts of food and as a consequence suffered from indigestion. In order to relieve his disorder, he consumed daily substantial quantities of 'theriac' (an antidote to poison).[17] His digestive difficulties convinced him that he had an intestinal infection and was really evacuating blood, but that the doctors were keeping the truth from him. He insisted on being shown his stools, and when he saw no blood, he accused the doctors of putting something in the bowl to disguise the blood. He also rejected any attention to his person with the result that his toenails grew very long, making it difficult for him to walk. He would not allow anyone to arrange his hair, which likewise grew very long and unkempt; his solution to this was to stick a wig on top of his unruly mop. In this condition, he refused to go out and consequently took no exercise. In early September, he went with Elizabeth and the court to stay for three weeks in Puerto de Santa María, but once there he refused to leave his residence. In those weeks, according to the French ambassador, he went out only six times. He would walk the 30 metres down to the river, and just stand there watching the water flow by. His favourite and virtually only entertainment was to go fishing by moonlight, but his fishing took a very special form, since Puerto de Santa María did not have the fishponds that existed in the Alcázar. He would sit out at night in the garden, and his attendants would place in front of him a large bowl with fish in it. He would then fish.[18]

Government ministers and courtiers had to adapt themselves to the unfortunate king's humours. When overtaken by his mental disorder, Philip became very sensitive; he would not allow others to make decisions for him, and tolerated no contradiction. In Seville he would wander round the Alcázar insisting repeatedly, to anyone he met by chance in the corridors, that 'je suis le maître' ('I'm in charge here'). The phrase seems to have given him reassurance that people were not doing things behind his back. Very frequently, he would refuse to accept tasks that other people did for him, on the grounds that they were challenging his capacity to make decisions. If Patiño placed before him a carefully arranged pile of papers that had to be signed in a certain order, he would surreptitiously change the order when Patiño was not looking, placing at the bottom papers that had been at the top.[19]

Working with a head of state on these terms was, obviously, very difficult. The king retained full control of business and policy-making, and always knew exactly what was going on. There was no question about the clarity of his mind. But this apparent normality functioned within a context that was completely abnormal. In Seville in January 1731 the French ambassador, the count of Rottembourg, confessed that the situation was 'incomprehensible'. Negotiating with the king was bizarre. He could talk to Philip only at night, usually in the early hours of the morning. And the problem affected all ministers. In September 1730 the king held his council meetings between 11 p.m. and 2 a.m., had his supper after the meeting, then went to bed at around 6 a.m. and got up from bed at 2 p.m., after which he heard his morning mass at 3 p.m. and then had lunch. In January 1731 Philip usually went to bed at 8 a.m., then woke up for his 'morning' mass at 4 p.m., and had lunch after it. At this stage of Philip's terrible illness, the queen, who always shared the king's bedroom, displayed her incredible resilience by attempting to lead a normal life and doing things at fairly reasonable hours; she heard her morning mass, for example, at 6 a.m. The ambassador, for his part, with good reason complained that he was quite exhausted by the hours he was required to keep. On one evening visit, he was kept talking by the king until 3.30 a.m. On another visit, at which Patiño was also present, the meeting went on until 6 a.m.

The discussions at Soissons were put into effect now through further agreements that complemented the treaty of Seville. The crucial event at the beginning of 1731 was the death, on 20 January, of Elizabeth's uncle the grand duke of Parma. His widow claimed to be pregnant, but this turned out to be incorrect, and the question of the succession therefore lay open. Spain had reason to expect that the international agreements in its favour would be implemented, but was alarmed by reports that the emperor had sent his troops in to occupy Parma and Piacenza. Obtaining no satisfactory response from the French, the king on 28 January issued a declaration saying that he felt 'not bound by the deceptions contained in the treaty, and completely free to adopt the solution most convenient to the royal interests'.[20] The consequence was a move towards an agreement with Britain. All the powers acknowledged that the question must be resolved once and for all, to avoid war. At Vienna in March 1731 Britain, Holland and Austria concluded a further treaty, which was followed by an agreement between Spain and Austria in July that year. By these accords, the emperor accepted the intentions of the treaty of Seville, and allowed Spanish troops to enter into Parma, Piacenza and Tuscany. The agreements were an important step forward in European diplomacy for they embraced once more most of the conditions that had been reiterated by the European powers from the time of the Quadruple Alliance to that of the congress of Soissons. They also stabilised the situation in Italy, which since the fifteenth century had been a bone of contention between the powers. Finally, they recognised the validity of Philip V's claims for his family in Italy, and therefore assured peace in the western Mediterranean.

Though it appeared that Spain had done well, the real winner was of course Britain, which secured protection for its commercial privileges and managed to exclude the question of Gibraltar from the diplomatic agenda. It remained the supreme power in the western Mediterranean, theoretically the *mare nostrum* of the Spaniards. And it was the English who supplied the fleet that put the international accords into effect.

* * *

The king's Andalucian interlude had a very real importance for Spain, because it shifted attention to one of the country's chief economic resources: America and its riches. For two centuries, Spain had been drawing on American wealth and exporting settlers to the New World. Trade to America was organised as a monopoly restricted principally to Castilians. The fleets would normally leave from Seville and then divide when they arrived in the Caribbean, where one part (called the 'fleet' or *flota*) would head for Mexico and the other (the 'galleons') would go to Portobelo and cartagena. Only merchants who were members of the trading guilds or *consulados* of Seville and the New World could participate in the trade. The monopoly made administration easier, but it was of course impossible to impose adequately; indeed, in the sixteenth century Seville became a boom town precisely because many other merchants, both Spanish and foreign, found ways of taking part in the theoretical monopoly. By the end of the seventeenth century the foreign merchants were in control of over three-quarters of the trade. Large quantities of silver continued to arrive, but most of it went to foreigners, the Spanish crown seldom obtaining more than 10 per cent of the precious metal.

The symbol of the change to foreign control was the city of Cadiz, which had been growing in size throughout the seventeenth century and soon became the effective point of departure for ships taking part in the American trade. The foreign traders preferred to live in Cadiz because of its proximity to the fleets. Finally on 12 May 1717 Patiño carried through the historic reform – which aroused both opposition and controversy – by which a royal decree transferred the bodies that controlled the American trade, namely the House of Trade and the Consulado, from Seville to Cadiz. At the same time the government was given direct control over trade to America, which was removed from the competence of the Council of the Indies and put under the control of the Navy minister.

The court's stay in Seville added fuel to the long-standing rivalry between that city and Cadiz. The latter was proud to have obtained control of the trade monopoly in 1717; by contrast the former had to be content with the pride it took in the presence of the court from 1729. Visits to Cadiz by the court were described in lavish detail by pamphlets there, and responded to with sarcastic comments by pamphlets published in Seville.[21] At the same time, Seville launched satires against

Patiño, holding him responsible for undermining its trade. For two centuries the cities had shared in the lucrative trade to the Indies, but gradually most of it came to be organised from Cadiz, which had the advantage of being a coastal port, and one from which the ships to America actually sailed.[22] After 1680, when Cadiz was fixed as the point of departure for all fleets taking part in the Indies monopoly, Seville was left with only the control of administration. The decision in 1717 to transfer the administration as well had an immediate negative impact on Seville's commercial position, and the famous Exchange (the Lonja), where merchants had jostled each other in their business dealings, turned into an abandoned and empty edifice.

   Patiño's measures to control the movement of ships to America were part of an attempt to improve the financial resources of the crown in terms of trade; but they had very little success. The main problem was the superior naval power of Britain and France. Foreign shipping accounted for 75 per cent of all the vessels taking part in the American trade, and foreign merchandise represented at least 50 per cent of all the goods traded to the New World. When Spanish vessels reached the ports of America, they found that foreign vessels had been there before them and flooded the market with produce which they had imported directly, without going through the monopoly system that operated from the peninsula. One of the most lucrative businesses was the slave trade, operated through a trading company registered in Spain, with a contract (an *asiento*) to send a fixed number of African slaves to the American market. During the War of Succession the French had operated the *asiento*. With the peace of Utrecht in 1713, the *asiento* passed to the British, together with the right to send one ship a year to the trade fair at Portobelo. In Spain there was an impression that the British were making huge profits as a result of their control of the *asiento*, and that foreigners were promoting contraband in America. It was an issue, as we shall see, that led to many disputes and eventually to war. In fact, the British found it difficult to make profits out of a trade system that was in total chaos. In the period up to 1732 they managed to supply only two-thirds of the contracted slaves, and sent only 40 per cent of the annual ships.[23] But when they did make profits, they made very healthy ones. At the Portobelo fair of 1731 the merchants of Peru spent half their money exclusively on the goods carried by the annual ship of the British South Sea Company. Patiño was therefore justified in believing that naval power was the secret to success. From 1722 he arranged for the financing of a squadron of fighting ships to police the Caribbean. Called 'coastguards' (*guardacostas*), they were a useful weapon in the constant struggle against smugglers and pirates. Nor was the chaos in American waters necessarily in the interests of Britain. In Seville in February 1732, Keene and Patiño signed an accord that attempted to deal with the situation.[24] However, commercial rivalry continued, and armed conflict between trading vessels in the Caribbean was constant.

*   *   *

The way in which discussions were conducted at court between ambassadors and the crown gives us remarkable insight into the relationship between Elizabeth and Philip. From the 1720s, Philip allowed the French ambassador immediate access to his private apartments, and would often receive him while he was in bed. Saint-Simon offers us the fascinating picture of being received in the morning by Philip in a bed draped with satin. It was always a double act by Philip and Elizabeth, in which the queen usually did a good part of the talking. From around 1730, when Philip was unwell and kept in the background, it was Elizabeth who spoke the most. But though the king spoke little he always controlled the act. In one exchange with the French ambassador in March 1731, Elizabeth became very angry over France's apparent indifference to her interests in the duchy of Parma, and seemed to be threatening the French. Philip murmured gently to her, 'I would not do anything against France'.[25] She immediately changed her tone.

The relationship between king and queen was only in appearance one in which Elizabeth dominated. In one of his more perceptive judgments, Saint-Simon observed that the queen had to use all her wiles in order to manage Philip. 'Her compliments, her flattery, her honeyed words, were continuous; she never let weariness or the burden of work show itself; she gave first place to everything that might make him contented, and did it with so natural an air that it seemed as if she were doing it for her own satisfaction.'[26] The queen had to contend with the fact that Philip combined apparent passivity, noted by all observers, with an inner firmness that was inflexible. During extensive periods of the king's illness, Elizabeth took over complete charge of decision-making. But she did so in the knowledge that her ideas (as she often insisted) were identical to those of Philip. It may be that she also welcomed the chance to act on her own, since Philip could be extremely stubborn. But when they performed together, she always made it clear that her wishes were exclusively those of her husband.[27]

In private, she was totally devoted to Philip. Saint-Simon in 1721 observed that 'she seems attached to the king to the point of forgetting about herself, and is so totally attentive to what he wishes that one might think that it is really what pleases her'. He was perceptive enough to see that Elizabeth deliberately sacrificed her own comfort for his.[28] Bearing in mind the wholly odd programme of hours followed by the king in the 1730s, one cannot fail to sympathise with and admire her patience. When he was depressed or out of humour, the king treated her outrageously. Their private quarrels in their chambers were very Italian: loud and wordy, and therefore faithfully reported by servants to other servants and finally to diplomats. During these moments of illness and stress, Philip could be particularly harsh with his personal insults to her. But the couple remained passionately united.

She endured much. In March 1731, reverting once more to his self-destructive urges, Philip seems to have hinted that he might abdicate again. In such circumstances Elizabeth always increased her vigilance, and had to watch him personally. This put intolerable pressures on her, since it meant she had to follow his bizarre timetable. She was fortunate, in these days, if she managed to sleep three hours out of twenty-four. One cold night she fell asleep exhausted at his side in bed. He got up, since these were his waking hours, and opened a window. She woke up frozen and complained of the cold air. When they began to argue, the attendants came in to help. 'Very well,' Philip conceded, 'close half the window for the queen and leave the other half open for me.'[29]

One evening in June 1731, when the French ambassador came for a scheduled visit he found that the queen was worn out and fast asleep in bed. The king, by contrast, had not been to bed for forty-eight hours; he was wandering about, but would not face the ambassador alone. The luckless diplomat therefore waited all night until at 7 a.m. the king and queen came to say they could see him – but not until 5.30 that evening. Philip was seriously indisposed during the entire first half of 1731. There was, finally, a severe crisis in July. At this point, he slept only about one hour in every twenty-four. 'His Catholic Majesty', according to Keene, 'seems to be trying experiments to live without sleep'.[30] He walked about the Alcázar with his mouth open and his tongue hanging out. His legs were grossly swollen. His doctor was convinced that the king was in the final stages of his illness, and about to die. Public opinion in Seville thought the same. The Seville crowds had seen little of Philip after 1729 for in 1730 he had spent Holy Week in Granada, and in subsequent years his illness prevented him taking part in the great public feasts. The royal family celebrated Holy Week 1731 quietly inside the Alcázar, an annalist commenting on 'the impressive silence in the palace, which is full of people but appears to be a desert'.[31] Philip managed to take part from a distance, that is to say from a balcony of the Alcázar, in the procession of Corpus Christi in 1731, when the route of the procession had to be specially changed for him. For all practical purposes, the illness cut him off from a normal life.

In these circumstances, it was inevitable and logical that Elizabeth should once again take over control of the court and government.

* * *

She took direct charge of the diplomacy during that crucial summer, since the king, though perfectly lucid, was in no condition to carry out his duties. The major event was the visit to Cadiz in August 1731 of a powerful fleet of sixteen English warships under Admiral Charles Wager, sent to put the international accords into effect. Wager sailed upriver to Seville to visit the court, and was in the city from 15 to 20 August, where he acquired personal experience of Philip's condition.

The king was happy to receive him, but Elizabeth could not persuade Philip to change his clothes for the occasion. 'The English will never make me do something I do not wish to do,' he said stubbornly.[32] So he received the admiral in a completely dishevelled state. Wager went on to Barcelona, where his fleet made its rendezvous with the Spanish vessels, which eventually totalled 25 warships, 7 galleys and 46 transport ships carrying the six regiments of soldiers for the garrisons of Parma.

The prince for whom this display of naval power was mounted, the Infante Charles, then aged fifteen, took leave of his family in Seville on 20 October. Partings of this nature were nearly always final, and the king and queen were deeply moved as the prince knelt before each of them to receive their blessing. He was escorted by his brothers to within a short distance from the city, from where he continued his journey accompanied by an escort of 100 cavalry.[33] Charles travelled by land towards the Mediterranean coast of Spain, passing through Ecija and thence on the route towards Albacete. At every stop he took the opportunity to indulge in his favourite sport, hunting. After Albacete he made a special visit to Almansa, where he visited the site of the battle that had secured Spain for the Bourbon dynasty. During the journey he kept in almost daily touch with his parents, exchanging letters with them (all written in French) by special messenger.[34] The day after his departure, Philip wrote to Charles: 'The only thing that consoles me for your absence, is the confidence I have that you will be happy in the country to which you are going.' For her part, Elizabeth was deeply distressed: 'We cannot get used to living without you, my dearest son', she wrote in the same letter. 'It was a miracle that I did not faint when you left, but God helped me and I was able to lie down on my chair next to the window, from which I saw your carriage go by. I drank three glasses of water to strengthen me.' Two days later she wrote in what was her second letter to Charles that day: 'When I see your brothers without you my heart breaks, and I cannot stop myself crying'. 'I am happy that you visited the battlefield of Almansa,' she wrote in November, 'and that you understood everything about it, for it was one of the things that assured the throne to your father, and brought you to where you are.' The fascinating correspondence also gives some insight into Philip's health, never directly mentioned by the queen to her son. Though the king's first letter to Charles was written in a firm, steady hand, his later letters have poor, shaky handwriting, the words are out of line, and ink blots show where his hand trembled. Philip's daily timetable was, moreover, now fixed in its new routine. King and queen were both still awake at three or four in the morning, to receive the messenger. 'It is 3.36 in the morning, my dearest son,' Elizabeth wrote on 29 November, 'and your courier has not yet arrived. I assure you that it causes both your father and me great worry, for you know that when one is far away one imagines all sorts of things.' On 19 December she wrote: 'Dearest son, we have received your letter from Salou, and the king was very pleased, I kissed his hand for you, it is not yet five o'clock in the morning and we have not yet had supper.'

Charles arrived at Valencia on 11 November and then took the coastal route towards Barcelona, where he spent two days, from 21 to 23 December, and was greeted with celebrations. In Perpignan on the 28th the French authorities gave him a festive welcome. His destination (after visits to Montpellier and Nimes) was the port of Antibes, where on 22 December he boarded the vessels of the joint Anglo-Spanish fleet under Wager and the marquis of Mari, and was escorted to Livorno. When they arrived four days later, the Spanish troops were allowed to occupy the duchies of Parma and Piacenza, and the Austrian garrisons withdrew. The settlement of Charles's inheritance promised peace for Europe, and seemed to fulfil all the aspirations of the king and queen. Many years of war, much money and very many lives had been expended in securing Spanish aspirations. As time would show, however, it was only the first of several moves in the diplomatic strategy of Philip V, and Charles did not remain long in Parma.

*   *   *

According to Benjamin Keene, during the spring of 1732 Philip was in good health and good spirits. During this hyperactive phase, and encouraged by the successful accession of Charles to the duchies, the king proceeded with a plan that he had been considering even before his son's journey. He intended to recover for Spain the African fortress of Orán, lost to the Muslims as a result of the defection of the commander of the Spanish galleys, the count of Santa Cruz, at a key moment during the War of Succession. The marquis of Mari was instructed, after finishing his work at Livorno, to take three warships to Genoa and pick up 2 million pesos deposited with banks there in the king's name, the money to be used to hire vessels for the Orán fleet. 'The king is of such a martial disposition,' Keene reported in May, 'that he is willing to make war upon his friends or foes.'[35] The Orán scheme was put into the hands of Patiño, who as usual carried it out with scrupulous efficiency. A military force of 30,000 men on 12 warships, 7 galleys and a large number of transport vessels, under the command of the count of Montemar, José Carrillo de Albornoz, sailed from Alicante on 15 June 1732 and crossed the straits to Africa. Information about its objective was kept secret until the moment of sailing, when Philip issued a decree in Seville confirming the operation. Resistance in Orán was minimal; both the fortress and the neighbouring town of Mazalquivir were occupied after a period of six days. News of the success arrived in Seville on 8 July, and gave rise to the inevitable festivities: the whole Giralda was lit up with fireworks. In mid-August, the overjoyed king bestowed the insignia of the Golden Fleece on the two architects of the expedition, Montemar and Patiño. It is doubtful, however, whether the acquisition was of any direct benefit to Spanish security or shipping. Keene, who as a diplomat was suspicious of the possible threat to British interests in Gibraltar and the Mediterranean, also doubted whether the campaign had really been successful, and put the loss of Spanish lives as high as 3,000 men. However, the affair gave enormous comfort to the king, who commissioned a series of paintings of the event, which he later hung in his palace of La Granja. By securing Orán, as he had secured Ceuta twelve years before, Philip V converted into reality one of the most permanent dreams of the Spanish political elite: the maintenance of an empire in north Africa.

*   *   *

The capture of Orán seems to have been the culmination of Philip's sense of personal achievement. With his son safely installed in Parma, and the last African fortress annexed, there appeared to be nothing more to do. From the end of the summer of 1732, he entered into another period of profound depression.[36] From the end of August he said that he preferred to remain in bed, even though he was not apparently unwell. He would lie there for several days, saying nothing, with his finger in his mouth. The situation continued for weeks. He refused to change his bed-sheets or his clothes, and would not allow himself to be shaved or have his hair combed or his nails cut. After a month of this, by the end of which the king both looked and smelled awful, Elizabeth became desperate and decided to take over. She nominated a ruling council consisting of seven persons including the prince of Asturias and Patiño. The king's hand was held for him to sign the decree setting it up. It was a wise move, for matters only got worse. 'We are now effectively without any government,' Benjamin Keene reported, 'for he has not seen either his ministers or his confessor for nearly twenty days.'[37] In the first fortnight of October, Philip refused to talk to anyone, except to say a few words to his wife and to Ferdinand. There was, according to him, logic in his apparent madness. His silence, he said, was because he was really dead and therefore could not speak. At other times, however, he explained that he was at fault for having resumed the throne. He had no right to be reigning, 'and the surest way of not reigning, is not to talk'. 'It must end in an abdication or in a change of ministry', was Keene's opinion.[38]

The evidence points clearly to a disorder centring on an obsession with the themes of succession and abdication. Elizabeth was right to believe that the wish to abdicate was always lurking in his mind. Equally obsessive was the preoccupation with his own succession to the thrones of Spain and France, and that of his sons to the Italian duchies. In October, after his refusal to talk to anyone, Philip decided that he would talk, but only to his *valet de chambre*. His conversation centred on the forthcoming – as he saw it – union of the crowns of France and Spain. Few *valets de chambre* have ever been thus privileged to receive the undivided attentions of a head of state explaining his future foreign policy.

In the middle of November, Philip insisted on conceding an audience to the count of Rottembourg. The startled count was presented with the spectacle of a king with his clothing completely disordered, with a long and filthy beard, and wearing no trousers or shoes, his legs and feet naked. The situation at court continued in this manner. Suddenly, on the day after Christmas, the king appeared like new: clean, shaven, well-dressed. He rose from bed at a normal time, 9 a.m., and dined not in bed but at table. But it was no recovery. Soon he was back in his bed, where he would lie immobile for hours, clutching his head with his hands and staring up at the ceiling, his mouth open. There was a rumour at court, reported by Keene, that on 30 December Patiño had gone to see the king who had beaten him and bruised his head. For the better part of 1732, the king had not been governing Spain. The situation continued into early February the following year, when the king was still inactive, refusing to see people or to deal with his state papers.

*   *   *

As it happened, it was a new international crisis, over the succession to a throne, that brought Philip back to the real world of everyday events.

In February 1733 the king of Poland, Augustus II, died. Poland had one of the few monarchies in Europe that was not hereditary but elected by its parliament, the Sejm. As soon as Philip received the news in Seville, his condition changed. 'He leaped from the bed', Keene reported, 'to which he was almost always confined by his hypochondriac illness, inattentive to public matters and even negligent of his own person. He now returned to the charge of government, took cognisance of even the smallest matters pending, and gave orders that the necessary preparations be made as soon as possible for entering on campaign.'[39] In the first week of March, a messenger was sent in secret from Seville to Warsaw to negotiate the possibility of the throne for the Infante Philip (then aged twelve) or even for Charles. His mind now firmly concentrated on a concrete issue, Philip had no time for his depression, and he began acting again with his old enthusiasm.

The decision was made to take the court back to Castile. Like everything else that the king did, it was decided suddenly and with no logic or adequate preparation. Philip announced the impending departure four or five days before it was to take place.[40] On 16 May, amid complete confusion, the move out of the Alcázar commenced at midday. To avoid protocol, delays and further expenses for everyone, Philip decided that he would pass through the least possible number of towns. Those in charge of the move therefore had the difficult task of plotting out a route that avoided large centres of population and cut straight across fields. The journey, planned to cover a span of eighteen daily stages, followed the route from Seville to Ecija, avoiding Córdoba, then going northwards through Andújar, Bailén, Valdepeñas and Tembleque.[41] The royal party arrived finally at Aranjuez, without mishap, on 12 June.

As soon as they arrived, Philip issued orders for the isolation – for a brief period – of the prince of Asturias and his wife. They were not to receive visitors, and could not go out in public, not even for a walk, restrictions apparently originating in resentment at the prince's attitude during Philip's illness. During the preceding years, schemes of all sorts had been prepared, by a number of people ranging from the grandees to the Portuguese ambassador, to take charge of affairs of state in the event of Philip's expected death. The schemes inevitably centred their hopes on the prince and princess of Asturias, and Philip could hardly have looked with approval on the plotting behind his back. Barbara of Braganza's links with Portugal also served to create tension between Philip and the Portuguese. Certainly they contributed, along with other factors, to the diplomatic break with Portugal that took place in 1735, when the ostensible cause was a minor incident involving the personnel of the Portuguese embassy in Madrid in February of that year.[42]

The differences between the king and the prince of Asturias serve to remind us of the problems of disunity within the royal family. It was traditional for the households of the royal children to be administered separately from those of the king and queen; they did not necessarily even live in the same palace. The masterly portraits of Philip's family painted by Ranc and Van Loo were formal montages and did not point to any common link between the personages other than that of dynasty. The interests of each royal household could be radically different, as was the case with that of Ferdinand and Barbara. One of Barbara's most important innovations during her stay in Andalucia had been the patronage she extended to the famous Italian composer Domenico Scarlatti, son of the Alessandro whose music had so delighted Philip V during his stay in Naples. Scarlatti had been her music teacher in Lisbon, and she brought him subsequently to Seville, where he entertained her court and took part in its regular journeys.

By the summer of 1733, the king seemed to be fully restored to health. He and Elizabeth installed themselves in La Granja, the only place where he felt completely at ease; but their official residence was the Buen Retiro, alternated with visits to the other royal palaces. He now entered on a phase of frenetic activity, stimulated by the idea of a war over Poland. Benjamin Keene reported in July 1733 that the king 'continues to apply himself to public affairs, to such a degree that the government seems to function regularly and in an orderly way. As for his health, I have never seen him so happy and expansive.'[43]

The Polish question had very little to do with Spanish interests, and the fantasies of the king and queen about a Spanish king in Warsaw were never taken seriously. Nevertheless, the problem certainly affected a wide range of issues, principally the rivalry between the French and Imperial candidates to the throne. This time it was France that needed the support of Spain, since the French candidate was Louis XV's father-in-law, Stanislas Leszczynski. Philip agreed to drop the candidature of his son in favour of the French candidate, and the marquis of Castelar was sent to Versailles to oversee negotiations there. Relying on the support of its other European allies, principally Savoy, France declared war on the emperor on 10 October.

The outcome of the conversations between France and Spain (those in Paris were interrupted by the death of Castelar) was the so-called first 'Family Pact' between the Bourbons, signed in the Escorial on 7 November 1733. French diplomacy, which had in the past worked hard to maintain the peace, now worked equally hard to persuade Spain to go to war against Austria, whose candidate was in possession of the Polish throne. In return, Fleury promised to support any Spanish enterprise against Naples and Sicily, and to obtain Gibraltar from the British. Philip and Elizabeth could not have hoped for more. In this way Spain found itself implicated in perhaps the most pointless war of the reign of Philip V, pointless because no Spanish interests were directly involved. 'Who would have thought', a puzzled Keene asked himself at the end of 1733, 'that the death of a king of Poland could have promoted matters into the state which they are now in?'⁴⁴

CHAPTER SEVEN

The Years of Crisis, 1734–1746

'WE DO NOT NEED ANYONE TO PROPOSE PROJECTS TO US, WE
OURSELVES WILL THINK OF THEM AND ORDER THEM TO BE
CARRIED OUT.'

ELIZABETH FARNESE TO THE FRENCH AMBASSADOR, MAY 1744

The War of the Polish Succession was, for Philip, exclusively a Mediterranean war. France fought the conflict principally in Germany, where in October 1733 an army under Berwick (who met his death later during the campaign) crossed the Rhine. A French army also crossed the Alps into Italy, under the command of the 82-year-old Marshal Villars; meanwhile the Spaniards sent troops under Montemar to northern Italy. By mid-February 1734 the forces of Villars and of Carlo Emanuele of Sardinia had occupied all the Milanese and part of Mantua. However, Spain's objectives in the zone conflicted with those of the French and Carlo Emanuele, and Philip consequently changed his policy. Since the enemy was Austria, it made sense to direct attention to Imperial possessions in the south of Italy. Montemar was informed that the objective was to be Naples and Sicily. Charles (now aged eighteen) had been named supreme commander of the army in October 1733 and took command of the forces in February 1734. In mid-January he wrote to his parents: 'Montemar arrived here yesterday. I shall leave on the first of next month for Florence, with the aim of carrying out Your Majesties' orders'.[1] From its naval bases in the western Mediterranean, Spain had little difficulty in backing up the military expedition; a large fleet of 20 Spanish warships, accompanying a force of 16,000 men, sailed from Barcelona for Italy. Patiño, whose job it was to find the money, the ships and the men, sardonically commented on the role of Philip in all this: 'The queen wants peace,' he said, 'but the king likes battles, and we have to humour him.'[2]

It was a rapid and wholly successful campaign. The passage of the troops through the papal states by means of a safe-conduct was arranged by Cardinal Belluga in Rome. The inhabitants of the south of Italy had never accepted Austrian rule and greeted the Spaniards with enthusiasm. Under such auspicious circumstances, on 14 March, in Neapolitan territory, Charles was able to issue a general pardon to all Neapolitans, confirm all their laws and privileges and promise to remove all taxes imposed by the Austrians. Seeing that their situation was hopeless, the bulk of the Imperial forces refrained from offering resistance. Hence, on 9 May, even before Charles had arrived there, the representatives of the city of Naples came to offer their obedience to the Spanish forces. Charles made his solemn entry into the city of Naples on 10 May and was proclaimed king. An Austrian force that invaded from the Adriatic later that month was defeated by Montemar. Meanwhile the Sicilians waited expectantly to be liberated from Imperial rule. Then, in August a force under Montemar sailed from Naples for Sicily, and on 1 September entered Palermo and proclaimed Charles king. All over the island the Sicilians rose in support. Charles crossed over to visit them in January 1735, only returning to Naples in July. The Spanish Bourbons were now in control of all southern Italy as well as Tuscany. It was an astonishing achievement carried out with remarkable speed and very little loss of life; Philip V's forces had recovered all the Italian territories lost at Utrecht, with the exception of Milan. In Naples, the Bourbons initiated a great new dynastic epoch.

Meanwhile, in northern Europe the Polish throne was confirmed to the Austrian candidate, and the various parties prepared to make compromises in order to arrive at a peace. To compensate the French candidate, an exchange of states was proposed, by which Leszczynski would be given the duchy of Lorraine, and the duke of this state would be given the grand duchy of Tuscany. France and the emperor came to an informal agreement in October 1735 without consulting Spain. Austria would give up Naples and Sicily (the two states were now known as the Kingdom of the Two Sicilies) to Charles, but would receive in exchange Charles's duchies in Parma and Tuscany. Both Elizabeth and Philip were furious at the proposed loss of Elizabeth's family patrimony, secured for Charles after many years and much cost. 'As long as I live', the queen said to Keene, 'I shall not have any contact with France.'³ There were various objections on all sides, and a firm agreement took years to arrange. A formal treaty between France and Austria was signed only in November 1738 in Vienna. Spanish envoys ratified the clauses concerning Spain, at Versailles in April 1739. In concrete terms, Spain gained through the confirmation of Charles as king of Naples and Sicily. The agreements also confirmed the emperor's sovereignty over Parma, a condition to which Spain objected strongly though with little success.

Throughout the war and after it, Spain's international negotiations were directed personally by Patiño. The marginalisation of Spain by the peace negotiators in 1735 made several Spanish diplomats consider it an appropriate time to abandon the links with France, and strengthen those with Britain. Walpole had refused to take his country into the recent war, and Patiño felt that the policy of peace was a reasonable one. In a letter to the director of the South Sea Company in 1735, he explained that 'the king's intention is not, and never has been, to support the war, into which he has been forced by the obduracy of the court of Vienna and the pressure and petitions of France'. He outlined Philip V's interests: 'His Majesty is concerned to propose a union of friendship for the maintenance of trade, and the security of the dominions that he assumes should remain to the king of the Two Sicilies'.⁴

The successes in Italy received Philip's closest attention. His deep pride in the achievement may be seen by the review of the army which he ordered to be held in September 1737 in the grounds of San Ildefonso. All the royal guards, all the troops that had been in Italy and all their generals participated in an enormous and unprecedented military exercise that lasted for seven days, from the 20th to the 27th of the month. The royal family was housed in a special pavilion, and on each day different units paraded before the king. Thousands of people came in from nearby cities to see the unprecedented display: 'The confluence of all kinds of people from Madrid, Valladolid, Segovia and other parts has been immense, both in the palace and in the grounds,' reported the *Gaceta*, 'and in the grounds the Captain General the marquis of Castelfuerte has put on a continuous and splendid reception for all the officers and persons of distinction, both by day and by night, with abundant and delicious refreshments in the afternoon, while the attendants of the royal household also served in style to those present all types of drinks in a large tent right next to that of His Majesty'. The weather remained perfect every day. In the course of the exercise, the king announced various promotions and a special increase in salaries. The celebrations were a deliberate effort by Philip to demonstrate the achievements of his monarchy:

> By His Majesty ordering that the fountains of the marvellous gardens of San Ildefonso be opened for the enjoyment of those who had had the fortune to serve him, it was made fully clear to everybody through these royal displays, that this simple artifice served to flatter their Sovereign, who had made his August Name respected throughout the world, to the great wonderment of Europe.[5]

*   *   *

After 1733, San Ildefonso was Philip's preferred retreat, but it tended to be reserved as a country house rather than a permanent residence, and one on which architectural work continued to be carried out. The main official residence was the Buen Retiro, used as the base from which the royal family made their excursions. Considerable sums of money had just been spent making the Alcázar of Madrid suitable for the return; government operated from this palace, where the councils were allotted specific rooms and the Despacho occupied virtually the entire main floor.[6] For five years the king had not been resident in

Madrid, but the capital slipped back quickly into its old routine. In December 1734, however, a major tragedy occurred. On Christmas Eve, a fire broke out in a wing of the Alcázar. The flames were spread quickly by the night wind, and went on to destroy the royal apartments, the south façade, the chapels and a large quantity of the art treasures of the palace. Personnel who had been sleeping in the palace made frantic efforts to rescue precious items, principally those kept in the royal chapel. But the flames were too fast: 'the archive, with documents of the whole monarchy and papers of all state business, was burnt in a very short time, to everyone's horror'.[7] Keene reported that the greater part of the archives of the councils of War, the Navy, the Indies and Finance, perished in the fire,[8] an incalculable loss for historians of the reign. The flames raged all the following day, Christmas Day: 'the fire formed a line along the entire square before the palace, and that evening and night continued to feed on itself'. A week later the workers demolished dangerous walls. 'All that remained of the palace was the façade on the square and of the Torre del Príncipe, as well as the Charles V section, which was barely touched; all the rest had to be demolished.' By one estimate, over 500 paintings by famous artists perished in the flames; a list drawn up at the time by Jean Ranc includes works by Rubens, Van Dyke, Tintoretto and Velázquez.

Within the week, Patiño wrote to the Spanish ambassador in Turin, saying that the king wished to invite a new architect to rebuild the palace. This was, Patiño wrote, 'the Sicilian architect, whose name we do not know, who built the cathedral in Lisbon' and who was then working in Turin. The king was evidently in such a hurry to locate the man that he did not even have time to find out his name. The architect in question was the priest Filippo Juvarra, born in Messina in 1678, who had for some time now been working in the Savoyard capital. Juvarra arrived at the court in Aranjuez in mid-April 1735 and immediately set to work drawing up plans for the new palace.

It was not a good moment, as we shall see, to be committed to more expenditure. Juvarra in November 1735 commented to Patiño that 'the treasury here always keeps putting obstacles in the way of executing Your Excellency's orders'.[9] While the architect prepared his plans, work continued on conserving what remained of the old palace. The scheme presented by Juvarra within a few weeks, following consultation with the king and Elizabeth, called for a huge building three storeys high, with several patios. But the work was never realised, since he died unexpectedly at the beginning of 1736. Patiño then made efforts to find a substitute architect in Rome, but without success. The project was taken over by Giovan Battista Sacchetti, a Turin architect, who changed the layout significantly; he now made the building twice as high, but with one single large patio. He also planned a whole series of buildings adjoining the palace.

The reconstruction of the royal palace confirms, like the construction some years before of La Granja, the enormously important contribution made by Philip and Elizabeth to the art of their time. But it required a lot of money. The recorded costs of the new building rose from 465,000 escudos in 1737 to 1,564,000 escudos in 1739 and 1,856,000 in 1741.[10] In 1740 the costs represented, as we can see from Diagrams 8 and 9, 2.3 per cent of state expenditure. Elizabeth conscientiously built up the art collection that decorated La Granja. At the same time, improvements were made at the palace of Aranjuez from around 1730, but a subsequent fire meant further renovation. This new work, carried out after 1744, was directed by the architect Giacomo Bonavia. There were also improvements in El Pardo, where in 1738 the French architect François Carlier, son of René Carlier who had planned the gardens of La Granja, constructed the chapel. At least in his gardens, Philip tried to re-create some of the environment that he had known in France: in 1736 he purchased 600 flowers bulbs from Paris for the Buen Retiro, and in 1741 imported 13 cases of trees for Aranjuez and La Granja.

Philip made use of Juvarra's stay in Madrid to have the architect also add touches to San Ildefonso. After him, Sacchetti remodelled the entire façade overlooking the garden: his estimate for the works amounted in August 1737 to 477,000 escudos.[11] The plan was personally approved by the king in September 1738 and put into effect in the following months. The extent of the works – involving above all the demolition of the garden façade – meant that Philip and Elizabeth could not reside there and had to live instead in Aranjuez if they wanted to be outside Madrid. The raw materials came principally from Italy: in October 1740 the royal treasurer was informed of the arrival of '58 cases of marble from Alicante for the façade of the palace', which had to be paid out of the 'small budget available for the works'.[12] Though La Granja was meant to be a retreat, it was designed by Philip as one surrounded by military glory; the scheme of paintings with which he asked Juvarra to decorate the building concentrated on the martial figure of Alexander the Great. The deeply personal contribution made by the two monarchs was complemented by the dedication of their leisure hours to art: the inventory drawn up at his death shows that Philip left 279 sketches done by his own hand while he was at San Ildefonso. In the same way, Elizabeth left many paintings, and pastels of twenty studies of heads.[13]

* * *

The strengthening of cultural links between Italy and Madrid extended, as we have seen, to all the arts and was felt particularly in music and the theatre. A symbol of this was the career of the *castrato* singer Carlo Broschi, better known as Farinelli. Born in the kingdom of Naples in 1705, he was already famous throughout Europe before he was invited to Madrid by Elizabeth Farnese in 1737. He was in London, where he had been performing since 1734, when he received the invitation. He asked for temporary release from his English contract, and on his way to Aranjuez passed through Paris and sang before Louis XV. When he arrived in Spain, he found Philip V sunk in one of his crises of depression. His first concert for the royal family, on an afternoon in mid-August 1737, was consequently performed in the king's absence. As the clear tones of his voice rose into the air, they penetrated to the bedroom where the afflicted Philip lay. The divine voice immediately resuscitated the king, who snapped out of his depression and began to attend once more to his work routine. Astonished by the therapeutic effects of Farinelli's music, the king and queen demanded that he sing for them every day.[14]

Thereafter he became an indispensable part of Philip's life. Within a few days he was named '*Músico de Camara* of Their Majesties', given the title of *'Familiar Criado mío'* ('my personal assistant'), ordered to give no public concerts but to sing only for the royal family, and given lodgings in the royal palace and the same high salary he had earned in London, but tax-free. The contract with his English employers was rescinded. In effect, Farinelli now became the king's physician. He had certainly not been prepared for the king's strange daily timetable, and found that he had to sing his repertoire at all hours. At midnight, he usually sang in the king's chamber accompanied by a trio of musicians from the royal chapel. He had to be available at any time in the night, and was allowed to withdraw to rest only when the king had had his 'dinner' at 5 a.m. In a letter of February 1738 Farinelli wrote: 'Since the day I came I follow the same routine, singing every night for the king and queen who listen to me as on that first day. I pray God to preserve my health in this manner of life; every night I sing eight or nine arias. I never rest'.[15]

Diplomatic gossip claimed that Philip had little taste for music, and that he demanded the same handful of arias from Farinelli every day. In reality, Farinelli's own papers show that the repertoire he sang for the king included hundreds of different pieces of music ranging from Pergolesi to Scarlatti and other composers. The singer's role was also not as limited as might appear. From his privileged position, he was given charge of the arrangement of music and spectacles in the court; he directed private entertainments for the royal family; and developed close personal ties with the royal children. The court, and Madrid by extension, experienced a growing interest in musical presentations and in the beginnings of opera. By inviting over from Italy noted performers in these arts, Farinelli played a key role in the development of cultural relations between Italy and Spain. As the singer himself claimed, 'my achievement is that I am considered not as mere Farinelli but as ambassador Farinelli'. His report on one opera that was presented in Madrid in February 1738 is enlightening: 'on Tuesday we produced the Italian opera. Heavens, what a fuss, what excitement it caused! The Spaniards, who are not accustomed to see such things, were so delighted that nothing remains to be said'.[16] It was only the beginning. Italian opera went on to achieve unbelievable success in Madrid society.[17]

Italian theatre too had begun its successes, with the arrival in 1708 of Francesco Bartoli, who operated from a small theatre in Madrid. Annibale Scotti in 1719 was given the responsibility of constructing a new theatre building, the Coliseo de los Caños, which was inaugurated on the Sunday of Carnival in 1738 with a performance of the opera *Demetrio*. That same year, however, preference began to be given to the theatre at the Buen Retiro, where operas were put on to celebrate the wedding, in May 1738 in Dresden, of Charles, the king of the Two Sicilies, to Maria Amalia of Saxony. The Buen Retiro building was enlarged and remodelled in time to celebrate, in October 1739, the wedding of the Infante Philip to Marie Louise of France. Such patronage extended by Philip to Italian opera is ample evidence that he played an active part in the cultural life of the capital; we learn from the *Gaceta* that in November 1739 'Their Majesties and Highnesses went at night to the opera in the new theatre of the Buen Retiro.'[18] Great pains were taken to bring over the best singers from Italy. So strong was his interest that from 1740 the king ordered money to be made permanently available for what was known as the 'little theatre', a small group of musicians and singers who were to accompany the court everywhere, to La Granja, to the Escorial, and to any other residence where Philip happened to be. Through Farinelli, the king had discovered at last, after many years of suffering, a satisfactory therapy for his disorder.

*   *   *

The death of Orendain, marquis of La Paz, in 1734, left the way open for José Patiño to assume full ministerial powers. Patiño had controlled the ministries of the Navy and the Indies since 1726, and that same year he was entrusted with the ministry of Finance. In 1730, when his brother Castelar went to France as ambassador, he took over Castelar's ministry of War. Now in 1734 he was given the ministry of State. As we have seen, for several years he had been directing many of the principal affairs of each and every one of these ministries, and it was by no means a mistake to place so much business in his hands. Decision-making became more rapid and efficient. Above all, the king and queen were delighted to find that they could make major decisions by consulting with one person alone. Patiño became, as foreign diplomats observed, an obedient instrument for their belligerent foreign policy. 'The king and I', Elizabeth informed Keene on one occasion, 'have trained Patiño in the science of foreign affairs. If we wish, we can direct the ship of state, and if not, we shall create other ministers'.[19] Despite the seeming naivety of her words, the queen fully realised that 'directing the ship of state' would have been impossible without so excellent a minister as Patiño.

An impartial view of Patiño's role was given in 1735 by the Venetian ambassador. According to him,

> Patiño is the man who has rendered himself necessary to the queen, to the aggrandisement of her sons, and to the kingdom. He is clear-sighted, ready in resource, untiring in labour, and disinterested. He may fitly be called first minister, though he has not been formally appointed, for he gives orders and forms decisions in every class of business, with full authority, and only communicates to the queen what he thinks most necessary.[20]

After his fundamental reforms in the administration of the army and navy, for which he had received the full co-operation of Alberoni, in his later years Patiño concentrated his attention on commerce and on the reform of state finances. Spain at the beginning of the century was effectively a colony of foreign commerce, a fact which all Spanish commentators recognised. Foreign nations exported more to Spain than they bought from it, with negative consequences for both the economy and treasury of the country.

As we have noted, Patiño's support came in part from his colleagues in the administration where he had served for two decades, in part from the queen. After the return of the court to Madrid, the tension between the king's government, represented by Patiño, and the political class, represented by the grandees and the 'Spanish party', became almost literally a fight to the death. The opposition backed the appearance of a series of satirical attacks on the minister (written, it was discovered later, by a Portuguese friar) that first appeared on Thursday, 8 December 1735 and continued to appear unfailingly every Thursday in

Madrid until June 1736. Titled 'El Duende' (that is, 'The Phantom') or
'El Duende Crítico', the pamphlets were in both prose and verse, and
written in a wide variety of styles. The first number stated:

> Yo soy en la Corte
> Un crítico duende
> Que todos me miran
> Y nadie me entiende.
>
> Cuando meto ruido
> En el gabinete
> Enfado a Patiño
> Y asusto a los reyes.

(I am, in Madrid, the phantom who criticises, everyone sees me but
nobody knows who I am. When I make a noise in the cabinet, I
frighten Patiño and startle the king and queen.)

Directed against the entire government team associated with Patiño,
including even the queen, the pamphlets claimed to be denouncing
corruption, but used the techniques of vulgarity and insult in order to
do so. Being unlicensed, they were obviously illegal, but it was difficult
to discover their authorship. When the governor of the Council of
Castile, Bishop Gaspar de Molina, was entrusted with the task of uncovering the author, he began to feature in the pamphlets as well.

Apart from sponsoring the appearance of a street press, the political
opposition represented by the 'Spanish party' was both ineffective
and impotent. 'They vent their displeasure in speculation, and long
speeches in their private assemblies, but none that I know has ability
or courage enough to go any further', commented Keene.[21] They tended
to support the wars in Italy, because they brought glory, but when
Philip decided that the Two Sicilies under Charles should be a separate kingdom, they complained bitterly that Spain was being denied its
imperial rights. When news arrived in Madrid that Charles had been
proclaimed king in Naples, only two grandees, both of them Italians,
went to La Granja to congratulate Philip on the achievement.

Patiño's unexpected death at the age of seventy on 3 November
1736 was preceded by a short illness. It is very likely that the cares of

office, and the unremitting campaign against him in the underground press, shortened his days. But Philip V, who had most to lose by the minister's death, was probably the person who contributed more than anyone to it. Visiting Patiño during his last illness, the king bestowed on him the rank of grandee, which drew from the dying minister the ironic comment that he was being allowed to cover his head[22] when he no longer had a head to cover. Philip was no doubt quite unaware of any responsibility for Patiño's poor health; however, a report from Benjamin Keene leaves us in no doubt about the situation:

> I cannot give you an idea of the extreme disorder that prevails here in the despatch of business because of the king's manner of life, nor the straits to which those who have to serve him are reduced. Patiño who has responsibility for everything, loses daily four hours in the palace: from two in the morning to six o'clock, he spends in conversation with Their Majesties. He hardly has time left to eat or sleep.[23]

The loss of Patiño forced Philip to take over personal control of government until he could find another suitable minister, but the king had never been fond of Patiño, and was unmoved by his death. Elizabeth, on the other hand, had always appreciated his talents and was much affected. Her reaction to the death was a brave comment to the French ambassador: 'The king and I are still here, and we are quite capable of seeing that everything continues to function well'.[24]

* * *

The period when the opposition mounted a pamphlet war against Patiño was also that in which many pamphlets directed their ire against Elizabeth. Ever since her marriage and the beginning of Italian influence, the grandees in Madrid who formed the 'Spanish party' had financed satires against her as they had financed satires against the French. A verse of 1736 commented:[25]

> Aquí considera a un rey
> De pasta por reina hecho.

(Consider here the case of a king dominated by a queen.)

On the basis of these satires, there is good reason to assume that the queen was unpopular in Madrid, though we should not infer that this attitude prevailed throughout Spain. The fact is that her entire situation condemned Elizabeth to an unpopular role. Since she was forced by Philip's illnesses to make many decisions for him, she was accused of dominating him and refusing to let him rule. When he was seriously indisposed, she forbade any access to him, which inevitably irritated both diplomats and members of the government. As a consequence, there is a virtual unanimity in their view of the queen. The reports of both the French and the British ambassadors coincide in attributing to her alone the wish to find thrones in Italy for her sons, when in reality Philip had always made clear that it was his policy even more than hers. Because the queen did most of the talking in diplomatic audiences, diplomats assumed that it was her will that prevailed.

Starting from the premise that the king could not be attacked and that everything he did was correct, the opposition pamphlets left themselves no option but to blame everything on the queen:

> Todo lo echó a perder
> Esta intrigante ambiciosa,[26]

(Everything has been ruined by this ambitious schemer)

went a satire that came out after the king's death. It was a viewpoint that prevailed at the time, and will possibly continue to prevail, because all the contemporary reports coincide. Elizabeth herself recognised that there was nothing she could do to protect herself against the calumnies. 'The Spaniards do not love me,' she said once to Saint-Simon, 'but I also hate them.' But her words reflected only the anger of the moment; all her other words and actions reflect clearly enough her satisfaction at being in Spain at her husband's side. She had no desires or ambitions that were not also those of her husband. Nevertheless, the implacable opposition of the political class in Madrid, as well as of most foreign diplomats, made her public life a constant struggle. Fortunately, there appears to have been some respite from the problems of Philip's illness in the last months of 1737. In the autumn they even went hunting, a sport that Philip had generally dropped in the period after his stay in Andalucia; and every evening they listened to Farinelli.

However, the mental disorder had not really gone away. Keene's report in December 1737 that 'the king is in perfect health, and most exceedingly inactive'[27] was ominous testimony to the persistence of Philip's malady. Commentators did not realise that Philip's lethargy was an integral part of his health problem.

*   *   *

Spain's friendship with Britain, meanwhile, was being put to the test by several small conflicts in the Americas. A quarter of a century of disputes, centring on Gibraltar, the *asiento* and illegal English trade to America, fuelled Spanish grievances. The English for their part complained of obstruction of their legitimate trade, and harassment by the *guardacostas*: according to the government of Robert Walpole, between 1713 and 1731 more than 180 English trading ships had been illegally confiscated or robbed by *guardacostas*. However, the incident that gained most notoriety was that involving Captain Robert Jenkins, who stated in the House of Commons in 1738 that seven years before, in 1731, his ship had been pillaged by the Spaniards in America, and he had been bound to the mast and had his ear cut off. As proof, he showed the House a bottle with his ear preserved in it. When asked what he had done then, he stated that he 'committed his soul to God and his cause to his country'. His speech stirred patriotic sentiments in England and convinced the Commons that war with Spain was the only solution. In April 1738 Benjamin Keene in Madrid was instructed by his government to demand compensation for the damage done to English shipping. Talks over the amount resulted in the Convention of the Pardo in January 1739, negotiated by Keene and the Spanish minister La Quadra. In reality, the Convention settled none of the major points in dispute, and the amount of compensation that Spain agreed to pay was offset by money that it demanded in return for the sinking of its fleet at Passaro.

The resentment against Spain among both politicians and traders in England after the failure of the Pardo negotiation made war inevitable and the Walpole administration was forced into action. Admiral Vernon was sent out to attack Spanish settlements in the West

Indies, and war was declared in London in October 1739, with the ringing of church bells and rejoicing in the streets. 'It is your war', the reluctant Walpole wrote to one of his ministers, 'and I wish you joy of it.' He had previously condemned any action against Spain as 'unjust and dishonourable'. Shortly afterwards he resigned. And the 'War of Jenkins' Ear' went on.

* * *

Spain, which declared war in November 1739, was not economically prepared for conflict.

Perhaps the most impressive achievement of Philip V's regime had been its efficiency in finding revenue to meet its needs. Government income had risen dramatically after the War of Succession, and the expeditions to Sardinia and Sicily had taken place without generating any financial crisis. But various war expenses in the 1730s, and the cost of maintaining the army and navy, created debts that ministers were not able to cover. Patiño's legacy, according to a subsequent minister of Finance, was negative. Most of the available income was spent, and in 1737 many government payments were seriously behind: 'the royal households with arrears of six and a half years, the government both inside and outside Madrid in the same situation, the troops both in Italy and in Spain with thirty salary payments outstanding, the Navy with bigger arrears and with no means for maintenance, and creditors of state with mounting difficulties'.[28] The report is confirmed by Benjamin Keene, who stated early in 1738 that 'the officers of the army have not received their pay for ten months, nor the king's household for five years'.[29] The annual expenses of the monarchy at that period (1737) totalled nearly 34 million escudos (see Diagrams 8 and 9), of which military and naval expenses accounted for some 45 per cent.[30]

After Patiño's death, the four posts he held were divided up among his colleagues, several of them (such as Casimir Uztáriz and Juan Bautista Iturralde) natives of Navarre and the Basque country. The effective chief minister, in the view of foreign diplomats, was Sebastián de la Quadra (created marquis of Villarias in 1739), who continued to serve as a principal minister for the next ten years. The attentions of ministers could not, however, prevent the development of a crisis in financial affairs.

It is difficult to imagine that the treasury had problems when we consider the sums of money spent in October 1739 by the royal court and the city of Madrid on the celebrations to mark the marriage of the Infante Philip to Princess Marie Louise of France. The crisis, however, was due not only to excessive expenditure but also to the inability of taxpayers to pay. From 1734, there were serious food shortages in different parts of the peninsula. Drought that year produced a very poor harvest in Mallorca, Valencia, La Mancha, Andalucia and Extremadura; the city of Granada referred to 'the unprecedented shortages'.[31] In 1735 the crops were good in some areas, less so in others. The following year, 1736, was the first of five successive years to experience bad harvests and widespread food deficits.[32] In Valencia and Andalucia, there was a particularly acute harvest failure in the period 1737 to 1739, with severe floods in 1739; as a result, the importation of grain was allowed duty-free into the ports of these provinces.[33]

At the same time the government was suffering the weight of accumulated debts, and had to borrow money and anticipate revenue from future years. The situation was so difficult that a decree of 21 March 1739 suspended all payments from revenue, while a subsequent decree of 8 April suspended all state pensions for two years.[34] In the middle of these hardships came war with Britain. The special committee appointed in 1739 to examine war finance reported that the war costs for 1740 alone would exceed the entire available revenue of the crown.[35]

The position looked even more serious when it was discovered that the immediate debts of the state at the end of 1739 were equivalent to about three years' normal revenue.[36] The Council of Castile refused to sanction further taxes, but it was overruled and decrees in December 1740 levied new taxes on salt, an increase in the *alcabala* tax, plus a special emergency tax of 10 per cent on all income. Such was the state of Spanish resources when Britain pushed Spain into the War of Jenkins' Ear, a conflict that aggravated Spain's position, reduced the volume of commerce and provoked a recession in the country.

*   *   *

Long before the formal declaration of war in the autumn of 1739, the British navy had taken up its positions. In the summer, a large war fleet was cruising off the coast of Portugal. In July Admiral Edward Vernon, as we have noted, sailed for the Caribbean with a squadron, and after consultation with the governor of Jamaica decided that the most suitable objective was Portobelo, focal point of Spain's trade in America and also the base from which the *guardacostas* operated. On 2 December with six warships Vernon bombarded and captured the port in an action that finally destroyed the Spanish trade system in America.

The death of the Emperor Charles VI on 20 October 1740 ushered in the last phase of foreign policy in Philip's reign. In accordance with the arrangements made by Charles, who had no male heirs, the crown was to go to his eldest daughter Maria Teresa, wife of the former duke of Lorraine who was now duke of Tuscany. The other European powers put forward other candidates for the Imperial throne, and once again preparations were made for war, the so-called War of the Austrian Succession. The British signed treaties of alliance supporting Maria Teresa. Over the same period, Spain made other important international agreements, among them a historic trade agreement with Denmark (July 1742).[37]

The European conflict over the Austrian succession drew Spain into war on two fronts, both in the Mediterranean and in the Atlantic. It was an impressive display of military power by a country that barely a generation earlier had had neither an army nor a navy. With hindsight the conflicts may be judged to have been both unnecessary and wasteful, but at the time Philip V felt that Spain was in some sense fighting for survival: it was defending its commerce against the British, and seeking guarantees for Spain's presence in Italy. After the outbreak of hostilities against Austria in 1740, Spanish expeditions (with the participation of the Infante Philip) landed in Italy in 1741 and 1742.

As in previous wars, however, Philip V found that it was difficult to make the entente between the Bourbons work. He made it perfectly clear to Fleury that Spain had limited interests: 'the main issue is the settlement of the Infante Philip' in the duchy of Parma. When Cardinal Fleury died in January 1743 the king wrote to his nephew Louis XV advising him to 'take no more chief ministers because I do not think you need to at your present age'. He proposed to Louis 'a perfect union between us' and asked him to uphold 'the honour of the house of Bourbon'. He also added, emphasising his current wish to place the Infante Philip in the duchy of Parma, that 'I can say in confidence that although I very much love all my sons, he is the one for whom I feel the most affection'.[38]

The French, however, were already trying to reach an agreement with Austria, and hoped that Britain would also make peace with Spain. When the French ambassador put forward the idea to the king and queen in February 1743, Philip could hardly believe his ears. As we have seen, in this period the queen tended to do most of the talking at diplomatic audiences. But this time Philip could not restrain himself. 'Did you hear what he said?' he burst out, turning to the queen. 'Did you hear what he said?' He then took up the issue with the ambassador. 'You want me to ask for peace with England!' he exclaimed. 'I have waged an honourable war, and you want me to make a shameful peace! It is against my own honour and that of the nation!' It was obvious that peace on French terms was unacceptable. Elizabeth entered the conversation by emphasising one essential condition: 'The king is determined not to make peace without at least obtaining Gibraltar'.[39]

In the event, Philip's stance was justified by the alliance made between Great Britain and Austria in September 1743 at Worms. The Bourbon reaction was to draw up the second Family Pact between France and Spain, signed at Fontainebleau on 25 October 1743. In this agreement, attention centred on Philip's claims in Italy, namely possession of the duchies of Parma and Piacenza, but this time also Milan; Spain wanted all three territories for the Infante Philip. The demand for the recovery of Minorca and Gibraltar was also repeated. The French soon found reason to disapprove of Spanish belligerence over Italy. The war there, the French ambassador felt, was being conducted by the king and queen alone, without the participation of ministers. 'Here nobody makes proposals, or examines matters. Those with experience are not consulted. The ministers do not dare to protest.'[40]

* * *

Patiño's ministry had hushed but not extinguished the voices in the state bureaucracy that wished to return to the previous system of government through councils, which they viewed as more effective. There were of course efficient ministers in charge of affairs in Madrid, but they were not able to control the heavy demands of war expenditure. The crucial ministry was that of Finance. Continuing military costs in the Mediterranean brought to prominence in 1741 two of the most important ministers of the king. One was the marquis of La Ensenada, Cenón de Somodevila, appointed in 1741 to take charge of the military expedition to Italy. The other was José del Campillo, who had served the king for twenty-three years in the intendancies and the army, and in 1739 presented a plan for financial recovery in the light of the bankruptcy of that year. On the basis of his proposals, in February 1741 Philip appointed him to be head of Finance. In October, he was also given the ministries of War and of the Navy. Between them Campillo and Villarias (who controlled the ministry of State during these last years of the reign) directed all the business of government.

Campillo's early death in April 1743, at the age of fifty, cut short a promising ministerial career. He had been responsible for many reforms during his period as intendant in Aragon, but when he became minister in Madrid his reforming ideas remained unfulfilled. Most of them never took off from the pages of the numerous essays he published. One of his last tracts was entitled, significantly, *España despierta* ('Spain, awake'). In the event, the king and queen were bitterly disappointed by the death of someone whom they had hoped might be another Patiño. 'We are in very great difficulty about finding someone to replace him', Elizabeth admitted.[41] In his place the king immediately appointed the marquis of La Ensenada, who was given full powers over government, with control of the three key departments of War, the Navy and Finance. 'Nobody was more familiar than Don Cenón', Philip was advised, 'with the plans and ideas of Campillo, nor more suitable for carrying them out.'[42]

Meanwhile the drain on expenditure continued as the wars dragged on. By 1745 France refused to carry on with the war. The French minister d'Argenson, who had taken over the direction of foreign affairs in November 1744, stated firmly that peace was necessary and that the treaty of Fontainebleau with Spain must be scrapped. His ambassador in Spain, Vauréal, was faced with the almost impossible task of selling this idea to the Spanish court, and trying to reason with a somewhat irrational king. Philip was reverting to his previous habit of saying nothing. In one audience with Vauréal (in November 1745) even Elizabeth grew impatient with the king. 'Speak, Sire,' she urged him, 'for you put me out of patience. It is always I who have to talk for you; everything falls on me, though I do nothing but repeat what you have determined.'[43] At another audience in the royal chambers, when the king and queen as was their custom received him while they were in bed, the queen again became impatient. Vauréal reported: 'she got out of bed half an hour before the usual time, and when the king said that it was too early she replied, "I want to get up, you can stay there if you like". The king seemed to feel awkward, and I thought it better to retire'. After several weeks, the ambassador somehow managed to convey his message. After that, he had to endure the storm. At an audience in January 1746 the queen was so angry that she refused even to talk. This time the king did all the talking; he too was so furious that, as Vauréal informed d'Argenson, 'I dare not repeat his expressions'.[44]

In order to put pressure on Philip and Elizabeth a special ambassador, the marshal duke de Noailles, who had served with the king in Catalonia during the War of Succession, was sent to Spain and arrived at court in April 1746. His instructions were to get the king to agree to peace terms. Philip was in no mood to accept the dictates of Versailles meekly. 'Are you going to tell me, Marshal,' he said coldly to Noailles, 'that the treaty of Fontainebleau is the fruit of anger and ambition?' The ambassador informed d'Argenson that 'Philip did nothing but attack the politicians and the generals, referring bitterly to what the two crowns could have achieved if they had acted together'. 'It was because I gave in to French pressure,' the king complained to Noailles, 'that I was dragged into the war of 1733. I declared war on the English in 1739 only because I counted on France's promise to send a substantial fleet to America.'[45] Philip went on to remonstrate that perhaps the most difficult decision imposed on him by France had been that of ceding Parma to Austria. 'My honour and my love for the queen' obliged him to ensure that as long as she lived Elizabeth could continue to enjoy her rights in the duchy. On these grounds, the king said, he refused to bow to French pressure and would continue to pursue his claims in Italy.

The wars in northern Italy dragged on, bringing little benefit. The Infante Philip, seeking his inheritance, scored notable successes in his joint campaign with the French armies, but triumphs in 1745 were reversed the following year. In June 1746, the Infante took his stand at Piacenza against the Austrian armies, but the Franco-Spanish forces suffered a resounding defeat. The news produced consternation in Madrid. Philip went to his desk and wrote to Louis XV. It was the last letter that he ever wrote.

*   *   *

In the years following his return from Seville, Philip worked conscientiously at his job as king. His mind was usually clear and lucid, he appears to have had no significant illnesses, and he had few serious relapses into instability. However, as time passed the relapses did become more serious. We have seen that in August 1737 Farinelli found the king in one of his crises. Although there was a rapid recovery when the tenor began his musical therapy, the basic symptoms did not disappear and Benjamin Keene early in 1738 referred to Philip as 'disordered in the head'. In August that year Keene reported that when the king 'retires to dinner, he sets up frightful howlings'. One such howling, at the end of July, 'lasted from 12 midnight till past 2 in the morning'. 'As the queen cannot be sure of his behaviour, she does not fail to keep him within doors. His behaviour at night is to hear Farinelli sing the same five Italian airs that he sung the first time he performed before him, and has continued to sing every night for nearly twelve months. . . . The king himself imitates Farinelli sometimes after the music is over, and throws himself into such howlings that all means are taken to prevent people being witness to his follies.'[46] As we have seen, it is not true that Farinelli always sang the same arias. The detail, however, is unimportant. Whether true or exaggerated, the reports suggest that the king was far from normal and that many people were well aware of it.

Philip never altered the bizarre timetable that he had followed in Seville. A report drawn up in 1746 confirms that the king usually had his dinner at 5 a.m., with the windows shut. He went to bed at 7 a.m., then woke up and had a breakfast refreshment at 12 noon. At 1 p.m. he got up and dressed, heard his morning mass at 3 p.m., and then had lunch shortly after. 'After lunch he did not take a siesta but stayed in his rooms, gazing out of the window, busying himself with the clocks, reading for a while or being read to, and in this way he passed the time until nightfall. At two o'clock after midnight, he summoned the ministers to business, and in this way the cycle repeated itself.'[47]

Attention should be paid to the impact this routine had on the government of Spain. In the summer of 1739, Keene reported that Philip 'troubles himself with no sort of affairs, and after his appearances in public he applauds himself to his queen for having behaved himself, as he says, *comme une image*'.[48] In May 1744 the queen commented frankly to the French ambassador about 'the manner of life that her husband the king obliges her to lead'.[49] During this period she seems to have dedicated herself exclusively to caring for his health and adapting herself to his timetable, leaving herself little opportunity to spend time with her children. The new routine of business by night and sleep by day inevitably took its toll on the king and on his role. His life and mind became completely interiorised. Up to and during the time that he went to Seville, he had been a lover of hunting and coursed almost daily. But after Seville he very seldom went out, gave up hunting almost completely, and spent his leisure time principally with his beloved books and in other cultural pursuits.

In April 1746 Marshal Noailles had his first official audience with Philip, at 3 p.m., just before the 'morning' mass. He subsequently sent the following report to Versailles.

> I have found the king of Spain altered to such a degree, that I would barely have recognised him had I seen him anywhere else than his own palace. He has swollen out terribly, and even seems shorter than before. He can hardly stand upright or walk, which may probably be attributed to a complete lack of exercise. His mental faculties seem unchanged, and his understanding as lucid as ever, and when state business is discussed with him and he takes the trouble to respond, he replies with great precision. He retains a perfect memory of what he has seen or read, and enjoys talking about events in the past. There is not a single hunting rendezvous in the woods at Fontainebleau that he does not recall exactly.[50]

Philip's death, long expected by those who were able to judge by his physical appearance or who understood the consequences of his daily routine, came quite suddenly and without warning in 1746. He had been working all night as usual in the Buen Retiro with his ministers, and went to bed at 7.30 a.m. on 9 July. He slept until 12 noon. At 1.30, he said to Elizabeth that he thought he was going to vomit. She immediately called for a doctor, but was told that the king's physician was out at lunch. Philip's throat started swelling, as did his tongue, and he fell back on the bed. Within seconds he was dead. It had been three minutes from the moment that he mentioned vomiting.[51] Neither priest nor doctor had been present at his passing; the time of his death was put officially at 'two in the afternoon'. He was aged just over sixty-two.

Philip's sudden demise was the consequence of a deterioration of both mind and body. He had not allowed himself to be bathed in a very long time, and the result of his condition was such that 'when his body was cleaned the sponges peeled off his skin, and they had to leave him unwashed'.[52] The body lay in state for three days in the Buen Retiro, while thousands of visitors filed past to pay their last respects. It was draped in cloth of silver and gold, and adorned with the collars of the Orders of the Golden Fleece and of the Holy Spirit. Masses were celebrated continuously at seven altars in the hall, until late in the evening of 14 July, when the body was escorted to the church of San Jerónimo, and then later transported to the church of San Ildefonso at La Granja. The procession arrived at its destination on the morning of 17 July, when the body was laid to rest in a tomb of black and white marble. He was the first ruler of Spain since the sixteenth century not to be buried in the Escorial. The prince of Asturias was proclaimed King Ferdinand VI.

Elizabeth never recovered from the death of her husband. He had been all her life to her. She had supported him against the whole world, had always subjected her will to his, and had accepted without complaint the wholly incredible lifestyle that he imposed on her. After he died the light went out of her. When, shortly after the funeral, she left the Buen Retiro to go into retirement, the French ambassador commented that she looked like 'a living person going to her own burial'.[53] She remained in Madrid until July 1747, but ceased to have any official role. Two mansions in the city, one belonging to the duke of Osuna the other to the Príncipe Pío, were allotted to her as a residence and structural alterations were contracted out to the architect Giacomo Bonavia.[54] Diplomats called on her out of courtesy; the Danish ambassador reported visiting her 'in the final antechamber of her apartments, where we were received; she addressed a few agreeable words to us and we engaged in small talk'.[55] She then withdrew to the estate of La Granja; Philip's testament had left her the palace, together with a large pension. She remained there for the twenty-one years that she survived her husband, still faithfully following the strange day and night routine that she had accepted from him. She returned to the capital very briefly in August and September 1759, to act as regent when Ferdinand died and until her son Charles III arrived from Naples. The Venetian ambassador, who visited her in 1754, reported that 'though she has no share in the business of the court, yet by her kindly and agreeable manners and by singular proofs of intellectual ability, it can be readily seen what she once was'.[56] She died on 20 July 1766 and was buried in San Ildefonso at the side of her husband.

One of the many malicious satires that emerged after Philip's death went:[57]

Requiescat: murió Philip
In pace ha quedado el reino
Amén dicen los vasallos
Jesús ¡a qué lindo tiempo!

(Philip died in peace, leaving his kingdom in peace; 'it was high time' say his subjects.)

In reality, the people of Spain had mixed emotions. Some remembered him with hostility, as the destroyer of their liberties. Others still preserved in their memory the image of the valiant king, the 'Animoso'. A pamphlet noted:[58]

Murió Philip el guerrero
Que su valor en campaña
Supo probar en España
Por el filo de su acero.

(Philip the warrior has died, who demonstrated to Spain his valour in campaigns and the sharpness of his steel.)

We hear the same sentiments expressed in the sermon given at the funeral honours in Seville, where the preacher saluted Philip as 'a prince who secured the throne with his sharp sword, who conquered what was his by right, and who twice possessed the crown of Spain'.[59] Nearly half a century had passed since that young, hesitant prince had ascended the throne, and converted himself into the militant warrior who overthrew the treaty of Utrecht and recovered for his dynasty the entire western Mediterranean. He had regained for Spain its international pride, and promoted within the peninsula the beginnings of a modern state. But during all those years he was unable to check the ravages of an illness that deprived him of his efficiency, of his reason and, eventually, of his life.

CHAPTER EIGHT

The Spain of Philip V

'DESPITE THE STATE OF DECADENCE IN WHICH SPAIN FINDS
ITSELF, THERE IS NO NATION THAT CAN RAISE ITSELF UP AND
RECOVER MORE EASILY, AND NOW MORE THAN EVER.'

BUBB TO STANHOPE, 9 FEBRUARY 1715

Philip V, despite the very serious problems posed by his illness, trav-
elled more through his territories and had more contact with his sub-
jects, both Spanish and Italian, than any Habsburg ruler since Philip
II. He seems not to have visited the north-west or the south-east of
Spain; but apart from those areas, he made extensive visits to most of
Castile, Extremadura, Andalucia, the Basque country and Navarre,
Aragon and Catalonia, and the whole area of the Pyrenees. The briefest
of his visits, because it was interrupted by war, was that to Valencia.
His longest visit, as we have seen, was to Andalucia, but he also loved
the solitude and mountain air of Navarre, where he spent several
months. In nearly all these areas, he made tourist visits to cathedrals
and monasteries, prayed at the principal shrines, and had some contact
with his subjects. His language did not cut him off from them: though
he always preferred to use French, he read and spoke Spanish, and
(as we have seen) he habitually employed it when annotating state
documents. He differed from the tastes of many in his unalterable

preference for non-Spanish culture – in food, in dress, in music and in literature; and though he participated with great goodwill in many aspects of entertainment, especially the popular culture of festivals (carnivals, bullfights), he seems not to have incorporated them habitually into his style of life. This fact may, of course, be seen as positive and creative, for thanks to his tastes the Spanish world began to open itself – as it had under Philip II – to aspects of European culture that it had hitherto avoided. His admiration for French and Italian art and architecture gave a firm impetus to tendencies that already existed among sections of the Spanish elite, where it was becoming the fashion to imitate foreign ways. The nobility at court began to dress in the French manner. The army also began to wear uniforms imitated from those of France. Madrid, along with a section of the ruling class, became conscious of European horizons. The success of Italian opera in Madrid was symptomatic. However, the Europeanisation of the dynasty, and of the society associated with it, had a negative side. In Habsburg Spain, the upper classes had for the most part shared in the culture of their people. In Philip V's Spain, a gap began to open up between the culture of the modernising elite and the traditional culture of the masses. This gap was emphasised by one section of the ruling elite – the 'Spanish party' – that identified itself with Old Spain and rejected what the Bourbons had brought with them. Philip's dynasty had to work hard to survive in a country where very many people, in both the upper and the lower classes, felt it had little place.

It is common practice to refer to Philip's regime as 'absolutist', but the term has very little meaning when used of Spain in the early eighteenth century, and it may be appropriate to abandon it. Historians have increasingly come to realise that the label 'absolutist' presents more difficulties than it resolves.[1] Philip's state was in substance a *Machtstaat*,[2] a 'power state'. The power consisted essentially in 'a permanent army capable of putting down any internal opposition, and a fiscal organisation which extracted the money and men required'. A devotee of war, Philip deployed most of his resources in financing the army and navy, which were responsible for all the great events of his reign. 'The state had a territory and claimed sovereignty within it. Legitimate state activity was extended to include regular taxation and law-making.' The army would continue to be, in Bourbon Spain, the basis of power.

But Philip's *Machtstaat* was different from other states of its time, such as Prussia, where a reformed administration strengthened central power. His Spain lacked, in general, the two other basic aspects of the modern state: effective political centralisation, and ideas of state power.

Philip's regime initiated political centralisation but did not proceed very far with it. The attempt to create a centralised state bureaucracy in the form of intendants was dropped after the opposition of Philip's ministers to the intendancies introduced in 1711 and 1718. The nobles who controlled the central government (which throughout the reign opposed both the army and the intendants) continued to dominate the administration, and consistently – though not always successfully – opposed the king's own officials. The old feudal elites and many regional elites continued to direct the political system, because a new bureaucratic class was only beginning to come into existence when Philip died.[3] In essence, the social structure remained largely unchanged from what it had been during the Habsburg dynasty. In the Crown of Aragon, as well as in Castile, the traditional nobility continued to control essential aspects of administration, justice and finance; the organisation of economic structures remained wholly feudal. Though the new state bureaucracy, appointed from Madrid, began to direct important sectors of political and fiscal business, day-to-day government remained regional rather than centralised. Nor were there the lineaments of a centralised state. In the north, the Basque territories and Navarre continued as completely autonomous provinces – virtually republics – within the state.[4]

Philip's regime is also notable for the complete absence of theories of power. The only relevant authority claimed by the king was 'sovereignty', a concept that appears in the text of the abolition of the *fueros*, and also in that of the Nueva Planta in Catalonia. No other significant ideas of political theory emerged either from the king's circle or from the group of advisers surrounding him. The only important political theorist of the reign, Melchor de Macanaz, left the country in 1715 and spent the greater part of his life in exile. As we can see clearly from the sources quoted in his writings, Macanaz was never an absolutist. His theories were purely 'regalist'; he argued that the crown in former times enjoyed privileges or '*regalías*' (over the Church and over the provinces of Spain) that it could legitimately revoke in the case of rebellion.[5] None of the ministers of the king, including Alberoni, believed in or practised 'absolutism'. The most important political writings of the reign did not devote themselves to theories of state or government, but rather to economic policy, as with the works of Gerónimo de Uztáriz and José del Campillo. A progressive thinker like Benito Jerónimo Feijoo was conservative in his political ideas, but even while supporting the supreme power of the king he emphasised that the king was subject to the 'public welfare', that is, the common good.[6]

Decisions of state were made within a context wholly free from any ideology of power. Though many historians view the abolition of the Aragonese *fueros* as 'absolutist', the fact is that the same 'absolutist' king also preserved the *fueros* of the non-rebel Basque provinces and Navarre, and in 1718 dropped the proposal to reform their autonomous customs barriers. It is interesting that one of the strongest critics of the abolition of the *fueros*, the Aragonese count of Robres, identified the abolition not with French absolutism but rather with Castilian centralism. With the decree of 1707, he wrote, 'arrived the moment so desired by the count duke of Olivares, for the kings of Spain to be independent of all laws save those of their own conscience'.[7] Another active critic, the exiled Count Amor de Soria, referred to the regime of Philip V as 'a government established on acts of violence and tyranny',[8] words that were emotive rather than a rational analysis of the mechanics of Bourbon power. In any case, Amor de Soria's own patrons, the Habsburgs of Austria, made no secret of their own absolutism. The absence of any active Cortes of the realm after the War of Succession may seem to be the firmest indicator of 'absolutism' in the regime. But it should be remembered that for nearly half a century before Philip's accession, no Cortes had been summoned in Castile. Like most European rulers of his time, Philip saw no need of a legislative role for the parliament, although he apparently accepted (in 1713) that 'when the realm meets in Cortes it constitutes one body with me'.[9]

Philip's own political ideas do not appear to have been absolutist, and in no way mirrored those of his grandfather. Like his brothers, he had been brought up under the tutorship of the famous archbishop of Cambrai, Fénelon, whose anti-absolutist ideas were well known at Versailles and coincided with those of Madame de Maintenon and the duke of Saint-Simon.[10] Fénelon attempted to advise him about his political duties when he became king of Spain. We have the text of a letter that the archbishop sent him in 1701, listing nine fundamental points of good government, of which one was that he should 'moderate in his own person the exercise of royal authority'.[11] Philip may have been influenced also by Fénelon's deep sympathy with spiritual contemplation, instanced by the archbishop's warm support for the mystic Madame Guyon. An undoubted influence was exerted on Philip by Fénelon's moral parable, *Télémaque* (1699), which the archbishop had written expressly for his pupils. The work, implicitly critical of absolute government, described the travels of the hero as he wandered through various countries and experienced various political regimes, while searching for his father Ulysses. Philip admired Fénelon enough to attempt to have the work translated into Spanish. He also commissioned a series of tapestries on the life of Telemachus,[12] and in 1734 tried to obtain from France a new edition of the work. The praise of the traditional pastoral way of life expressed in *Télémaque* may have coincided with Philip's own profound wish for solitude and his attachment to La Granja, where, as we have seen, the symbolism expressed no cult of absolute monarchy. In 1701 the duchess of Orléans commented that 'the king of Spain takes Telemachus as a model'. If this was true, as it seems to have been, then we can accord due importance to the assertion of Fénelon, made in the year of Philip's accession to the throne, that

France cannot treat the Spanish nation like the king treats his grandson the king of Spain. Not all Spaniards are in agreement about accepting tutelage; they wanted to obtain help, not subject themselves to servitude. Absolute authority over the Spaniards cannot be maintained indefinitely.[13]

Philip's complete lack of interest in absolutist theory can be seen most clearly in the political testament he drew up for his son Luis in 1724.[14] At no point does he insist on the powers of the monarchy. Instead, the document offers advice on foreign policy and on aspects of domestic policy ('keep the Catalans, Valencians and Aragonese under control, and do not give them back their *fueros*, for they are turbulent people, especially the Catalans'). The king must 'try to encourage the arts and sciences, for it is the way a king gets loved by his subjects'. Surprisingly, the testament shows a concern for the Native Indians of America: 'he must try to help the poor Indians and do what he can to spread religion through those vast lands'. Luis must also 'give audiences and listen to others, for the king is father to the poor and he must listen to them and give them justice'.

Philip's contact with French ideas and influences was a novelty, not shared by most of the ruling class in Spain. The continued isolation of the nobility from European influences can be seen also in the conduct of the country's foreign affairs. Spain's new aggressive stance in European politics was directed by personnel who, if they were Spaniards, had little or no experience of the world outside the peninsula. The ministers of the department of State in the 1730s, for example, were a closed circle of Basques and Navarrese who had risen through the bureaucracy rather than through their experience of diplomacy.[15] When important negotiations had to be undertaken, they were put in the hands of persons who had been formed outside the peninsula, such as Baltasar Patiño, Ripperda, or the duke of Liria. In the first years of Alberoni's influence, the ambassadors of Spain in The Hague, London and Paris were all Italians.[16] Only these people, for instance, had any knowledge of foreign languages, and in particular of French, the tongue used by all diplomats to communicate among themselves.

Spain under Philip was a traditional society in process of change, a classical world where structures appeared to be immobile but where movement and flux were always present. The War of Succession accelerated this change, and gave greater momentum to the various forces at work in society. Philip made an active contribution to changes, and also accepted willingly all the trends that had already been forming. Passive by nature, he was inflexible over what he saw as political rebellion in the eastern provinces of the peninsula, but flexible in everything else. The marquis of San Felipe saw the king's passive role in a favourable light. Surrounded for years by rebellion and treason, 'he has not shed a drop of the blood of so many people guilty of disaffection, nor has he acted against them, and he has pardoned an infinite number'.[17] Afflicted for many years with an incurable mental condition, the king tried to follow his own strange timetable while the world around him was following another. His periodic incapacity produced one of the strangest monarchies of the century; very seldom in modern Europe had a realm been governed from a sickbed. A pamphlet of the time, *Sueño de España, letargo del Rey* ('Spain's dream and the lethargy of its king') presented Philip as a king asleep. Another, dated around 1730, addressed the king and warned him of impending dangers:

Despierta, señor, y verás
A España. . . .[18]

(Awake, Sir, and you will see Spain. . . .)

The king may have been sleeping, but his kingdom was waking up.

*   *   *

It awoke, above all, to the glorious liberty of uncontrolled publishing.[19] In other European countries the development of the popular press in the last decades of the seventeenth century had given rise to attempts to impose censorship. Spain too had seen the beginnings of political pamphleteering during the internal controversies of the reign of Charles II.[20] The government of Philip V made no attempt to carry out the impossible task of imposing the official rules of censorship,[21] trying, where it could, only to prohibit publications of which it disapproved. However, the War of Succession encouraged a flood of pamphlet literature that issued from both sides in the conflict and was difficult to control. 'The cities and the countryside', reported the Abbé de Vayrac, who was in Spain at the time, 'were inundated by manifestos and pamphlets'.[22] During the war, 'gazettes' (*gacetas*) were employed principally to spread false news (such as exaggerations of enemy casualties in battle) and to stir up support. The public acquired a taste for them. Literacy rates in Spain continued to be abysmal, but the contents of pamphlets were communicated by those who could read to those who could not, and in this way a form of propagandist literature was brought into existence. It was wholly new. 'Fifty years ago, or perhaps less,' observed Father Feijoo towards mid-century, 'there were no voices raised in criticism even in the most sophisticated circles, yet now even the villages are full of critics.'[23]

Pamphlets cannot strictly be termed 'clandestine', because in fact they circulated openly and were read by everybody, including those in power; it is more correct to call them 'unlicensed'. For more than a century, in the political struggles in England, Germany and France, unlicensed pamphlets had been the chief medium of propaganda,[24] and Spain was no different. Philip V's Spain was a chaotic society with few controls and little possibility of systematic repression. The pamphlets (many remained only in manuscript and were never published) circulated freely, expressing the opinions and conflicts of the groups who controlled the printing presses. They were not in any real sense 'popular': it is true that they were accessible to the reading public, but they arose almost exclusively out of polemics within the political class that ruled the country.[25] Nor were they in any real sense a 'press', for they lacked the essential element of the press, namely periodicity. There was no real press in Spain in the first third of the century. The first step forward in the evolution of one was the appearance in 1737 in Madrid of the *Diario de los literatos de España*, a journal that owed its genesis in part to Philip V, who had in 1723 suggested to his librarian Juan de Ferreras the idea of publishing information about books written in Spain.[26]

The pamphlets were also an important indication of a new trend: the awakening of political consciousness in Spain. The monarchy, we have observed, had no conscious political theory of any sort, and all Philip's ministers without exception were – as we have seen – destitute of a theoretical apparatus. By contrast, the failings of Philip's government system gave rise within Spain to some serious reassessments of the constitution. The conflicts of his reign helped Spaniards to regain some sense of their primary identities within their regions and their local societies. As in any time of crisis, people looked into themselves and tried to define who they were. Two obvious cases stand out: that of the Catalans, and that of the Castilians.

The Catalans had already experienced a major crisis in the middle of the seventeenth century, when the events of 1640 had brought to the surface issues relating to the role of Catalonia within Spain. The problem became attenuated during the later century, but surfaced again during the revolt of the peasants (known as *Barretines* from the cap or *barretina* they wore) around 1690. The defeat of the Habsburg sympathisers in the principality in 1714 provoked a crisis that affected all Catalans, regardless of which side they supported, for the historic political institutions of Catalonia were swept away, leaving an enormous emotional gap in the popular mind. Which way could Catalans turn if they wanted to affirm that the spirit of their people still survived? The propaganda leaflets of the war years are some guide to the way that ideas were beginning to take shape.[27] The loudest voices, quite logically, were those that criticised the English for their betrayal. The 1734 pamphlet 'Via fora als adormits' ('Sleepers, awake!') was typical of these writings that began to define a specifically Catalan point of view.[28] The exiled Juan Amor de Soria also made a specifically pro-Habsburg contribution in his unpublished work on the 'Chronic and perilous sickness of the realms of Spain'. Nevertheless, a long time would pass before any well-ordered thinking on the problem of a Catalan identity would emerge.

The Castilians also had their problems. Though historians have long been aware of the fact, the wider public often forgets that Castilians felt very disadvantaged by the Habsburg monarchy that came to Spain in 1516. The revolt of the Comuneros in 1520, a revolt limited exclusively to Castile, demonstrated that Castilians feared the implications of a European destiny. Over the next two centuries, Castilians complained repeatedly that they were receiving few benefits from empire and that everyone else was benefiting from Castile. Valencians, Basques and Portuguese could hold office in Castile, they complained, but Castilians had no rights to hold office in those realms.[29] During the seventeenth century, complaints against the burden of empire became shriller, and Olivares represented part of a movement that wished both the burdens and the rights to be shared equally among all Spaniards.

The Bourbon succession, greeted with such enthusiasm by Castilians, turned out to be as much of a disappointment as the Habsburg succession had been. Philip V created a nation in which Castilians played (according to critics) no recognisable part. Their traditional government institutions were overturned, their famous Cortes rendered impotent, their aristocracy undermined. Their armies were commanded by foreigners. Up to 1715 Frenchmen had the leading voice in public affairs, after 1715 Italians were substituted for them. Very little of these changes affected the daily life of the towns and villages of Castile. But at government level the Castilian elite harboured deep resentment.

The consequence was the emergence of a strong political feeling that based itself firmly on an appeal to 'Castile' and to 'Spain'. The crystallisation of this feeling can be identified, as we have noted in a previous chapter, with the rise of the 'Spanish party',[30] a phrase that refers not to a defined group of people but rather to a tendency of opinion that was identified as such by the British ambassador in 1716 and by the French ambassador in 1746. The tendency was shared exclusively by a section of the traditionalist Castilian aristocracy, some of whom supported the archduke in the War of Succession. These aristocrats felt that they had been deprived of their proper role in the state. As the admiral of Castile proclaimed in 1702 when he took refuge in Portugal, 'justice and good government have been cast aside, there has been only contempt and disdain for the respect due to blood, authority and the most exalted lineage'.

It would be a mistake to dismiss such opinions as the swan song of a barren elite. Though many individual nobles were ruined, imprisoned or died in exile, the aristocracy as a class survived. They continued to play a significant part in the court, in the administration and in Spanish society. They also directed a good part of the pamphlet literature of these years. At all times, they attempted to keep alive the idea that their tendency represented the true interests of Castile and of Spain. As a result, they were a serious obstacle to the government of Philip V throughout his reign. As Marshal Tessé observed to Elizabeth Farnese in 1724, 'everything that is considered typical of Spain – the councils, the committees, the confessors, the theologians, the priests, the friars – will always be hostile to your interests'.[31] In the political circumstances of the time, the 'Spanish party' concentrated its hostility on foreigners, and backed a conservative attitude of 'Spain for the Spaniards'. After 1724, as we have seen, the 'party' added to its programme the demand for 'legitimacy', and began questioning the basis on which the Bourbon monarchy ruled in Spain.

* * *

Spain awoke, under the first Bourbon, to economic stability. The reigns of the last Habsburgs had been plagued by an uncontrolled rise in prices, but from the 1680s, monetary and price inflation was drawing to an end, a trend that became confirmed after the 1720s.[32] Although prices rose during the War of the Succession, they stabilised in subsequent decades. The government of Philip V took steps to achieve a stable national coinage, essential in view of the monetary confusion in the peninsula, where Castilian, French, Catalan, Valencian and Aragonese coins all circulated. One of the basic tasks of the new intendants was to check against false coins in circulation. Confidence in the coinage helped to control prices, even in periods of crisis. The result was that 'it would be difficult to find a fifty-year period of more stable prices in the history of any country' other than Spain between 1700 and 1750.[33]

Spain awoke to demographic stability, which (historians now agree) can be dated from the 1680s. The War of Succession was, like all wars, destructive; but it had little negative impact on the population of the peninsula. For example, in the city of Girona, which was always in the middle of a war area, there was no significant increase in mortality or any observable loss of population.[34] Spain prepared itself to share in the demographic growth of Europe's eighteenth century, though in a modified way. Plague, the great bringer of

mortality that had afflicted the peninsula severely in previous generations, disappeared completely from the Mediterranean after 1720.
There were no further obstacles to population increase, which followed
three regional models of growth in Spain: the north-west, the centre,
and the Mediterranean. In the north-west, where the growth pattern
was very irregular, population (according to the most optimistic
historians) may have risen by 20 per cent during the reign; in the
centre, the increase may have been even higher, up to 40 per cent in
Castile and León; and in the Mediterranean the highest increases
were registered.[35] However, we should be cautious about accepting
these high estimates. In reality, mortality levels in Spain remained very
high, and it has recently been suggested that the population increased
more slowly, at an average annual cumulative rate of little more
than 0.43 per cent.[36]

Spain awoke to adequate food supplies. Agrarian production, the
fundamental sector of the economy, increased all over the peninsula.
Valencia had been very severely damaged by the war, but grain output
there rose steadily throughout the reign of Philip V.[37] Higher grain
output[38] supplied food for the growing population; in Galicia and
Cantabria the cultivation of maize solved constant problems of cereal
output. The growth in the agrarian economy, however, did not mean
development. While in northern Europe social and technological
improvements boosted agrarian growth, in the peninsula a number of
serious obstacles blocked the way to progress.[39]

The most convincing evidence of the adequate level of subsistence
in the peninsula is the absence of significant popular agitation. Apart
from strictly local discontent, as during the *matxinada* in the Basque
country in 1718, Philip V's Spain was surprisingly free of social crises
caused by economic distress. This situation in its turn contributed to
the security of the upper sections of society. Ironically, however, it was
sections of the privileged class that now began to participate actively in
political opposition. In Catalonia, for example, the great economic
advances achieved during the eighteenth century left many of the
ruling elite dissatisfied, for after the abolition of their political institutions they were unable to enjoy the political privileges that normally
accompanied economic success.

The almost continuous wars of Philip V had the positive consequence of stimulating the economy. Apart from the conflict of 1705–14,
they were wars of limited duration, paid for exclusively out of the
central treasury and without raising exceptional taxation. The conflicts,
like many similar wars of pre-industrial Europe, stimulated production
in secondary sectors that served military activity. Industry represented
only a small part of the economy and of economic output, but
significant steps forward were made. With good reason, the textile
factory at Guadalajara[40] has been seen as the symbol of the effort made
under Philip V, though in reality substantial production here occurred
only in the second half of the century. A sector associated with textile
production was that of wool, which experienced a resurgence in output.
Though the exact figures are in dispute, there is little doubt about the
steady rise in wool production after the war and the associated increase
in wool exports from Castile.[41]

Despite these positive aspects, it is not possible to offer a wholly
optimistic picture of the military recovery of Spain under Philip V.
Unlike other contemporary states such as Prussia, where great care
was taken to build up an infrastructure to support military activity,
Spain did not develop an adequate war machine. Money was raised,
men recruited and ships built, only for specific enterprises. If the
enterprises failed, everything was lost and the whole process had to
be started again. The clearest example is Spain's naval resurgence,
referred to repeatedly above. Spanish naval expansion under Philip
was phenomenal. But most of it went to waste. Over two-thirds of the
warships built in the reign were sunk shortly after being launched: the
disaster of Cape Passaro was typical of the great fragility of Spain's
naval role.

Philip V's advisers were unanimous that the way forward for Spain
was through its commerce, and that the most profitable way was through
the establishment of trading companies. From Macanaz onwards, ministers were agreed that two fundamentals must be pursued: the opening
of American trade to all Spanish ports, and the creation of companies
like those operated by the English. The ideas can be seen in Macanaz, in
Patiño, in Alberoni, and in Campillo. Gerónimo de Uztáriz, in an
influential treatise of 1724, was the first to explore the theme in detail.[42]

Miguel de Zabala y Auñón, in a treatise addressed to the king in 1732, emphasised the idea.[43] Bernardo de Ulloa, in a voluminous work of 1740,[44] returned to the subject. Campillo's study of the subject was not published until the end of the century. All these writers have with reason been described as 'mercantilists', that is, they advocated the intervention of the state in the formation of economic policy. The state, in their view, would enrich itself through promoting trade and through developing industrial goods for export. In practice, little was achieved in these matters by the state during this reign. The government made serious efforts to direct and subsidise sectors of the economy, through a controlling body called the Junta de Comercio (Board of Trade), but there were always obstacles in the way of success.

The efforts of the mercantilist writers, in fact, demonstrate the continued commercial backwardness of Spain. For generations, the famous wealth of the Indies had belonged not to Spain but to the trading nations of northern Europe. Foreign interests and foreign merchants dominated Spain's trade. Under Philip V the French and the English, as we can see from Diagrams 2 and 3, imported a quantity of raw material from the peninsula but sent a far greater quantity of manufactured goods to it, thereby creating a trade pattern which put Spain into the category of a dependent nation. The entry of English goods was sharply interrupted only by the military intervention in Spain in 1719 and by the War of Jenkins' Ear in 1739. The importation of French goods, likewise, declined only during periods of war, but maintained their superiority throughout the reign.[45]

* * *

Philip V's active patronage of art, theatre, architecture and music had little impact on Spanish culture beyond the ambit of the court.[46] He was not one of the great patrons of culture,[47] in large measure because of his character and his unfortunate illness. But his modest contribution was significant. 'The court of Philip V', it has been pointed out, 'both in art and in many other fields represented a decisive breakthrough, one that is always desirable in a country that has the inclination to close in on itself, and imperative in a period of national reconstruction'.[48] He established the acceptance of European tastes among the educated elite. Artists and writers had always looked towards Italy; his reign now encouraged the new trend of looking towards Paris.

The king's patronage in intellectual matters was always indirect and there existed already a tradition of continuity in intellectual matters from the reign of the last of the Habsburgs. Members of the educated elite, drawing on their experience of extra-peninsular culture, profited from the European horizons of the new century to establish discussion groups. For example, as a result of the cultural salons held in the residence of the marquis of Villena, he and his colleagues proposed to the king in 1713 the founding of an academy to 'work together to examine and determine the words of the Castilian language in their most correct, elegant and pure form'. Close members of the king's household were present at the founding meeting in July 1713, and one may therefore suppose some royal involvement.[49] The consequence was the establishment by decree on 3 October 1714 of the Royal Academy of Language, made up of twenty-four members. From 1726 the Academy began to publish its *Diccionario*. The king took a personal interest in its work, and in 1734, for example, received the entire Academy in the Buen Retiro and graciously accepted the fourth volume of the *Diccionario*.[50] The next significant foundation was that of the Academy of History, approved by the king in 1738. During this reign, an exceptional interest in the writing of history was provoked by the polemical events of the War of Succession. The works of the Bourbon sympathisers San Felipe, Robres and Belando are perhaps the best known, though they are surpassed in quality by a work that the regime suppressed, the great *History of Catalonia* by Narcís Feliu de la Penya. There were during these decades several regional academies active; among the best known was the Valencian Academy, founded by Gregorio Mayáns in 1743, and the Academy of Letters of Barcelona, which received royal approval in the next reign.

The intellectuals who contributed to the formation of academies had, of course, been active prior to the reign of Philip V. They had in that earlier period contributed much to a rising interest in medicine and science, and had initiated the early Scientific Revolution in Spain. Already under Charles II, the Royal Society of Medicine in Seville had pioneered the way for scientific academies; among its successors in the peninsula being the Madrid Medical Academy, established in 1734. The enormously important contribution to intellectual development made by small groups like these, and by individuals of the calibre of the Benedictine monk Feijoo in Asturias and the intellectual Gregorio Mayáns in Valencia, is well known. Feijoo's *Teatro crítico universal*, published in seven volumes from 1726 to 1739, based itself heavily on French writings, and by its critical attitude prepared the way for the Enlightenment in Spain. Mayáns's intellectual development, based to a great extent on his contacts with Italy, perhaps best reflects the new horizons that the Bourbon monarchy favoured.[51]

The continuous contact with foreigners gave rise to one of the more significant foundations of the period. In 1728 in Madrid an Englishman, the duke of Wharton, a well-known Jacobite, founded in association with a group of other English gentlemen ('who reside at the moment in Madrid and in other cities of Spain') the first lodge of Masons in the country's history.[52] Madrid, in effect, became the recipient of the principal changes inaugurated by the new dynasty. French styles in dress, as we have noted, were imitated by high society. The white wig, typical of Louis XIV's France, began to be worn by both men and women. High-society women began to wear large bows and flowers – what they called a 'garden' – on their heads.

Philip's patronage contributed, finally, to one of the great scientific enterprises of the century. In 1734 he gave his permission for an expedition to South America that was led by the great French scholar La Condamine, and included two young Spanish officers with scientific qualifications, Jorge Juan and Antonio de Ulloa. From 1735 to 1743, the two Spaniards made a historic and fruitful series of journeys through the American continent, in the course of which they accumulated an enormous amount of new data and measured the dimensions of the earth.

* * *

Historians have with good reason seen in the reign of the first Bourbon the beginnings of the modern Spanish state, but it was a state that, like all others in Europe, paid very little attention to the needs of the mass of the people so that among the themes to which writers under Philip V paid attention was that of the extensive poverty in the country. Feijoo noted of Asturias that 'the agricultural labourers are the most under-nourished and unprotected people in these lands', and Moya y Torres in 1730 stated that in the Spanish countryside 'I found only continuous laments, hunger, poverty, depopulation and emigration'.[53] The opinions may have been exaggerated, but the fact was that few solutions existed for poverty at that time. The marginal population, in both town and country, was seen as basically 'idle' and sent off to join the ranks of military conscripts. 'Idle', for example, were the schoolteacher condemned in the middle of the century 'for the little attention he gives to teaching', the philosophy student from Alcalá condemned 'for not studying', and the workman from El Ferrol condemned 'for not working enough'.[54] Their 'idleness' was decided, of course, not by the state but by the local town mayor and the parish priest. The unfortunate 'idle' represented, in fact, the gradual dissolution of traditional society, and the rise of the modern proletariat of marginalised persons. The 'vagrants' or unemployed, thousands of whom were rounded up from all over Castile in order to serve in the army – nearly 9,500 in 1759 alone[55] – were classified by the authorities as 'given to vice', 'lazy', 'bad workers', 'useless'. One unfortunate was classified as 'not given to vice, but of no use in his village', a description that qualified him immediately for useful public service in the army. Of the vagrants rounded up between 1730 and 1746, about 10 per cent were sent to serve in the navy and 90 per cent in the army. The latter was also a useful place to send offenders accused of drunkenness and wife-beating.

Social discipline of this type could not be applied to the large numbers of indigent poor in the towns and cities of Spain. One guide to the problem comes from the statistics of the Brotherhood of Refuge and Piety of Madrid, a body that had been founded in 1618 and enjoyed official protection. In the streets of the capital, this Brotherhood aided some 5,000 persons a year in the decade 1701–10, over 5,000 a year in 1721–30, and over 6,000 a year in 1731–40.[56] Since this was a reign of reasonable harvests and no severe subsistence crises, apart from the problems caused by the war at the beginning and the bad harvests after 1734, the consistently high figure for poor receiving assistance demonstrates the existence of a real social problem. Bernardo Ward, an experienced government official of the period, estimated that in the mid-eighteenth century the poor in Spain made up 20 per cent of the country's population.[57]

There is no clear way of measuring poverty nor do censuses of the 'poor' exist, but if we guide ourselves by the levels of poverty elsewhere in Europe, we can be certain that 20 per cent is an underestimate for Spain in that period. The lower classes in the Spain of Philip V had an insecure existence, with low life expectancy, the agrarian sector, representing the greater part of the economy, being the most insecure. 'It is lamentable', wrote the official Zabala y Auñón in 1732, 'to see a poor labourer perspiring at his work like a slave, for a miserable wage, yet in Spain these are the majority, who with their daily wage have to sustain their household.' Those who earned their living in the non-agrarian sector of the economy could hope to earn a wage only on the basis of a working year of 180 days[58] (taking into account that nearly half the days in the year were holidays). At least in Madrid, the popular diet was made up of bread, pulses (particularly chickpeas), olive oil, and small quantities of pork for soups and stews. Meat and fish appeared very rarely, except among the well-to-do.[59] In times of low wages or poor harvests those who had incomes would suffer; those who had no income would perish. The Church worked heroically to relieve the poor, and Philip V, like other kings, played his part. But Philip's own policies were not (despite the concern he expressed in his political testament of 1724) calculated to help the poor. Cardinal Belluga, in a pamphlet written towards 1730, *Manifiesto universal de los males que España padece* ('Manifesto on the ills that Spain suffers'), complained that the war policies of the government had raised taxes and worsened the economic situation of the country. It was a perfectly justifiable criticism of a government that had devoted little attention to the needs of the majority of its subjects.

*   *   *

The frail shoulders of a young and tormented Philip V bore on them the weight of a new dynasty and a new beginning in the life of his adopted country. He was not one of the heroes of Spain's history, and nations tend to be unforgiving with such rulers. Criticised by both French and Castilians, he was distrusted by the provinces of the Crown of Aragon that identified him as the source of their ills. The last warrior king of the peninsula, he took his duties and obligations seriously, and participated actively in all the tasks of government. Problems of health and personality, however, undermined his public role and distorted his perspectives, particularly in foreign policy. His five-year absence in Andalucia undermined the respect of his subjects. However, as the first Bourbon, he coincided with and gave his support to all the major developments that created modern Spain. Melchor de Macanaz, writing from exile in Paris, expressed the opinion that Philip had been 'the greatest king that we have had in two centuries',[60] an interesting verdict, by a prominent political expert, on all the kings who had succeeded Philip II.

Thrown brutally into the maelstrom of European politics by the War of Succession and the ensuing wars of Elizabeth Farnese, Spaniards were caught up in a series of wholly new choices that dictated both the good and the bad in their subsequent history. Philip's Spain was one in which the economy, population and production flourished; one in which intellectuals, scientists and historians began to have vigorous interchanges with each other and with other Europeans. But it was also a Spain where the centralised state was beginning to become the sole arbiter, and where that state – fully in accord with developments in the rest of Europe, whether in Britain, France or Prussia – was conceived in national and not in regionalist terms. It is interesting that the best-known intellectual of the reign approved wholeheartedly of these two distinct aspects. Spokesman of a forward-looking and critical approach to the sciences, Feijoo was a conservative in political matters. He praised the new Bourbon polity as 'that body of state where, under a civil government, we are united by the bonds of the same laws. Thus, Spain is the authentic object of a Spaniard's love.' The pre-Bourbon polity of autonomies had been, he felt, 'the root of civil wars and revolts against the sovereign'.[61] The uncompromising verdict of Feijoo is evidence that the legacy of Philip V was rich and fruitful, but also both polemical and conflictive.

1. War expenditure of Spanish state, 1703–1718 (thousands of escudos)

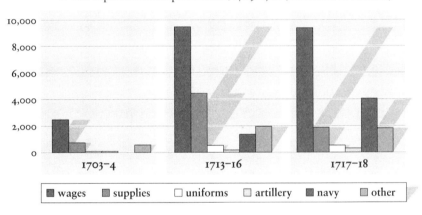

source: *Kamen*, War of Succession, *table 10, p.229.*

2. Trade between Spain and Britain, 1703–1748 (thousands of pounds)

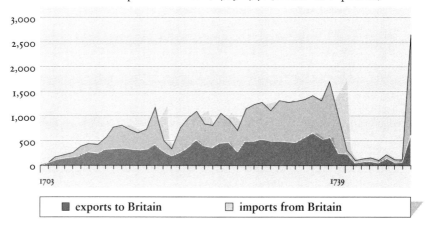

source: McLaclan.

3. Trade between France and Spain, 1716–1750 (millions of francs)

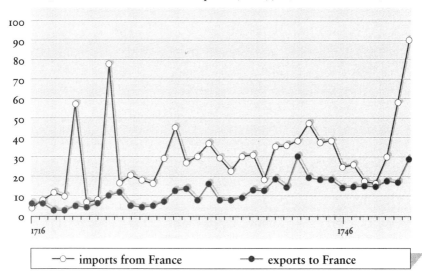

source: Vicen Vives.

4. Main sources of revenue of the Spanish government, 1713–1741 (thousands of escudos)

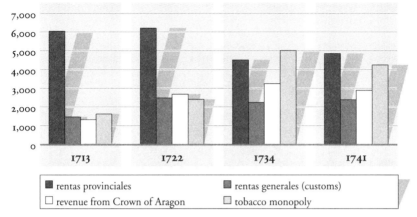

source: documentation in AGS Secretaría de Hacienda.

5. Spanish military expenditure, by region, 1734 (thousands of escudos)

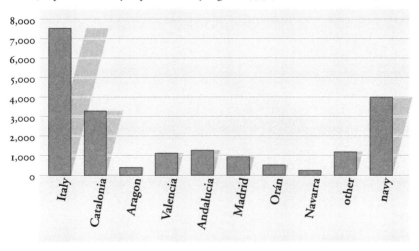

source: AGS Secretaría de Hacienda

6. Army costs, 1739

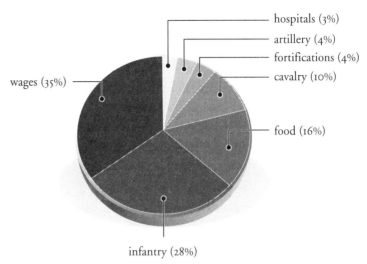

hospitals (3%)

artillery (4%)

fortifications (4%)

cavalry (10%)

wages (35%)

food (16%)

infantry (28%)

source: AGS Secretaría de Hacienda.

7. Sources of tax revenue, 1741

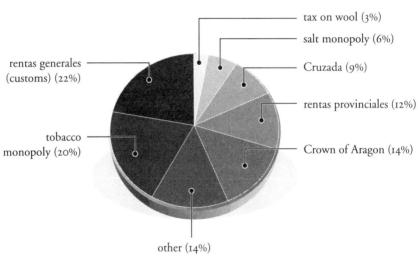

tax on wool (3%)

salt monopoly (6%)

Cruzada (9%)

rentas generales
(customs) (22%)

rentas provinciales (12%)

tobacco
monopoly (20%)

Crown of Aragon (14%)

other (14%)

source: AGS Secretaría de Hacienda.

8. State expenditure, 1740

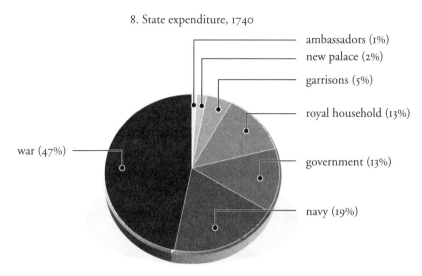

ambassadors (1%)

new palace (2%)

garrisons (5%)

royal household (13%)

war (47%)

government (13%)

navy (19%)

source: AGS Secretaría de Hacienda.

9. Annual government expenditure, 1734–1741 (thousands of escudos)

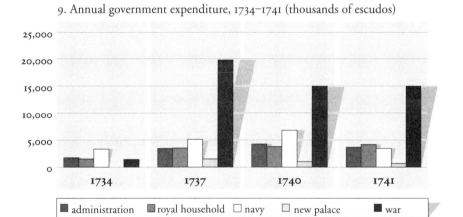

■ administration ■ royal household □ navy □ new palace ■ war

source: documentation in AGS Secretaría de Hacienda.

ABBREVIATIONS

ACA:CA	Archivo de la Corona de Aragón: section Consejo de Aragón
AE:CPE	Archives du Ministère des Affaires Étrangères, Paris: Correspondance Politique (Espagne)
AGI	Archivo General de Indias, Seville
AGS	Archivo General de Simancas
AHN	Archivo Histórico Nacional, Madrid
AN:AE, B^I	Archives Nationales, Paris: section Affaires Étrangères, fonds B^I
BN	Bibliothèque Nationale, Paris
BNac	Biblioteca Nacional, Madrid
BUV	Biblioteca de la Universidad de Valencia
Guerre A^I	Dépôt Général de la Guerre, Vincennes, Paris: fonds A^I
PRO:SP	Public Record Office, London: State Papers

CHAPTER ONE: THE DISPUTED SUCCESSION

1. Kamen, *Later seventeenth century*, p. 391.
2. Letter of 6 May 1666, PRO:SP 94/50/199.
3. Cited in Kamen, *War of Succession*, p. 5.
4. 'Explicación de los motivos que ha tenido el Rey', Madrid, 20 Feb. 1719, AHN Estado leg. 2819.
5. *Crónica*, p. 31.
6. Ibid., p. 32.
7. Louville, I, 26.
8. Cited by Bottineau, p. 154.
9. In Dec. 1700, cited in Baudrillart, I, 41.
10. Ubilla y Medina, *Succession del Rey*, p. 165.
11. Louville, I, 124.
12. There is a good outline of the reforms in Bottineau, p. 195 ff.
13. AE:CPE 102 f.68.
14. Louville, I, 154.
15. Ibid., 134.
16. Louville to Torcy, May 1701, in Louville, I, 133.
17. Cited in Egido, *Opinión*, p. 92.
18. Blécourt to Louis XIV, AE:CPE 91 f.187.
19. The wife of Vittorio Amedeo, Anne-Marie, was daughter of Philip of Orléans (1640–1701) and sister of Philip II of Orléans (1674–1723). Her eldest daughter, Marie Adelaide, was wife of the duke of Burgundy, brother of Philip V.
20. François Combes, *La princesse des Ursins: essai sur sa vie et son caractère politique*, Paris 1858.

21. Letter from the Príncipe Pío, 20 July 1701, AHN Estado leg. 2793.

22. Robres, *Historia de las guerras civiles de España*, p. 62.

23. *Crónica*, p. 40.

24. *Dietari*, vol.XXIII, p. 239.

25. Quoted by Eva Serra, 'Les Corts de 1701–1702', in *L'Avenç*, no.206, 1996, p. 24.

26. *Dietari*, vol.XXIV, pp. 8–9.

27. *Crónica*, p. 44.

28. AE:CPE 104 f.264.

29. Cited in Manuel Danvila y Collado, *El poder civil en España*, 6 vols, Madrid 1885, III, 369.

30. Cited by Charles Weiss, *L'Espagne depuis le règne de Philippe II jusqu'à l'avènement des Bourbons*, 2 vols. Paris 1844, II, 371, n.1.

31. Ibid., p. 55.

32. Henry Kamen, 'The decline of Castile: the last crisis', *Economic History Review*, 2nd series, XVII, 1 (1964).

33. See especially the two chapters by Pere Molas, 'Reactivación económica y cambios sociales en los países de la Corona de Aragón' and 'Reactivación económica y cambios sociales en los países de la Corona de Castilla', in *Historia de España Menéndez Pidal*, vol.XXVIII, Madrid 1993.

34. James Casey, *The kingdom of Valencia in the seventeenth century*, Cambridge 1979.

35. *Copia de Carta que un Cortesano remitió a Barcelona a mano de un Ministro*, in AE:CPE 102 f.408.

36. Baudrillart, I, 103.

37. Ibid., 107.

38. Ubilla y Medina, *Succession del Rey*, pp. 466, 507.

39. Count of Marcin to Louis XIV, July 1702, in Baudrillart, I, 110.

40. Ubilla y Medina, *Succession del Rey*, p. 572.

41. Ibid., p. 577.

42. Ibid., p. 594.

43. San Felipe, p. 50.

44. *Crónica*, p. 50.

45. Louville, II, 50, 99.

46. On the political role of Marie Louise, see Chapter 3.

47. Cited in Bottineau, p. 301.

48. Morán, *Imagen*, pp. 81–3.

49. Bottineau, p. 197.

50. BN fonds Espagne 378; there are several copies of this in Spain.

51. C. Fernández Duro, *El último Almirante de Castilla*, Madrid 1902.

52. A. Rodríguez Villa, *Don Diego Hurtado de Mendoza y Sandoval, Conde de la Corzana (1650–1720)*, Madrid 1907, p. 197.

53. AE:CPE 114 f.281.
54. Noailles, II, 158.
55. Robres, *Historia de las guerras . . .* , p. 228.
56. Details in Kamen, *War of Succession*, pp. 96–7.
57. Saint-Simon, *Mémoires*, VIII, 153.
58. San Felipe, p. 51.
59. Noailles, II, 186.
60. A. Morel-Fatio and H. Léonardon, eds, *Recueil des instructions données aux ambassadeurs*, vol.12, *Espagne*, Paris 1898, p. 8.
61. Baudrillart, I, 167.
62. Amelot to Louis XIV, 22 June 1705, AE:CPE 147 f.190.
63. Amelot to Louis XIV, 27 May 1705, AE:CPE 147 f.64.
64. A.M. de Boislisle, ed., *Correspondance des Contrôleurs Généraux des Finances avec les Intendants des Provinces*, 3 vols, Paris 1883, II, 499.
65. 'Mémoire du Roy concernant le Commerce', AN:AE, B¹ 771.
66. AE:CPE supplément II f.215.
67. Amelot to Torcy, 21 Nov. 1707, AE:CPE 171 f.69.
68. Louis XIV to Amelot, 18 Feb. 1709, in Girardot, *Correspondance*.
69. Parnell, *The War of the Succession*, chap. 3.
70. AGI Indiferente legs. 2530, 2634.
71. See Henry Kamen, 'The destruction of the Spanish silver fleet at Vigo in 1702', reprinted in *Crisis and change in early modern Spain*, Aldershot 1993.
72. Francis, *Peninsular war*, chap. 3.
73. Bottineau, p. 299.

CHAPTER TWO: THE WAR IN THE PENINSULA, 1704–1709

1. 'Reconnoissance de l'État present des Troupes', AE:CPE 119 ff.276–9.
2. AE:CPE 119.
3. Guerre, A¹ 1786 f.235.
4. Guerre, A¹ 1884 f.126.
5. Chamillart to marquis of Ribas, 26 Aug. 1704, Guerre A¹ 1786 f.125.
6. Letter of 23 Aug. 1703, in Saint-Simon, *Mémoires*, XII, 531.
7. Details in Kamen, *War of Succession*, pp. 62–7.
8. Cited in Noailles, II, 274.
9. Letter to duchess of Noailles, 28 July 1703, in M.A. Geffroy, ed., *Lettres inédites de la princesse des Ursins*, Paris 1859.

10. Albert-Octave de T'Serclaes Tilly (1646–1715) served in Spain from 1703, the year he became colonel of the Royal Guard. He was created grandee in 1705, and died in Barcelona of an illness in 1715.

11. Francisco Ronquillo Briceño, count of Gramedo, was president of the Council of Castile in 1705. His elder brother, Antonio, died in battle in 1710. On the Ronquillo family, see Janine Fayard, *Les membres du Conseil de Castille à l'époque moderne (1621–1746)*, Paris 1979, p. 277.

12. Cited in Noailles, II, 245.

13. Louis, count of Toulouse, was son of Louis XIV by Madame de Montespan; in this year he was aged twenty-seven.

14. The elder Schomberg, a Protestant, emigrated from France after Louis XIV revoked the Edict of Nantes in 1685 and settled in Ireland.

15. Petrie, *Berwick*, p. 176.

16. Francis, *Peninsular war*, p. 147.

17. Toby Bourke to Chamillart, 28 Aug. 1705, Guerre, A¹ 1886 f.295.

18. Narcis Feliu de la Peña, *Anales de Catalunya*, Barcelona 1709, III, 492.

19. Nuria Sales, *Senyors Bandolers*, Barcelona 1984, p. 158.

20. Audiencia of Catalonia to the Council of Castile, 29 Aug. 1697, ACA:CA 470.

21. Cited by F. Fernández-Armesto, in *Visiones de fin de siglo*, Madrid 1999, p. 80.

22. Joaquim Albareda, *Els catalans i Felip V. 1700–1705*, Barcelona 1993. See the same author's summary in *Història política, societat i cultura dels països catalans*, vol.5, Barcelona 1995, pp. 148–9.

23. Robres, *Historia de las guerras . . .* , p. 249.

24. AHN Consejos legs. 7240, 7243, 7244.

25. Fray Nicolás de Jesús Belando, *Historia civil de España desde el año de 1700 hasta el de 1733*, 3 vols, Madrid 1740–4, I, 207.

26. Archbishop to José de Grimaldo, 30 Sept. 1705, AHN Estado leg.264 f.6.

27. Melchor de Macanaz, *Regalías de los Señores Reyes de Aragon*, Madrid 1729, pp. 124–6.

28. José Manuel Miñana, *De bello rustico valentino*, in three books, translated into Castilian in the *Revue Hispanique*, 55 (1922), p. 456.

29. Cf. Kamen, *War of Succession*, pp. 275–8.

30. Villagarcía to José de Grimaldo, 17 Dec. 1705, AHN Estado leg.279 f.23.

31. The fall of Lleida can be followed in the letters of the bishop of Lleida and others in AHN Estado leg.264 ff.2, 4, 8, 28, 36.

32. Cited by Domínguez Ortiz, *Sociedad y estado*, p. 95.

33. Ibid., p. 47.

34. Letters of the king to Berwick, in AHN Estado leg.2460² no.8.

35. Tessé, *Lettres et Mémoires*, II, 220.

36. Parnell, *The War of the Succession*, p. 156.

37. Ibid., p. 169.

38. The total eclipse, of course, would have lasted only about two minutes.

39. Kamen, *War of Succession*, p. 291.

40. San Felipe, p. 107.

41. Baudrillart, I, 254, 262.

42. Tessé, *Lettres et Mémoires*, II, 164.

43. See Danvila y Collado, *El poder civil en Españā*, III, 536.

44. Details in Kamen, *War of Succession*, chap. 4.

45. The technical details of the changes are summarised in the useful essay by José Antonio Escudero, 'La reconstrucción de la administración central en el siglo XVIII', in his *Administración y estado en la España moderna*, Valladolid 1999.

46. Letter of 20 Aug. 1705, in Girardot, *Correspondance*.

47. AE:CPE 149 f.149.

48. AE:CPE 149 f.134.

49. AE:CPE 159 f.207.

50. Saint-Simon, *Mémoires*, XIII, 56.

51. Francis, *Peninsular war*, p. 226.

52. The three were the duke of Béjar, the count of Peñaranda and the count of Colmenar.

53. He was appointed head of the archduke's government in Barcelona, where he died in December 1707.

54. There are more names in 'Memoria de las personas que acompañaron el Estandarte del señor Archiduque', in A. de Valladares, *Semanario Erudito*, vol.7, p. 96.

55. Amelot to Louis XIV, 29 July 1706, AE:CPE 160 f.112.

56. Amelot to Louis XIV, 3 Aug. 1706, AE:CPE 160 f.151.

57. San Felipe, p. 116. San Felipe's anecdotes are not always to be believed.

58. Philip to Louis XIV, 27 Sept. 1706, Aranjuez, AHN Estado leg.2574 no.6.

59. She arrived in Guadalajara in May 1739. Immediately, Philip V arranged to see her (she was aunt of the queen, Elizabeth Farnese), and they spent three days together in the palace of the archbishop in Alcalá: *Crónica*, p. 202. She died the following year, 1740.

60. Marie Louise to Madame de Maintenon, Nov. 1706, Baudrillart, I, 272.

61. Baudrillart, I, 287.

62. Petrie, *Berwick*, p. 215.

63. *Crónica*, p. 64.

64. San Felipe, p. 140.

65. Letter to Torcy, 4 Mar. 1708, in M.A. Geffroy, ed., *Lettres inédites de la princesse des Ursins*.

66. Saint-Simon, *Mémoires*, XVIII, 70.

67. Philip to Louis XIV, 18 July 1707, and 6 Aug. 1708, in AHN Estado leg.2460² no.7.

68. Cited in Parnell, *The War of the Succession*, p. 257.

69. Berwick to Amelot, 21 May 1707, AE:CPE 176 f.103.

70. Baudrillart, II, 58 n.2.
71. Cf. Virginia León Sanz, *Entre Austrias y Borbones. El archiduque Charles y la monarquía de España (1700–1714)*, Madrid 1993.
72. 'Copia de los manuscritos de Macanaz', BUV MS.24.
73. Louis XIV to Amelot, 27 June 1707, in Girardot, *Correspondance*.
74. Ozon to Torcy, 17 Sept. 1704, AE:CPE 105 ff.50–4.
75. Cited in letter from Amelot, June 1707, AE:CPE 176 f.279.
76. Henry Kamen, *Philip of Spain*, London and New Haven 1997, p. 232.
77. This is not the place for a full or adequate discussion of this important law and its implications; see Kamen, *War of Succession*, chaps 10–13; and there are several recent studies in Spanish on the subject.
78. Archbishop to José de Grimaldo, 16 July 1707, AHN:E leg.320¹.
79. Some of the propaganda of the war years is studied in M.T. Pérez Picazo, *La publicística española*.
80. Isidre Planes, 'Sucessos fatales de esta Ciudad y Reyno de Valencia', BUV MS.456 f.12 vo.
81. Marquis of Villadarias to José de Grimaldo, Feb. 1714, AHN Estado leg.456.
82. San Felipe, p. 132.
83. On Xàtiva, see Kamen, *War of Succession*, pp. 294–5.
84. Carlos Sarthou Carreres, *Datos para la historia de Játiva*, 3 vols, Xàtiva 1933–5, I, 343–5.
85. Miñana, p. 511 (II, vii).
86. Cited in F.X. Borrull y Vilanova, *Fidelidad de la ciudad y reyno de Valencia*, Valencia 1810, p. 100.
87. Amelot to Louis XIV, 14 Jan. 1709, AE:CPE 189 f.38.
88. See Kamen, *War of Succession*, pp. 254–360.
89. San Felipe, p. 167.
90. There is an outline by Teófanes Egido in R. García-Villoslada, ed., *Historia de la Iglesia en España*, vol.IV, Madrid 1979, pp. 162–71.
91. Louis XIV to Amelot, 3 June 1709, in Girardot, *Correspondance*.
92. Letter of 30 July 1709, in Léopold-Collin, ed., *Lettres inédites de Mme la Princesse des Ursins à M. Le Maréchal de Villeroy*, Paris 1806.
93. AE:CPE 229 f.113.
94. Saint-Simon, *Mémoires*, XVIII, p. 81.
95. Letter of 1 Sept. 1709, in Geffroy, *Lettres inédites*.

CHAPTER THREE: THE LATER WAR YEARS, 1709–1715

1. Baudrillart, I, 341.
2. Louis XIV to Amelot, 26 June 1709, Girardot, *Correspondance*.
3. Baudrillart, I, 350.

4. Philip to Bergeyck, 24 Mar. 1710, AHN Estado leg. 2574 no.15.

5. Coxe, II, 24.

6. Ibid., II, 32.

7. In AGS Gracia y Justicia leg. 1021 antiguo, there are copies of letters from Medi-naceli to the ambassador of Tuscany (a supporter of the archduke) in the United Provinces; they could have been the reason for his arrest.

8. Letter written in Genoa in Aug. 1710; AHN Estado leg. 2989.

9. Marie Louise to Louis XIV, Madrid, 1 Aug. 1710, AHN Estado leg. 2574 no.35.

10. Coxe, II, 37.

11. Bottineau, p. 320.

12. King to Marshal Noailles, Corella, 27 June 1711, AHN Estado leg. 2460¹ no.20.

13. San Felipe, p. 20.

14. *Crónica*, p. 78.

15. Morán, *Imagen*, p. 50.

16. Ibid., p. 49.

17. Baudrillart, I, 503.

18. Ibid., 273, 435.

19. Cited Egido, *Opinión*, p. 94.

20. *Respuesta de un amigo a otro que le pregunta por el fin que vendrán a tener nuestros males en España*, printed by V. Palacio Atard in *Anuario de la Historia del Derecho Español*, XVIII, 1947.

21. Cf. Escudero, *Administracíon*, pp. 147–8.

22. The twenty-eight cities in the Cortes included two from Valencia and five from Aragon. For Valencia, the towns were Valencia and Peñíscola; for Aragón, they were Saragossa, Tarazona, Calatayud, Borja, Fraga; see P. Molas, 'La Cortes de Castilla y León en el siglo XVIII', *Las Cortes de Castilla y León en la edad moderna*, Valladolid 1989.

23. Cf. Escudero, *Administracíon*, pp. 149–56.

24. AE:CPE 228 f.130.

25. The document, which is still unpublished, can be seen in BN MS.10.745; there are various copies.

26. 'Regalism', in a Church context, refers in Spain to the affirmation of royal power over the Church: see the studies by A. Domínguez Ortiz and by Teófanes Egido, in chapters 2 and 3 of the *Historia de la Iglesia en España*, ed. R. García-Villoslada, vol.IV, Madrid 1979.

27. There is a useful summary of this document by Teófanes Egido, in the *Historia de la Inquisición en España y América*, ed. J. Pérez Villanueva and B. Escandell Bonet, Madrid 1984, I, pp. 1237–47.

28. Macanaz to Grimaldo, 14 Mar. 1722, BNac MS.767 f.1.

29. 'It is not possible to speak unequivocally of Catalan support for the archduke': J.M. Torras i Ribé, 'Reflexions sobre l'actitud dels pobles i estaments catalans durant la Guerra de Successió', *Pedralbes*, 1, 1981, p. 191.

30. Ibid., p. 198.

31. The best study of the question is by J.M. Torras i Ribé, *Els municipis*. Cf. also Albareda in *Història política*, p. 149: 'One cannot speak of pro-Habsburg or of pro-Bourbon municipalities. Specific local conditions determined the attitudes people took.'

32. Cited by Albareda, in *Història política*, p. 167.

33. 'The uprising of 1705 was not anti-Castilian': ibid., p. 149.

34. Núria Sales, *Els Botiflers 1705–1714*, Barcelona 1981.

35. Cf. Rosa Mª Alabrús, 'La publicística de la guerra', *L'Avenç*, 206, Sept. 1996.

36. Cited in Francis, *Peninsular war*, p. 363.

37. Ibid., p. 364.

38. Coxe, II, 102.

39. Lynch, *Bourbon Spain*, p. 43.

40. Cited in Petrie, *Berwick*, p. 252.

41. Berwick to king, Perpignan, 30 June 1714, AHN Estado leg. 2733 no.2.

42. Baudrillart, I, 653.

43. Philip V to Louis XIV, 2 Apr. 1715, ibid., I, 654.

44. The figures are Berwick's.

45. Albertí, *L'Onze de Setembre*, p. 373.

46. Petrie, *Berwick*, p. 257.

47. J. Albareda, 'Repressión y disidencia en la Cataluña borbónica (1714–1725)', in *Disidencias y exilios en la España moderna*, Alicante 1997.

48. Cited in Bottineau, p. 190.

49. *Crónica*, pp. 48–9.

50. Baudrillart, I, 101.

51. Marie Louise to Philip, 1 Sept. 1702, in Louville, p. 325.

52. Cited in Philippe Erlanger, *Philippe V d'Espagne. Un roi baroque esclave des femmes*, Paris 1978.

53. Gramont to Louis XIV, AE:CPE 146 f.235.

54. Notably by Baudrillart, whom other historians have followed. The image of Philip in Lynch, *Bourbon Spain*, p. 67, is also based on Baudrillart; he says that the king was 'driven by two compulsions, sex and religion, he spent his nights, and much of his days, in constant transit between his wife and his confessor, torn between desire and guilt, a comic figure easily subject to conjugal blackmail'.

55. Coxe, II, 58, 65.

56. Egido, *Opinión*, p. 96.

57. Saint-Simon, *Mémoires*, XI, 223.

58. Baudrillart, I, 258.

59. Marie Louise to Vittorio Amedeo, 31 Jan. 1708, AHN Estado leg. 2574 no.27.

60. Marie Louise to Louis XIV, 28 Nov. 1710, AHN Estado leg. 2574 no.30.

61. See the comments by Gregorio Marañón on the medical reports, in Danvila, *El reinado relámpago*, p. 444.

62. Louville, I, 173.
63. Saint-Simon was not in Spain at that time, and knew nothing of the circumstances of the death of Marie Louise. Unfortunately the portrait of Philip V offered by Lynch in his fine book, *Bourbon Spain*, pp. 67–9, is based almost wholly on the exaggerations of Saint-Simon.
64. Coxe, II, 127.
65. Brancas to Torcy, AE:CPE 228.
66. AE:CPE 237 f.99.
67. Francesco Giudice, prince of Cellamare, was born in Naples in 1647, became cardinal in 1690 and interim viceroy of Sicily in 1701.
68. The extracts cited here come from the original letters in AHN Estado leg. 2460² no.5.
69. Baudrillart, I, 622.
70. Robinet to José de Grimaldo, 6 July 1712, AHN Estado leg. 413.
71. Bottineau, p. 398 n.111.
72. Asso, *Historia*, p. 207.
73. Archbishop to José de Grimaldo, 26 Sept. 1705, AHN Estado leg. 264 f.4.
74. The case is documented in Ramón Castel de la Virgen María, *Mi patria. Apuntes geográficos e históricos de Arén*, Lleida 1923.
75. Vicente Pérez Moreda, *Las crisis de mortalidad en la España interior, siglos XVI–XIX*, Madrid 1980, p. 329.
76. Miguel Rodríguez Cancho, *La villa de Cáceres en el siglo XVIII*, Cáceres 1981, pp. 80–1.
77. Ramón Sánchez González, *Economía y sociedad en al Antiguo Régimen. La comarca de La Sagra en el siglo XVIII*, Toledo 1991, p. 31.
78. Príncipe Pío to Miguel Fernández Durán, 7 Mar. 1716, AGS Guerra Moderna leg. 1614.
79. Archivo del Ministerio de Hacienda, Consejo de Castilla, impresos, vol.6549 f.8.
80. Cited in Cepeda Adán, *El Madrid de Felipe V*, p. 8.
81. Vilar, *La Catalogue*, I, 671.
82. Pierre Vilar, *Le manual de la Companya Nova de Gibraltar*, Paris 1963, p. 80.
83. Gaspar Melchor de Jovellanos, *Informe de la Sociedad Económica de Madrid . . . en el expediente de Ley Agraria*, Palma 1814, p. 6.
84. Pedro Rodríguez de Campomanes, *Discurso sobre la educación popular de los artesanos y su fomento*, Madrid 1775, p. 421.

CHAPTER FOUR: ELIZABETH FARNESE, 1715–1723

1. Cited in Armstrong, *Elizabeth Farnese*, pp. 21–2.
2. Ibid., p. 40.

3. Bottineau, p. 368.
4. See, for example, the opinion of the Grand Duke of Tuscany in the reign of Charles II, in Angel Sánchez Rivero, ed., *Viaje de Cosme de Médicis por España y Portugal (1668–1669)*, 2 vols, Madrid, n.d.
5. Cited Bottineau, p. 367.
6. For the analysis that follows, I am grateful for the information supplied during conversations with medical friends. A comprehensive guide to depressive disorders, on which I have drawn, is available at the moment on the Internet at http://www.pslgroup.com/DEPRESSION.HTM.
7. This is the suggestion of Gregorio Marañón, in a letter on the case of Philip V to Elías Torme, cited by the latter in his article, 'Centenario de Felipe V', pp. 415–17. In his analysis, Marañón mentions only the aspect of 'melancholy, inherited through his family, with a final phase of madness'.
8. Coxe, II, 191. George Bubb served as minister for Britain in Spain until 1717; from the year 1720, when he came into an inheritance in England, he changed his surname to Dodington.
9. Escudero, *Administracíon*, p. 161.
10. José Patiño was born in Milan in 1666; he and his brother Baltasar (later marquis of Castelar) began their careers in the service of Spain during the War of Succession.
11. Cited in Escudero, *Administracíon*, p. 161.
12. Coxe, II, 189.
13. Ibid., 151.
14. Ibid., 177.
15. James III was the son of James II, the Catholic king who lost the throne of Britain in the Revolution of 1688; his dynasty, the Stuarts, continued to claim their rights to the throne.
16. 'Jacobite' comes from the Latin for James, 'Jacobus'.
17. Coxe, II, 214.
18. Bubb to Stanhope, July 1716, in Coxe, II, 170.
19. Coxe, II, 187.
20. Ragnhild Hatton, *George I*, London 1978, p. 225.
21. Ministerio de Hacienda, Ordenes Generales de Rentas, vol.2 f.423.
22. Bernardo de Ulloa, *Restablecimiento de la fábricas y comercio español*, 2 vols, Madrid 1740, I, 123.
23. Marquis of Villadarias to Grimaldo, 19 Feb. 1714, AHN Estado leg.456.
24. J.M. Torras i Ribé, 'L'etapa de provisionalitat institucional borbònica en els municipis catalans durant la Guerra de Successió (1707–1716)', *Pedralbes*, no.2, 1982, p. 146.
25. Philip to Louis XIV, El Pardo, 2 Oct. 1714, AHN Estado leg. 2460² no.5/1.
26. Príncipe Pío, marquis of Castelrodrigo, to the government, 31 Dec. 1715, AGS Guerra Moderna leg.1614.

27. 'Estado de los pagos del exercito de Cathaluña', AGS Guerra Moderna leg.1610.
28. Nicolás Hinojosa to José de Grimaldo, 6 Oct. 1715, AGS Guerra Moderna leg.1811.
29. Patiño to Miguel Durán, 8 Apr. 1715, AGS Guerra Moderna leg.1815.
30. Report from the intendant Pedrajas, 5 Feb. 1717, AGS Guerra Moderna leg.1622.
31. Letter of 28 May 1718, AGS Guerra Moderna leg.1636.
32. Budgets in AGS Guerra Moderna leg.2362.
33. Enrique Giménez López, 'La nueva planta y la corona de Aragon', *Torre de los Lujanes*, 38, Feb. 1999, p. 86.
34. H. Kamen, *The Phoenix and the Flame. Catalonia and the Counter Reformation*, London and New Haven 1993, p. 373.
35. See the pages on this subject in Manuel Ardit, Albert Balcells, Núria Sales, *Història dels Països Catalans, de 1714 a 1975*, Barcelona 1980, pp. 39–46.
36. In Valencia, 'the decline of Catalan as a literary language derives from the sixteenth century': *Història del País Valencià*, ed. Manuel Ardit, Barcelona 1990, p. 172.
37. J.M. Rodríguez Gordillo, 'Una aportación al estudio de la expansión de la renta del tabaco en el siglo XVIII', offprint from *Historia, Instituciones, Documentos*, Seville 1978.
38. 'The establishment of Intendants in early Bourbon Spain', in Henry Kamen, *Crisis and change in early modern Spain*, Aldershot 1993.
39. AE:CPE 119 f.213.
40. AGS Guerra Moderna leg.2362, 'Gastos generales de los ejércitos'.
41. Bergeyck to Pontchartrain, 3 Apr. 1713, AN: AE, B¹ 776.
42. For example, the contract cited by Mercader, *Felip V*, p. 220. Pages 217–32 of his book give an excellent picture of the contracts negotiated by Patiño.
43. Coxe, II, 199.
44. Ibid., 177.
45. Cf. M.A. Alonso Aguilera, *La conquista y el dominio español de Cerdeña (1717–1720)*, Valladolid 1977, pp. 49–56.
46. Cited by D. Ozanam, in *Historia de España Menéndez Pidal*, XXIX, i, 589.
47. Dr M. Weissman, 'The changing rate of major depression', *Journal of the American Medical Association* (2 Dec. 1992), vol.268 (21), pp. 3098–105.
48. Baudrillart, II, 248.
49. Coxe, II, 221.
50. Armstrong, *Elizabeth Farnese*, p. 109.
51. It was not, of course, a 'party' in the modern sense of the word, but simply a number of people who shared a certain political tendency.
52. See Egido, *Opinión*, p. 278.
53. Antonio Giuseppe del Giudice, 3rd prince of Cellamare and 3rd duke of Giovenazzo: see Ozanam, *Les diplomates*, p. 276.
54. Baudrillart, II, 328.

55. *Enciclopedia General Ilustrada del País Vasco. Cuerpo A. Diccionario*, San Sebastian 1982, vol.XIII, p. 200.

56. Petrie, *Berwick*, p. 323.

57. Alberoni to the Grand Duke of Parma, Jan. 1719, in Armstrong, *Elizabeth Farnese*, p. 118.

58. 'Declaration faite par le roy Catholique', AHN Estado leg. 2819.

59. A. Meijide Pardo, *La invasión inglesa de Galicia en 1719*, Santiago 1970.

60. Ibid., p. 29.

61. James to Philip, La Coruña, 21 Apr. 1719, AHN Estado leg. 2478 no.3.

62. Bruce Lenman, *The Jacobite risings in Britain 1689–1746*, London 1980, p. 191.

63. Alberoni went to Italy, where he entered the papal service, and drained the marshes of Romagna; he died in Rome in 1752 aged eighty-eight.

64. Baudrillart, II, 415.

65. Egido, *Opinión*, p. 129.

66. San Felipe, p. 319.

67. AHN Estado leg. 2732 nos 1–32.

68. 'Il est de l'intérêt des Espagnols de la [Ceuta] bien défendre, car sans elle le prétexte de la Bulle de la Croissade cesserait et avec elle le profit immense qu'elle rapporte au Roi': *Voyage du Père Labat en Espagne 1705–6*, Paris 1927, p. 232.

69. Coxe, II, 192. This is my only authority for the king's presence at an *auto de fe*.

70. Louville, I, 124.

71. *Crónica*, p. 100.

72. The best analysis of these events is by Teófanes Egido, in the *Historia de la Inquisición en España y América*, ed. J. Pérez Villanueva and B. Escandell Bonet, Madrid 1984, vol.I, pp. 1394–404.

73. AHN Inquisición legs. 4755–8.

74. Hatton, *George I*, p. 225.

75. In 1741, talking to the French ambassador: Baudrillart, V, 43.

76. Cited by Lynch, *Bourbon Spain*, p. 80.

77. The timetable given by Alberoni refers to the year 1715 and is given in Baudrillart, II, 416, n.1. The timetable given by Saint-Simon is in Saint-Simon 1880, p. 365. There are small discrepancies between the two timetables.

78. Coxe, II, 176.

79. According to Alberoni, the king in 1715 had supper at 8 p.m. and went to bed at 10.30 p.m.

80. Saint-Simon 1880, pp. 202, 357.

81. Ibid., p. 357.

82. Ibid., pp. 178, 227, 297.

83. *Crónica*, p. 109.

84. Saint-Simon 1880, p. 392.

CHAPTER FIVE: ABDICATION AND SECOND REIGN, 1724–1729

1. Baudrillart, II, 472.
2. AHN Estado leg. 2460² no.3.
3. AHN Estado leg. 2460¹ no.17. This text, from the original document, does not agree with that published in some books.
4. Cited by Egido, *Opinión*, p. 144 n.190.
5. This is the convincing argument of Baudrillart, III.
6. AHN Estado leg. 2460² no.6.
7. Baudrillart, II, 563.
8. Dr Myrna Weissman, in the *Journal of the American Medical Association*, 12 May 1999.
9. Cited in Armstrong, *Elizabeth Farnese*, p. 160.
10. *Crónica*, p. 90.
11. Cited in Bottineau, p. 419.
12. M.J. Quesada Martín, in *Historia de España Menéndez Pidal*, XXIV, ii, 348.
13. George Kubler and M. Soria, *Art and architecture in Spain and Portugal and their American dominions, 1500–1800*, Harmondsworth 1959, p. 44.
14. Morán, *Imagen*, pp. 61–6.
15. Stanhope, a distant relative of James, earl of Stanhope, served briefly in 1717–18 as British minister in Spain, and from 1720 as ambassador in Madrid until 1727; he returned in 1729 to negotiate the treaty of Seville. In 1730 he was created earl of Harrington.
16. Cited in Lynch, *Bourbon Spain*, p. 80.
17. According to a note written by the king, 'Liste de gens qu'il nous faudra avec nous', in AHN Estado leg. 2460² no.11, he required in all only twenty-four staff to accompany himself and the queen into retirement. In another note, the queen added that they would also need twenty guards for the grounds and perhaps some men to help the gardener.
18. José de Grimaldo, from Vizcaya, was born in 1660, became secretary for War in 1705 and marquis in 1714.
19. Baudrillart, III, 26.
20. Egido, *Opinión*, p. 146.
21. Coxe, II, 322.
22. *Crónica*, p. 120.
23. Egido, *Opinión*, p. 142.
24. Cited in Lynch, *Bourbon Spain*, p. 83.
25. Egido, *Opinión*, p. 145.
26. Danvila, *Reinado relámpago*, p. 301.
27. Baudrillart, III, 53.
28. Barcelona, Tarragona, Lleida, Girona, Tortosa and Cervera.

29. AHN Estado leg. 2530 no.139.
30. Cited in Egido, *Opinión*, p. 282.
31. Cf. Egido: 'The loss of respect for king Philip, who had been sacred till then, was the central fact marking the change of direction in criticisms made against the government', ibid., p. 148.
32. Baudrillart, III, 126.
33. The role of Gibraltar in the Spanish diplomacy of the period is studied by D. Gómez Molleda, *Gibraltar. Una contienda diplomática en el reinado de Philip V*, Madrid 1953. She observes that 'the recovery of Gibraltar became for Philip an obsession'.
34. AHN Estado leg. 2676: Louise's household costs in 1725 in Vincennes amounted to 255,343 livres a year.
35. Armstrong, *Elizabeth Farnese*, p. 184.
36. Cited in Béthencourt, 1954, p. 32, n.9.
37. Egido, *Opinión*, p. 153.
38. In Lynch, *Bourbon Spain*, p. 89.
39. Coxe, III, 32.
40. Cited in Lynch, *Bourbon Spain*, p. 89.
41. Coxe, II, 73.
42. See the discussion in Baudrillart, I, 509.
43. Ibid., III, 357.
44. Ibid., 279.
45. Coxe, III, 9.
46. Baudrillart, III, 359.
47. Estado leg. 2672.
48. *Crónica*, p. 140.
49. Coxe, III, 44.
50. What follows comes from Baudrillart, III, 415.
51. This documentation is in AHN Estado leg. 2460^1 no.16.
52. Article by Dr Beebe, 'Bulimia nervosa and depression: a theoretical and clinical appraisal', *British Journal of Clinical Psychology* (Sept. 1994), vol.33, pt 3, pp. 259–76; also the study by Dr Simpson and other researchers from Johns Hopkins University, 'Bipolar II affective disorder in eating disorder inpatients', *Journal of Nervous and Mental Diseases* (Nov. 1992), vol.180 (11), pp. 719–22.
53. Cited in Baudrillart, III, 423.
54. Coxe, III, 84.
55. Baudrillart, III, 467.
56. AHN Estado leg. 2460^2 no.14 doc.19.
57. Coxe, III, 85.
58. 'Memorias' of José del Camporaso, in San Felipe, p. 441.

59. Coxe, III, 88.
60. 'Memorias' of José del Camporaso, in San Felipe, p. 441.

CHAPTER SIX: ANDALUCIAN INTERLUDE, 1729–1733

1. There is a summary in José Jurado Sánchez, 'La visita de Philip V y su corte', *Actas II Congreso Historia de Andalucia*.
2. León, *Lustro real*, p. 20.
3. Francisco Aguilar Piñal, *Historia de Sevilla: Siglo XVIII*, Seville 1982, p. 18.
4. AHN Estado leg. 2572 no.59.
5. Cited in Aguilar Piñal, *Historia de Sevilla*, p. 21.
6. 'Memorias' of José del Camporaso, in San Felipe, p. 444.
7. Coxe, III, 129.
8. Some details in Walker, *Spanish politics*, pp. 95–9.
9. Egido, *Opinión*, p. 163.
10. Cited in Lynch, *Bourbon Spain*, p. 125.
11. Stanhope was rewarded in 1730 for his work on the treaty with the title of earl of Harrington.
12. In March 1730: Baudrillart, IV, 25 n.1.
13. Ibid., 29.
14. 'Jornada de los Reyes a la frontera de Andalucia', AHN Estado leg. 2551 no.10.
15. *Crónica*, p. 172.
16. Jurado Sánchez, 'Los viajes reales . . .', p. 556.
17. For some information on 'theriac', see the entry 'Theriak', in *Lexikon des Mittelalters*, Band VIII, Munich 1997, p. 678.
18. Baudrillart, IV, 53.
19. Ibid., 54.
20. Béthencourt, 1954, p. 58.
21. J. Cebrián García, *La sátira política en 1729*, Jérez de la Frontera 1982, p. 45.
22. A brief but unsuccessful attempt to return the Casa de la Contratación to Seville was made in 1725: A. García-Baquero, *Cádiz y el Atlántico (1717–1778)*, 2 vols, Seville 1976, I, 108.
23. Cited in Lynch, *Bourbon Spain*, p. 150.
24. Béthencourt, 1958, p. 50.
25. Baudrillart, IV, 79.
26. Cited in ibid., II, 415.
27. Coxe, III, 84.
28. Saint-Simon 1880, p. 357.
29. Baudrillart, IV, 85.
30. Cited in Lynch, *Bourbon Spain*, p. 72.

31. Cited by León, *Lustro real*, p. 100.
32. Baudrillart, IV, 109.
33. Danvila y Collado, *Reinado de Charles III*, vol.I, Madrid 1892, p. 50.
34. The original letters of Philip and Elizabeth to Charles are in AHN Estado leg. 2732 nos 61–109.
35. Keene to Newcastle, 14 May 1732, in Armstrong, *Elizabeth Farnese*, p. 273.
36. Baudrillart, IV, 150–1.
37. Cited in Lynch, *Bourbon Spain*, p. 71.
38. Keene to Newcastle, 24 Oct. 1732, in Armstrong, *Elizabeth Farnese*, p. 289.
39. Coxe, III, 104.
40. 'Memorias' of José del Camporaso, in San Felipe, p. 506.
41. *Crónica*, p. 180.
42. Béthencourt, 1998, p. 379.
43. Cited in Coxe, III, 105.
44. Armstrong, *Elizabeth Farnese*, p. 295.

CHAPTER SEVEN: THE YEARS OF CRISIS, 1734–1746

1. Danvila y Collado, *Charles III*, I, 95.
2. Armstrong, *Elizabeth Farnese*, p. 313.
3. Coxe, III, 114.
4. Cited in Béthencourt, 1954, p. 81 n.14.
5. *Crónica*, pp. 195–8.
6. Desdevises du Dézert, *L'Espagne de l'Ancien Régime*, I, 178.
7. 'Relato del incendio del Alcázar' by the marquis of la Torrecilla, printed in Cepeda Adán, *El Madrid de Felipe V*, pp. 35–40.
8. Keene, 27 Dec. 1734, cited in Armstrong, *Elizabeth Farnese*, p. 322 n.1.
9. Juvarra to Patiño, 9 Nov. 1735, *Filippo Juvarra a Madrid*, Madrid 1978, p. 21.
10. Bottineau, p. 597.
11. *Filippo Juvarra a Madrid*, p. 74.
12. Ibid., p. 82.
13. Bottineau, p. 478.
14. See the excellent study by Margarita Torrione, 'Farinelli en la corte de Felipe V', *Torre de los Lujanes*, 38, 1999, p. 123.
15. Ibid., p. 126.
16. Ibid., p. 131.
17. Farinelli continued his career with Ferdinand VI and Barbara of Braganza, left Madrid in 1759 when Charles III succeeded to the throne, and retired to Bologna, where he died in 1782.
18. A. Martín Moreno, *Historia de la música española. IV: Siglo XVIII*, Madrid 1985, p. 353.

19. Cited in Escudero, *Administracíon*, p. 169.

20. Cited in Armstrong, *Elizabeth Farnese*, p. 323.

21. Keene to Newcastle, 12 May 1734, in ibid., p. 325.

22. The distinctive privilege of a grandee was being allowed to keep his hat on in the king's presence.

23. Coxe, III, 127.

24. Baudrillart, IV, 369.

25. Egido, *Opinión*, p. 116.

26. Ibid., p. 117.

27. Armstrong, *Elizabeth Farnese*, p. 340.

28. Real Academia de la Historia, Madrid, MS. Est.24 gr.5ª. B no.128 f.31.

29. Cited by Lynch, *Bourbon Spain*, p. 113.

30. J. Canga Argüelles, *Diccionario de Hacienda*, 2 vols, Madrid 1833–4, I, 495.

31. Granada to the Council, 12 Oct. 1734, AGS Secretaría de Hacienda leg.87.

32. '1734–1739 were the biggest subsistence crises in the whole century': Ramón Sánchez González, *Economía y sociedad en al Antiguo Régimen. La comarca de La Sagra en el siglo XVIII*, Toledo 1991, p. 71.

33. AGS Secretaría de Hacienda leg.2.

34. BN MS.6952 f.24.

35. AGS Secretaría de Hacienda leg.396.

36. 'Deudas hasta fin de 1739', 31 Jan. 1740, in AGS Secretaría de Hacienda leg. 398.

37. J.M. Alegre, *Las relaciones hispano-danesas en la primera mitad del siglo XVIII*, Madrid 1978, pp. 213–37.

38. Baudrillart, V, 131.

39. Ibid., 134.

40. Ibid., 207.

41. Ibid., 145.

42. Cited in Escudero, *Administracíon*, p. 171.

43. Armstrong, *Elizabeth Farnese*, p. 374.

44. Ibid., p. 382.

45. Coxe, III, 193.

46. Cited in Lynch, *Bourbon Spain*, p. 72.

47. MS of the Biblioteca Nacional, Madrid, cited by Carlos Seco in San Felipe, p. xxxi n.96.

48. Cited in Lynch, *Bourbon Spain*, p. 72.

49. Baudrillart, V, 211.

50. Ibid., 409.

51. Ibid., 441.

52. Marañón, in Torme, 'Centenario de Felipe V', p. 416.

53. Baudrillart, V, 445.

54. AHN Estado leg. 2511.

55. Alegre, *Las relaciones hispano-danesas*, p. 278.
56. Armstrong, *Elizabeth Farnese*, p. 392.
57. Egido, *Opinión*, p. 113.
58. Egido, *Sátiras políticas*, p. 234.
59. Aguilar Piñal, *Sevilla*, p. 31.

CHAPTER EIGHT: THE SPAIN OF PHILIP V

1. For a recent discussion, see R.G. Asch and H. Duchhardt, *Der Absolutismus – ein Mythos? Strukturwandel Monarchischer Herrschaft in West- und Mitteleuropa (c.1550–1700)*, Cologne 1996.
2. Cf. Gunner Lind, in Wolfgang Reinhard, ed., *Power elites and state building*, Oxford 1996, pp. 139–40.
3. Much of our information on the new administrative class comes from the researches of Pere Molas.
4. Desdevises du Dézert, *L'Espagne de l'Ancien Régime*, I, 18–25; Kamen, *Later seventeenth century*, pp. 14–15.
5. See Henry Kamen, 'Melchor de Macanaz and the foundations of Bourbon power in Spain', *Crisis and change in early modern Spain*, Aldershot 1993.
6. Zavala, *Clandestinidad*, p. 141.
7. Agustín López de Mendoza y Pons, conde de Robres, *Historia de las guerras civiles de España* (written in 1709), Saragossa 1882, p. 367.
8. Cited Egido, *Opinión*, p. 262.
9. Cited by Molas in 'Las Cortes de Castilla y León', p. 169.
10. According to Fénelon, 'the power of the king must be limited by the Estates General, the nobles and the leading citizens': Roland Mousnier, 'Les idées politiques de Fénelon', in *La plume, la faucille et le marteau*, Paris 1970, p. 85.
11. In Louville, I, 55.
12. P. Junquera, 'Las aventuras de Telemaco. Tres series de tapices del Patrimonio Nacional', *Reales Sitios*, 1977, no.52.
13. Cited Bottineau, p. 185.
14. 'Ce qu'on doit recommander au Prince quand il sera Roy', AHN Estado leg. 2460² no.4.
15. Didier Ozanam: in *Historia de España Menéndez Pidal*, XXIX, i, p. 447; Pere Molas in *Historia General Rialp*, X-2, p. 106.
16. The marquises of Beretti-Landi and of Monteleón, and the prince of Cellamare. On these and other diplomats of the period, see the excellent work by Didier Ozanam, *Les diplomates espagnols*.
17. San Felipe, p. 355.
18. Egido, *Opinión*, p. 168.

19. The best study on the subject is by Iris Zavala, *Clandestinidad*.

20. Kamen, *Later seventeenth century*, p. 318.

21. 'During the reign of Philip V an infinite number of leaflets on political themes was published, but none appears to have been censored': Zavala, p. 316.

22. Abbé de Vayrac, *État présent de l'Espagne*, 3 vols, Amsterdam 1719, I, 31.

23. Cited by Egido, *Opinión*, p. 31.

24. See Henry Kamen, *Early modern European society*, London 2000, chapter 9.

25. 'It was not the popular classes that dedicated themselves to the task of "popular" criticism', Egido, *Opinión*, p. 46.

26. Paul-J. Guinard, *La presse espagnole de 1737 à 1791*, Paris 1973, p. 115.

27. The thesis by Rosa Maria Alabrús Iglesias, on 'Pensament politic i opinió a la Catalunya moderna 1652–1759', dated 1995, on this theme, should shortly be published.

28. See the interesting study by Ernest Lluch, *La Catalunya vençuda*, p. 55; the book extends its survey to the first half of the eighteenth century.

29. Examples cited in I.A.A. Thompson, 'Castile, Spain and the monarchy', in R.L. Kagan and G. Parker, eds, *Spain, Europe and the Atlantic world*, Cambridge 1995, p. 139.

30. Egido, *Opinión*, section 3.

31. Cited in ibid., p. 283.

32. Earl J. Hamilton, *War and prices in Spain 1651–1800*, Cambridge, Mass., 1947, pp. 136–51.

33. Ibid., p. 150.

34. J. Nadal Farreras, *La introducción del catastro en Gerona*, Barcelona 1971, pp. 92–3.

35. Details in *España en el siglo XVIII*, ed., Roberto Fernández, pp. 35, 306, 446–9, 637.

36. See the fundamental discussion by Francisco Bustelo, in *Historia de España Menéndez Pidal*, Madrid 1993, vol.XXVIII, pp. 509–12, 531–3.

37. Manuel Ardit, in *Història del País Valencià*, Barcelona 1990, pp. 55–8.

38. See the graphs in G. Anes, *Las crisis agrarias en la España moderna*, Madrid 1970.

39. Cf. the comments of Fernández, in *España en el siglo XVIII*, p. 39.

40. Agustín González Enciso, *Estado e industria en el siglo XVIII: la fábrica de Guadalajara*, Madrid 1980.

41. There are figures in C.R. Phillips and W.D. Phillips, *Spain's Golden Fleece*, Baltimore 1997, appendix 1.

42. *Theórica y práctica de comercio y marina*, Madrid 1742. There is an excellent recent study by Reyes Fernández Durán, *Gerónimo de Uztáriz (1670–1732). Una política económica para Felipe V*, Madrid 1999.

43. *Representación al Rey N. Señor D. Phelipe V, dirigida al mas seguro aumento del real erario*, Madrid 1732, p. 174.

44. *Restablecimiento de las Fábricas y comercio español*, 2 vols, Madrid 1740.

45. Gaston Rambert, 'La France et la politique commerciale de l'Espagne au 18e siècle', *Revue d'Histoire Moderne et Contemporaine*, 6, 1959.

46. There is a good summary of these themes in chapter 5 of Bottineau, *Les Bourbons*.

47. 'Faltan casi por completo en la legislación de aquel monarca, normas y estímulos': Domínguez Ortiz, *Sociedad y estado*, p. 116.

48. Bottineau, p. 678.

49. Cf. ibid., pp. 331–2.

50. *Crónica*, p. 183.

51. In a biography like this it is not possible to enter into discussion of the importance of Mayáns, who has been studied in several magisterial works by Antonio Mestre.

52. Cited in Cepeda Adán, *El Madrid de Felipe V*, p. 26.

53. Both cited by Zavala, *Clandestinidad*, pp. 143, 362.

54. Cited in María Rosa Pérez Estévez, *El problema de los vagos en la España del siglo XVIII*, Madrid 1976, p. 66.

55. Ibid., p. 207.

56. William J. Callahan, *La Santa y Real Hermandad del Refugio y Piedad de Madrid 1618–1832*, Madrid 1980, p. 106.

57. Cited in ibid., p. 14.

58. Pierre Vilar, 'Structures de la société espagnole vers 1750', in *Mélanges à la mémoire de Jean Sarrailh*, Paris 1966, p. 440.

59. V. Palacio Atard, 'Algo más sobre el abastecimiento de Madrid en el siglo XVIII', *Anales de Madrid*, 1970, p. 255. Cf. also Callahan, *Santa*, p. 14.

60. Macanaz to Ferdinand VI, Paris, 4 Aug. 1746, AHN Estado leg. 2721.

61. Cited by Antonio Mestre, 'La historiografía española del siglo XVIII', *Coloquio Internacional Carlos III y su siglo. Actas, tomo I*, Madrid 1990, p. 39.

alcabala	Castilian sales tax, normally levied at about 10 per cent of value
arbitrista	a writer, mainly of the seventeenth century, who drew up *arbitrios* or proposals for economic and political reform
asiento	a contract, usually in finance; used here specifically of the contract agreed by the Spanish government allowing the British to send an annual trading ship to America
brazo real	the noble estate in the Cortes of the realms of the Crown of Aragon (*braç reial* in Catalan)
Consell de Cent	the city council of Barcelona
conseller en cap	chief councillor of the city council of Barcelona
conversos	Christianised Jews or their descendants
Cortes	the provincial parliaments of the realms of Spain ('Corts' in Catalan)
Despacho	select committee of ministers in charge of government
Diputació	the government of Catalonia before 1714, consisting of deputies (Diputats) appointed from each estate of the Corts
escudos	originally a gold coin, in this period the standard unit of account in royal finances (in 1734 an escudo was worth 2s. 6d. of English money of the time)
fueros	the laws and privileges of towns and provinces, used here specially of the laws of the provinces of the Crown of Aragon
Infante/a	form of address for children of the Spanish royal family
jurat en cap	in Catalonia, chief town councillor
regalism	political doctrine stressing the privileges of the crown
tercios	Castilian troop formation

SELECT BIBLIOGRAPHY

In the last few decades of the twentieth century considerable progress was made in research on the previously neglected reign of Philip V, but a great deal remains to be done. The documentary sources are very rich – mainly in French, Italian and Spanish archives, but also in state archives of other European states (Great Britain, Austria) – and virtually unexplored. French scholars, notably Baudrillart and Bottineau, have made a fundamental and pioneering contribution; without their work, the present biography could not have been written. The old work by William Coxe, based mainly on British diplomatic papers, continues to be essential (because the original English edition is unavailable in Spain, the quotations used in my book are translated from the Spanish version, which is the work cited in the footnotes). Valuable work has been done by Spanish historians on the internal history of Spain. The most useful general survey of the period is that by Domínguez Ortiz; in English the best survey is that by John Lynch. Pere Molas, in the items listed below, offers an up-to-date summary of political and administrative history, themes to which he has made a fundamental contribution. In several studies that are cited throughout this book, on politics, the press and the Church, Teófanes Egido has established himself as the leading specialist on the history of the early eighteenth century. The politics of Catalonia has been studied in important books by Joan Mercader Riba, Josep Maria Torres i Ribé, Joaquim Albareda and others. Among books published during the reign of Philip V the best known is that of the marquis of San Felipe, which should be used with great caution since much of his information is wrong. The edition of the *Gaceta de Madrid* by Margarita Torrione, *Crónica festiva de dos reinados*, has been of great help in fixing the movements of the king.

The following short list is limited to principal items or to works cited frequently in the notes; it is not a statement of the books consulted for this study, nor in any way a bibliography of Philip V's reign. A few works on specific themes are mentioned in their relevant place in the notes, and do not appear in this listing.

Albareda, Joaquim, *Els catalans i Felip V: de la conspiració a la revolta (1700–1705)*, Barcelona 1993.

Allonville, Charles-Auguste d', marquis de Louville, *Mémoires secrets sur l'établissement de la maison de Bourbon en Espagne*, 2 vols. Paris 1818 (cited in the notes as 'Louville').

Armstrong, Edward, *Elizabeth Farnese, the Spanish termagant*, London 1892 (a good study that makes use of original Italian documentation).

Asso, Ignacio de, *Historia de la economía política de Aragón*, Saragossa 1798.

Baudrillart, Alfred, *Philippe V et la Cour de France*, 5 vols. Paris 1890–1900 (a fundamental work, based on the correspondence of the French ambassadors; cited in the notes as 'Baudrillart').

Béthencourt y Massieu, Antonio de, *Patiño en la política internacional de Felipe V*, Valladolid 1954.

Béthencourt y Massieu, Antonio de, *Relaciones de España bajo Felipe V. Del tratado de Sevilla a la Guerra con Inglaterra (1729–1739)*, Las Palmas 1998.

Boix, Vicente, *Historia de la Ciudad y Reino de Valencia*, 3 vols. Valencia 1845–7.

Bottineau, Yves, *El arte cortesano en la España de Felipe V (1700–1746)*, Madrid 1986 (a revised version, translated into Spanish, of *L'art de cour dans l'Espagne de Philippe V, 1700–1746*, Bordeaux 1960); (cited in the notes as 'Bottineau', this fundamental study is the best modern work on Philip V).

Bottineau, Yves, *Les Bourbons d'Espagne 1700–1808*, Paris 1993.

Carlos III y su siglo. Coloquio Internacional, Actas, 2 vols. Madrid 1990.

Castagnoli, Pietro, *Il Cardinale Giulio Alberoni*, 3 vols. Rome 1929–32.

Cepeda Adán, José, *El Madrid de Felipe V*, Madrid 1979.

Coxe, William, *Memoirs of the kings of Spain of the House of Bourbon . . . 1700 to 1788*, London 1815 (Spanish trans. *España bajo el reinado de la Casa de Borbón*, 4 vols. Madrid 1846; cited as 'Coxe', note references are to this edition).

Crónica festiva de dos reinados en la Gaceta de Madrid (1700–1759), Madrid 1996 (a very useful edition, edited by Margarita Torrione).

Danvila, Alfonso, *El reinado relámpago. Luis I y Luisa Isabel de Orleans (1707–1742)*, Madrid 1952.

Danvila y Collado, Manuel, *El poder civil en España*, 6 vols. Madrid 1885–6.

Delpy, G., *L'Espagne et l'esprit européen: l'oeuvre de Feijóo (1725–1760)*, Paris 1936.

Desdevises du Dézert, G., *L'Espagne de l'Ancien Régime*, 3 vols. Paris 1897–1904 (still the best survey of the subject).

Dietari de l'Antich Consell Barceloní, vol. XXIII (1698–1701), Barcelona 1970.

Domínguez Ortiz, Antonio, *Sociedad y estado en el siglo XVIII español*, Barcelona 1976.

Egido, Teófanes, *Opinión pública y oposición al poder en la España del siglo XVIII (1713–1759)*, Valladolid 1971.

Egido, Teófanes, *Sátiras políticas de la España moderna*, Madrid 1973.

Escudero, José Antonio, *Administración y estado en la España moderna*, Valladolid 1999.

España en el siglo XVIII. Homenaje a Pierre Vilar, ed. Roberto Fernández, Barcelona 1985 (concerned only with economic history).

Francis, David, *The first peninsular war 1702–1713*, London 1975.

Girardot, M. le baron de, *Correspondance de Louis XIV avec M. Amelot, son ambassadeur en Espagne 1705–9*, Nantes 1864.

Hamilton, Earl J., 'Money and economic recovery in Spain under the first Bourbon', *Journal of Modern History*, 15, 1943.

Hamilton, Earl J., *War and prices in Spain 1651–1800*, Cambridge, Mass. 1947.

Jurado Sánchez, José, 'Los viajes reales en la edad moderna. La visita de Felipe V y su corte a Badajoz y Andalucía (1729–1733)', *Actas del II Congreso de Historia de Andalucía, Córdoba 1991. Historia moderna, vol.III*, Córdoba 1995.

Kamen, Henry, *The War of Succession in Spain 1700–1715*, Bloomington and London 1969.

Kamen, Henry, *Spain in the later seventeenth century 1665–1700*, London 1980.

León, Aurora, *Iconografía y fiesta durante el lustro real: 1729–1733*, Seville 1990.

Lluch, Ernest, *La Catalunya vençuda del segle XVIII*, Barcelona 1996.

Louville, *see* Allonville.

Lynch, John, *Bourbon Spain 1700–1808*, Oxford 1989 (the most useful survey of the politics of the reign).

Macanaz, Melchor de, *Regalías de los Señores Reyes de Aragón*, Madrid 1879.

Marañón, Gregorio, letter to Elías Torme, printed in Torme, 'En el centenario de Felipe V', *Boletín de la Real Academia de la Historia*, 120, 1947.

McLachlan, Jean, *Trade and peace with Old Spain 1667–1750*, Cambridge 1940.

Mercader Riba, Joan, *Felip V i Catalunya*, Barcelona 1968.

Molas, Pere, in *Historia General Rialp de España y América, tomo X-2, La España de las Reformas*, Madrid 1984, pp. 3–39, 87–143.

Molas, Pere, in *Historia de España Menéndez Pidal*, tomo XXVIII, Madrid 1993, pp. 553–655.

Morán, Miguel, *La imagen del rey. Felipe V y el arte*, Madrid 1990.

Morel-Fatio, A. and Léonardon, M., eds, *Recueil des instructions données aux ambassadeurs de la France en Espagne*, vol.II, Paris 1894–9.

Mounier, André, *Les faits et la doctrine économiques en Espagne sous Philippe V: Gerónimo de Uztáriz (1670–1732)*, Bordeaux 1919.

Noailles, duke of, *Mémoires du duc de Noailles*, 2 vols. Paris 1828 (cited in the notes as 'Noailles').

Ozanam, Didier, *Les diplomates espagnols du XVIIIe siècle*, Madrid 1998.

Parnell, Arthur, *The War of the Succession in Spain during the reign of Queen Anne 1702–1711*, London 1905 (the definitive military history of the war in the peninsula).

Pérez Picazo, María Teresa, *La publicística española en la Guerra de Sucesión*, 2 vols. Madrid 1966.

Petrie, Sir Charles, *The Marshal Duke of Berwick*, London 1953.

Pulido Bueno, Ildefonso, *José Patiño*, Huelva 1998.

Robres, López de Mendoza y Pons, conde de, *Historia de las guerras civiles de España*, Saragossa 1882.

Rodríguez Villa, Antonio, *Patiño y Campillo*, Madrid 1882.

Saint-Simon, Philippe de Rouvroy, duc de, *Mémoires*, ed. A. de Boislisle, 45 vols. Paris 1879–1930 (this edition is a fundamental source for the period, less because of the memoirs than for the rich original documentation used).

Saint-Simon, Philippe de Rouvroy, duc de, *Papiers inédits du Duc de Saint-Simon. Lettres et dépêches sur l'ambassade d'Espagne*, introduction by E. Drumont, Paris 1880 (cited as 'Saint-Simon 1880').

San Felipe, Vicente Bacallar y Sanna, marquis of, *Comentarios de la guerra de España e historia de su rey Felipe V, el Animoso* (Biblioteca de Autores Españoles, vol.99), Madrid 1957 (cited as 'San Felipe').

Syveton, G., *Une cour et un aventurier au 18e siècle: le baron de Ripperda*, Paris 1896.

Tessé, Maréchal de, *Lettres et Mémoires du Maréchal de Tessé*, 2 vols. Paris 1806.

Torras i Ribé, Josep Maria, *Els municipis catalans de l'antic regim, 1453–1808*, Barcelona 1983.

Ubilla y Medina, Antonio de, marqués de Ribas, *Succession del rey D. Phelipe V, Diario de sus viages*, Madrid 1704.

Ulloa, Bernardo de, *Restablecimiento de las fábricas y comercio español*, 2 vols. Madrid 1740.

Uztáriz, Gerónimo de, *Theórica y práctica de comercio y de marina*, Madrid 1742.

Vilar, Pierre, *La Catalogne dans l'Espagne moderne*, 3 vols. Paris 1962, cited as 'Vilar'.

Villars, maréchal de, *Mémoires*, ed. De Vogüé, Paris 1884–1902.

Walker, Geoffrey J., *Spanish politics and Imperial trade, 1700–1789*, London 1979.

Zavala, Iris M., *Clandestinidad y libertinaje erudito en los albores del siglo XVIII*, Barcelona 1978.